Preface

Facility & Property Management includes a large number of distinct activities, skills and roles – that's what makes the profession of facility and property management complex, challenging and compelling.

In this book, I've chosen to deal with more of the strategic and management elements of the profession, since there are many books which focus on specific technical or tactical areas, such as project management, maintenance & operations, space management and more. A list of related books is provided at the back of the book and I encourage you to read them, too.

Facility management professionals are strategically important to the organizations they serve and need to do more to ensure that value is formally recognized. My objective is to help FM professionals build on their existing strengths with strategies, approaches and leading practices that let you leverage your other skills to their fullest value and help you get the best results for your company while also advancing your own career.

I believe that constant learning and involvement in the industry are critical to the success not only of the profession, but also of your own career. That's why I've included a listing of national and international associations, designations and magazines at the back of the book. There is something for almost any facility type, service or specialty, however don't limit yourself to your own current building type – there's a lot to learn from Facility and Property Managers who are responsible for other types of buildings, so read other magazines and get involved with umbrella conferences and associations.

This book is designed to make it easy for busy Facility and Property Managers to read and use. It's divided up into subject areas, each of which includes a number of stand-alone sections. Each of the sections deals with a specific strategic, leadership or management approach. As a result, you can read only those that interest you and you can read them in any order.

Michel Theriault

Table of Contents

Management and Leadership

Introduction

Facility Management is an increasingly complex and important profession. The industry has placed a strong emphasis on technical skills, and rightly so. But even though the technical side of facility and property management is important, those skills can only carry your career-and the profession-so far. Indeed, no matter how you choose to break down the real cost of housing people and processes, the risks associated with real estate markets and the impact of raw economics on productivity, these separate entities all combine to demand much more than technical expertise.

Today, management and leadership skills need to be emphasized in order to leverage the technical expertise and address the more complex business issues that are increasingly part of the profession. And that's why this book begins where it does. Regardless of whether you are just entering the profession, building your career or already at the top, you've got to be prepared to use the management and leadership skills in your FM tool belt.

1

Defining Facility Management

It's a complex role

"We shape our buildings; thereafter they shape us."
- Sir Winston Churchill

The International Facility Management Association re-wrote its definition of Facility Management, but in 23 words, it can't possibly tell the whole story.

Before we look at what it takes to be a leader in FM, it makes sense to look at what FM involves. According to International Facility Management Association (IFMA), facility management is *"... a profession that encompasses multiple disciplines to ensure functionality of the built environment by integrating people, place, process and technology."*

That definition works, but doesn't go far enough. FM is a complex profession made up of many different titles with varying scope and responsibility. It is about keeping the doors open and the lights on. But it's also about ensuring the company gets the best value for its investment in the buildings, whether it's the rent it pays or the return on investment it receives as an owner.

Admittedly, FM is largely a supporting role; one that allows the real show–the occupant or tenant's core business–to go on without a hitch. But it's the wide variety of things that come together to support the built environment that makes facility management difficult to define. This is why so many individuals, often associated with as many different titles, are now associated with the FM profession. Indeed, IFMA's own definition talks about "multiple disciplines" within the profession. These multiple disciplines have developed as the complexity of modern facility management has increased and the scope of activities that need to be involved in maintaining the built environment expands.

Increasing Sophistication

With a broad range of facility types and uses and a varied scope and size of portfolio, it's natural that specialties and focus have developed within the profession. This is partly to deal with the large scope of portfolios and responsibilities as well as the increasing sophistication, requiring specialization.

Of course, this has also meant expanding facilities departments to deal with the issues and complexities. Along with this has come a higher requirement for good management and leadership skills for facility managers, particularly when they are managing other specialists within FM.

It's this sophistication that has changed the industry itself. To a certain extent, it has resulted in convergence and a blurring of the lines between the traditional roles of the property manager and the facility manager. The increasing presence of professional FM outsourcing companies that provide a varying scope of service to their clients has also changed the industry. Even traditional property managers must now support their employers and tenants with a broader understanding of facilities issues.

Traditionally, property managers dealt with the technical aspects of buildings for owners, typically as an investment. Often, the property management function is for day-to-day operations of the building, including managing service providers for grounds, preventive maintenance, life safety and other asset-related requirements. They are the ones interfacing with occupants and tenants about technical, service and comfort issues. Facility managers, on the other hand, traditionally represented the occupant, dealing with moves, furniture, office functions and other logistical issues.

In some buildings, you will find a property manager working for the building owner and a facility manager working for the tenant. Where the tenant also owns the building, a facility manager oversees both.

A More Strategic Role

In some cases the facility manager has shouldered a broader set of responsibilities compared to the property manager. And while some facility managers manage tenant space for an employer with no responsibility for the traditional building management functions, they must be keenly aware of those functions in order to conduct their business successfully.

The end result is that the traditional roles and the strategic focus of each of them tend to be different in some cases and merged into one function in others. Property managers are responsible for the building functions and asset value over the long term, while facility managers are responsible for the more strategic management of the people in that built environment. The facility and property management roles can be performed by different people or the same person, depending on the portfolio size and whether the organization is a tenant or owner. Increasingly, it involves a team of individuals with expertise in different specialties.

Remember, too, that titles are not always clear indications of responsibilities. Asset management, for instance, may be performed by the facility manager, property manager, or increasingly, by another individual with the asset manager title.

If you look closely at the definition of facility management developed by IFMA, it is clear they are defining a profession and not a job title. Some of the confusion comes from the fact that the title of "Facility Manager," which often implies responsibilities for the full scope, is also used in the industry to identify individuals who manage a portion of the full scope of services.

As a result, the definition itself suggests that the profession comes together at a senior level within an organization, depending on the size of the company. This senior position would have overall responsibility for the many different activities required to provide the functionality of the built environment, and reflects the multiple disciplines that IFMA describes.

Connectivity at a Senior Level

The FM connection to a senior management position underlines the need for FM professionals at the top of their organizations to be able to see the whole picture. That vantage point is essential to their efforts to provide strategic direction to the company on managing and using the physical assets. While only the senior FM position may get that "big picture" point-of-view, we start to see why individuals looking to advance their careers in FM must seek that same vantage.

If you separate the roles and consider the property manager as the primary title within commercial property management and the facility manager as the primary title for a corporate facility environment, the profession as a whole can still be defined as including both these positions.

In fact, going back to the importance of that "big picture" perspective, FM would also include a number of other positions, including asset manager (which is found in both the corporate and commercial environments), as well as project manager, office manager, designer, planner, and a whole host of other positions.

Focus on Management & Leadership

The reality of the facility and property management industry is that most managers and staff have strong technical skills but less experience and training in management and business. That's a problem, since the skills and expertise associated with those areas are essential to the skill set they need to fully benefit from their technical knowledge so they can benefit their employers, advance their profession and improve their careers. The need to focus on non-technical aspects of facility and property manager skills is confirmed by two industry reports.

The International Facility Management Association's (IFMA) 2007 report, *Exploring the Current Trends and Future Outlook for Facility Management Professionals*, lists the top decision drivers that facility management professionals should address as "linking facility management to strategy."

APPA, the association for universities in North America, released its *Thought Leaders Series 2007*, which identifies the top ten critical facilities issues for 2007/08. There, the top issue noted was the need to improve communications. Also on the list is balancing and articulating expectations, focusing on the customer and aligning facilities planning with institutional goals.

Both of these organizations are putting non-technical skills ahead of the traditional technical skills, suggesting a shift in emphasis from swinging a wrench to driving a desk. Is it because these "soft" skills are more important? Sort of. There is already a wealth of strong technical skills in the industry. Non-technical skills, like management and leadership in particular, however, appear to need more emphasis as they enable the existing technical knowledge to be leveraged for the organization's benefit. Taking that argument a step farther, we see that these are also the skills facility managers need to advance in their careers and develop the industry as a true profession in the eyes of their employers.

Quick Summary

Key Points	➡ There are many different titles and roles within FM, all with different sets of responsibility. Together, they encompass the profession.
	➡ Developing skills beyond technical areas will enhance your career and improve results for your organization.
Executive Tips	➡ Communicating about and promoting the profession is one way to improve the visibility of FM as a profession.
	➡ You have to be a leader in addition to a manager to successfully deliver results.
Traps to Avoid	➡ Don't be hung up by titles or definitions. It's the function you provide that matters.

2

Facility Management Competencies

Facilities as a Profession, not as a Job

"A man who works with his hands is a laborer; a man who works with his hands and his brain is a craftsman; but a man who works with his hands and his brain and his heart is an artist"
— Louis Nizer

The definition of FM, as currently used primarily for corporate environments, applies to facilities of all types, whether these are owner-occupied or serve as an investment to a commercial landlord. The goals of both types of ownership are ultimately the same, even if they are approached differently.

The convergence of these two professions as outlined in IFMA's definition of facilities management ensures functionality of the built environment. It doesn't matter what the title is, since the profession itself is encompassed by the term "Facilities Management."

IFMA's Eleven Core Competencies

Unlike some professions, FM encompasses many different roles and skills. Not all facility or property managers are responsible for all of these roles, while others oversee all these roles through other subject-matter experts. Regardless, it's important to have a working knowledge of each one so you can effectively deal with your colleagues, manage staff or interface with external resources.

This is further expanded when you consider typical portfolios, which can range from a single building to a regional or national portfolio and even an international portfolio of properties. Like many other profession, the larger the scope, the more people involved at different levels. Where a smaller property may have a single Facility Manager, a large portfolio may have a Vice President, Facilities, with several hundred staff under them.

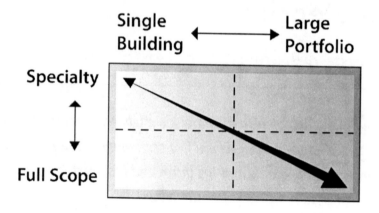

According to the International Facilities Management Association (IFMA), there are eleven competencies involved in FM based on their global job task analysis (GJTA) completed in 2009. This is a change from the original nine core competencies, with the addition of Environmental Stewardship and Sustainability and Emergency Preparedness and Business Continuity, two areas that have emerged as separate and distinct competencies. IFMA also reconfigured some of the existing core competencies as a result.

Since FM is a very broad profession, not all of these competencies are necessarily covered by each FM professional. Nevertheless, it is important to identify these competencies, understand the specific activities related to them and use that knowledge to improve your ability to manage these factors, particularly as you advance in your career and become responsible for specialists in these areas.

The 11 competencies are listed below in no particular order, followed by my commentary and interpretation about the importance and application of the competencies. You will note that not all competencies are covered in this book. As discussed earlier, the focus is on the overall leadership, management and strategy of FM, not specific skills or knowledge for activities such as leasing, maintenance, IT services, budgeting, energy conservation, environment, emergency preparedness or project management. Instead, the strategies and leading practices discussed in this book will make you more successful when you apply those specific competencies.

Competency: Operations and Maintenance

This competency is especially important if your organization owns its own properties and you are responsible for the physical infrastructure. Even if you aren't directly involved, understanding the operations and maintenance of buildings enables you to interface better with colleagues who are responsible for these functions, or to deal with your landlord about operations and maintenance issues that affect you as a tenant. Specific activities related to operations and maintenance include:

➡ Plan and manage preventive maintenance activities, including trades or contractors.

➡ Receive and act on occupant requests for services or maintenance requirements.

➡ Plan and organize the replacement or repair of building systems and components.

➡ Manage services such as janitorial, grounds, snow removal, mail, fleet and other services required by your organization.

Competency: Real Estate and Property Management

This is a very diverse area. Some look at "Real Estate" as buying and developing property, but in fact, it involves oversight of the physical asset and the environment for the occupants as well. Real estate involves space planning to enable flexibility and effective space use for your organization.

Some of the responsibilities include developing processes and procedures for the elements identified below. Others are strategic initiatives that help you maximize the use of the company's assets. The competency targets the FM's need to:

➡ Develop, manage and implement occupancy planning for their organizations.

➡ Manage real estate as an assets.

➡ Implement leasing strategies and conduct negotiations for space.

➡ Interface with landlords and tenants for services and to ensure expectations are met.

➡ Conduct assessments and develop capital renewal plans and business cases for funding.

Competency: Project Management

Project management skills and techniques position you well for the times when you will need these skills. While some FM professionals may not see a strong need to develop their ability to manage projects, these skills give you a definite advantage as you progress in your career or are responsible for overseeing internal or external project managers. As some issues that require project management skills arise with little warning, your ability to bring good ideas to the table will also bode well for your career.

Minor moves, adds and changes to space requirements can be frequent, while medium and large projects, such as major construction and relocations, are less common. Project management skills include:

➡ Manage programming and design.

➡ Plan and manage all phases of projects.

➡ Manage moves and relocations.

Competency: Leadership and Strategy

This is a non-technical skill set that is increasingly important in FM, regardless of your position in the organization. For career growth, however, it is even more important than it used to be. To successfully oversee a large facilities department, you need more than technical knowledge and skills, you need and a well-developed set of management and leadership skills as well as an ability to develop strategy and sell your initiatives within your organization. The FM professional needs to know how to:

➡ Develop strategic plans and initiatives to meet your organization's needs.

➡ Plan and organize the facility function in innovative ways.

➡ Lead, motivate and manage personnel within your group.

➡ Gain agreement from and develop cooperation with others.

➡ Implement processes and quality improvement for services.

Competency: Finance & Business

The ability to understand, manage and control costs for your organization also makes you more valuable to an organization that already needs your technical or facilities-related knowledge. Understanding how FM decisions financially impact the organization, how to get and use financial information, knowing where to balance risk and cost, how to organize and manage functions to minimize costs and how to analyze and audit costs to avoid waste will give you more visibility in your organization. Learn to:

➡ Manage the finances of the facility function.

➡ Effectively budget report and conduct financial analysis

➡ Develop and implement procurement initiatives.

Competency: Quality

These days, it's not good enough to do the job, you've got to do the job better. The ability to build quality assurance and management into your processes and to select and implement systems that provide you with the information you need will help you improve results. Skills and knowledge about how to effectively benchmark to improve results and to network with other facility managers, get involved in associations and attend tradeshows will help you innovate by learning the leading practices from others and by sharing your leading practices. If you're serious about quality assessment:

➡ Establish customer requirements and manage service delivery to meet those needs in the context of the overall organization's resources.

➡ Develop processes to assess the satisfaction of occupants and the quality of service delivery.

➡ Conduct benchmarking and assessments for continuous improvement.

➡ Audit service delivery to validate adherence to processes.

Competency: Communication

Whether it's with your staff, peers, occupants or your boss, being able to communicate and get your message across, get acceptance for business cases and initiatives and get compliance with policies and notices will make a difference. This is a soft skill that delivers hard results. To enhance your communication skills:

➡ Communicate effectively with Internal and External stakeholders.

➡ Understand how to use varied media to best achieve their purposes.

Competency: Technology

Professional FM departments use technology to do a better job, whether it's improved efficiency, better information to make decisions, or reduced costs. They may also be responsible for technology that the organization requires to conduct their core business or for the physical space that houses their organization's technology. Understanding technology is necessary for you to support your organization and enable it to be flexible and competitive. Whether it's managing space, work orders, preventive maintenance, furniture and equipment inventories, key control, board room booking, security or communications, you need to stay up-to-date with technology. Meeting this requirement requires you to:

➡ Understand and implement effective technology tools for the delivery of FM services.

➡ Provide or support technology requirements of the organization.

Competency: Human Factors

The work environment provided and managed by FM professionals has an impact on the productivity, satisfaction, health and safety of the organization's employees. Understanding and meeting the needs of a modern workplace, including legislative requirements, is as important as the technical and process related services. Productive space and layouts, ergonomic furniture, compliant indoor air quality (IAQ), effective security and a workspace free from physical risks and hazards is a fundamental requirement:

➡ Develop and implement occupational health & safety.

➡ Assess and mitigate workplace risks and hazards.

➡ Proactively assess and maintain IAQ.

➡ Implement space plans, workspace layouts, workspace furniture ergonomics and access / accommodation requirements to meet legislative and organizational needs.

Competency: Emergency Preparedness and Business Continuity

This has always been part of the FM responsibility as a result of the impact of facilities on the organization's ability to do its business. Whether you are leading or participating with others in your organization, you need to understanding how to effectively plan for and then manage emergency events that impact your facilities. Emergency preparedness includes having processes, resources and backups in place to manage, mitigate and restore services in the event of an emergency. Business continuity is both ensuring your own services and operations can continue to function in the event of an emergency and helping ensure your organization's business can also continue to operate. This competency requires you to:

➡ Develop facility specific emergency preparedness and response plans for all types of potential events and disasters.

➡ Develop your department's business continuity plans to ensure continued services

➡ Participate with your organization to support their business continuity plans and to develop effective emergency response plans.

➡ Test, evaluate and revisit plans regularly.

Competency: Environmental Stewardship and Sustainability

Any negative environmental impacts or costs associated with the facilities and real estate we manage carry increasingly negative social connotations which have a negative effect on the reputation and stature of the organizations we work with and for. From design through to the management of buildings, the FM has an opportunity and a responsibility to help reduce those negative impacts. The processes to achieve this, the technological solutions available and the cost impacts require a full understanding of the business and technical issues needed to improve the work environment for occupants and reduce the environmental impact of the workplace. This competency requires you to:

➡ Identify, develop, sell and implement initiatives to reduce consumption and unit costs of all forms of utilities.

➡ Develop internal communication plans to encourage occupants to participate in your initiatives and take their own action to conserve.

➡ Review and adjust your supplies, materials and work processes to reduce the environmental impacts, including meeting legislation.

➡ Establish procurement practices that encourage or require environmentally friendlier services and supplies.

The FM Pie

Since Facilities Management includes so many different skills and responsibilities, it's easiest to represent it with a pie-shaped diagram. This shows the full range of FM responsibilities. Depending on your role, you may be responsible for all these elements or just a few. You may also oversee them all, but have other experts on your team who focus on a specific aspect of the role. Some of these specific areas are actually represented by their own professions when performed as a distinct, separate role.

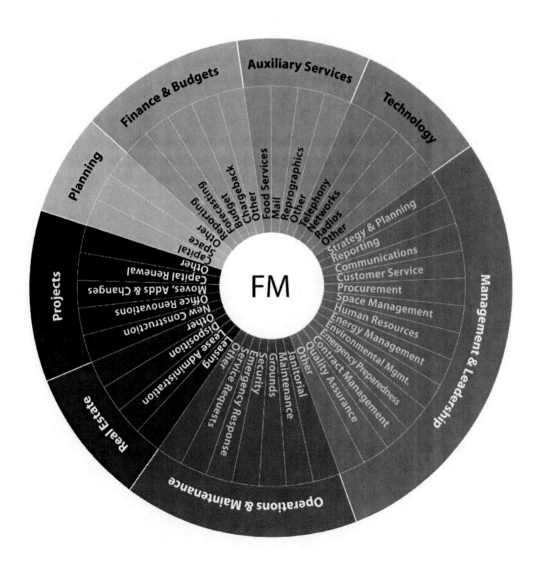

Quick Summary

Key Points

➡ Understand the full range of responsibilities and skills that makes up the FM profession.

➡ Develop a full range of skills and expertise.

Executive Tips

➡ Access information and training in all areas, whether they are currently within your responsibility or not.

➡ Encourage interaction between specialists within FM and with other departments/occupants.

Traps to Avoid

➡ Don't treat other competencies or skills as something others are responsible for – understand their drivers and impacts on your own activities so you can influence them better.

3

Promoting Facilities Management in your Organization

Advancing FM and your career with visibility

"To establish oneself in the world, one does all one can to seem established there already." - François de La Rochefoucauld

Facilities represent a large part of any organization's assets and expenses, yet don't typically receive the attention other parts of the organization receive. Having a professional facility management resource to provide strategic direction and stewardship is critical to getting results, lowering costs and minimizing risk.

In most organizations, FM doesn't get as much recognition as other departments or groups. It's time that changed. Part of the reason is that FM appears to play a supporting role. It is essential to the core business of the organization, yet relegated to something less. It is as if the organization exists entirely apart from its built environment. In fact, facilities can represent up to 32% of the organization's cost base and 85% or more of the total cost of ownership of a typical facility over its life.

Regardless of whether FM's contribution is measurable, facilities make a key contribution to the organization's productivity as they support everything from the staff who sits in the buildings to the output of services or products from the facilities.

Facility managers are usually not focused on promoting what they do–and why their work is so important to an organization's financial bottom line. The profession is arguably growing in status, as is indicated by the increasing number of industry designations and college and university programs with a focus on FM. Still, key perceptions of the role remain focused on a building operator at work in the boiler room; a perception that ignores the critical, and increasingly strategic, nature of the modern facility manager's role.

That problem appears rooted in the fact that the demands of the role leave most facility managers feeling as if they are on a treadmill and don't have time for planning and communication. This is evident when they aren't able to properly prepare their message and arguments to influence others in meetings. By failing to see face-to-face sessions as occasions to educate other senior managers and colleague about professional FM roles and responsibilities, facility managers devalue their own work and forego important opportunities to promote FM interests.

Without time to plan, communicate and promote, you will stay in the background. There are a few things you should do to improve your profile, both as individual facility managers and as members of FM departments.

Consider This

FM issues are often not heard or identified until there is a problem, meaning you and the value you provide are largely invisible and essentially taken for granted. And that's why the first thing you need to do is simple: get out of the boiler room.

Develop Communication Tools

Many facility managers agree they don't usually communicate very well about what they do or the value they provide. Believe it or not, the solution is relatively easy as there are many things you can do to promote your FM department and services.

That process begins with an assessment of what you do. If you work through the points listed below, you will get specific ideas about what you can do to change your organization's perception of FM. Some of the ideas will not be appropriate for your environment. Others can be adapted to your own needs. The main point is critical: perception is reality. If you are concerned about the perception of FM within your organization, you can change it.

To raise your profile and influence in the organization, consider doing the following:

- ✓ Develop a Mission, Vision and Value Statement.
- ✓ Develop your internal network with semi-regular One-on-One meetings/coffee with the decision makers in each department.
- ✓ Establish a decision maker summit for senior members of all the departments.
- ✓ Hold an Occupant Awareness / Appreciation Day for occupants
- ✓ Produce a newsletter (via email or paper)
- ✓ Distribute posters / brochures with info on how to reach you, services, etc.
- ✓ Distribute stickers with your help desk number.
- ✓ Develop your own logo to brand all your communications so it's clear that it's from you and is easily recognized.
- ✓ Move your offices to a more visible location. If you are in the basement, it's time to move!

Develop your Mission, Vision and Value Statement

If you don't already have one for your department and your team, develop a Mission, Vision and Values (MVV) statement that shows what your objectives are and how you support the organization's core business. Link it directly to your own organization's MVV statement to demonstrate how you support it. If other departments have their own statements, review them as well and see how yours will support theirs.

When you create it, be sure to involve your team so they understand and embrace it. Facility managers who approach this as a meaningful exercise in team building will have a MVV statement they can use to anchor a strategic plan and improve organizational communication. More information on developing your own MVV is discussed in the Communicating to Influence section later in the book.

Develop your Internal Network

When you're occupied with the day-to-day issues of FM, it's hard to stop and network with your colleagues in the profession, much less within your organization. That doesn't change the value of communication, nor subtract from the fact that the best communication strategies depend on direct one-on-one interaction with the decision makers, colleagues and customers within your organization.

It takes time and a certain amount of consideration, but facility managers who are serious about developing their internal network must formally identify the decision makers and other individuals who have influence or are regularly impacted by your services.

Once you've established who is in your network, you can take steps to understand their issues, see how you can help and educate them about FM. This is a strategic way to build a network of allies who will support your initiatives down the road.

Schedule short meetings with these individuals, perhaps over coffee, to find out what their pressure points are, what they think about your services, what their plans are and how you can help them be more successful. If you carefully manage the discussion, you can also give them insight into FM issues, including the potential need for additional resources or support for specific initiatives where your needs intersect with theirs. As an added bonus, this approach will also increase your visibility and influence within the organization.

If the departments hold regular meetings, conferences or other gatherings, try to be added to the agenda so you can speak to them about your initiatives and most importantly, your accomplishments.

Consider This

You may never get into the executive boardroom, but small group meetings and one-on-one interactions give you a chance to influence those at the boardroom table. By figuring out who the decision makers and key players are, you can foster critical relationships with people who are at that table. Where possible, always bring solutions, develop consensus and proactively support their operations. By talking their language (time and dollars) and providing facts, figures, data and evidence that what you do makes a difference, you are preparing for the times you need to call on these people for support with an FM initiative.

Establish a Decision Maker Summit

If possible, you should organize an annual FM meeting with all key decision makers, such as the senior representative of each department. Make it interesting by providing good information about what you're working on and what you plan to do in the future that may impact or benefit them. You should also provide coffee/lunch for their time.

This is a good place to give decision makers advance notice about your activities, including occupant awareness days, projects, policies and other key issues that will impact them. Always give them something to take away with them, whether it's a brochure of your services, a concise explanation of upcoming initiatives or samples of environmentally-friendly products you will be implementing.

Where possible, use these summits to talk about your approach to the issues you learned about through your one-on-one discussions. Always provide them with an opportunity to ask questions of you and your staff and encourage solutions-based discussions about the common building or occupancy issues they are dealing with. Always follow-up with a summary and an invitation to the next summit.

Hold an Occupant Awareness/Appreciation Day

Most occupants take their environment for granted and few understand what it takes to maintain it and manage it.

To increase awareness and make connections within the organization, hold an awareness or appreciation day once a year. Host the event in a central area, like the main lobby, so attendance is convenient and everyone entering the building will see you and your staff.

Invite all occupants and personally invite decision makers. Show them what you do and be sure to make it interesting for them by highlighting the functions that keep their departments running smoothly.

By providing interesting facts about the building, you can educate them about what is takes to keep a built environment functioning well. To make the event memorable, you could also work with the local newspaper to distribute free papers, or even use the opportunity to kick off a campaign and distribute information about an innovative FM project. If it involves environmental initiatives, you could distribute eco-friendly coffee mugs or light bulbs.

Include some displays on energy, projects, furniture, etc. and ask your staff/suppliers to be present. Work with them beforehand to develop specific talking points and recognize the event as an opportunity to reveal new plans or initiatives, whether for environment, energy, furniture or office move plans. Immediately after the event, conduct a kind of post-mortem to address things that worked and what you'd like to change next year. Factor the event into next year's budget to make sure it happens.

An event like this is also a good time to offer building tours for the occupants to visit the mechanical rooms or floors. Have your staff or subcontractors talk about how it works in terms the visitors will understand. You want them to learn how it impacts them and to discuss system limitations and issues so they understand more (and may complain less).

Produce a Newsletter

A newsletter is another valuable tool and it can be easy to develop and implement as long as you keep it small and don't promise an issue each month. You can either produce your own newsletter or contribute articles to your company's internal newsletter.

It's important to keep the items interesting and be strategic in what you say; the purpose is to gently promote your FM group, not provide dry, useless information.

Writing effective newsletter items, with interesting and eye-catching headlines, is important if you want people to read it. More details about writing newsletters are provided in the *Communicating to Influence* section that follows.

While the newsletter can be electronic instead of paper based, you should consider distributing paper copies to key people in your organization and posting copies on notice boards. You can also communicate more regularly by releasing information about a single topic (versus an entire newsletter). Here, the principles of effective writing remain the same; the article/bulletin must be topical, well-written and impart information that sheds positive light on your work in FM.

Distribute Posters/Brochures

It's surprising how many occupants don't know what their facilities department does or how to contact them for services or issues. It's also common for occupants to lack good information about important occupancy initiatives or issues ranging from economic cost-control projects to greening initiatives such as recycling and other services.

Posters in the lobby or elevator cabs can convey program and service information. Always include the help desk phone number and promote successful initiatives by sharing news about energy savings or recycling rates.

The key with posters is to make them a "single issue" communication tool that is very visible and easy to read in the very short time they have to look at it, especially if it's in an elevator cab. Use the techniques discussed in the *Communicating to Influence* section.

Brochures can provide more detailed information about your entire range of services or a single service, like Moves, Adds & Changes (MAC). Here, you can use the brochure to identify the process, lead times, information requirements, interfaces, approval process and more.

In all cases, decide on your message and focus on the specific audience. The brochure for MACs for instance, may be directed at the senior department representative or at each department's administrative support person, depending on who typically is responsible for initiating the requests in the department.

Distribute Help Desk Stickers

If you have a formal process like a help desk or self-serve website for work requests, complaints and issues, you should publicize it. While it may seem to make your life more difficult when you get more calls, you should encourage occupants to call and document issues. In addition to facilitating direct interaction with occupants and decision makers, you will have more information to use when making decisions, managing suppliers and reviewing processes.

You can use simple stickers that can be affixed to the phone, or a larger sticker/card to be stuck on other surfaces or pinned up on message boards, depending on your organization.

Consider This

One FM department printed its help desk number on telephone cord de-tanglers and distributed them to each occupant as part of the kick-off for their newly-implemented help desk.
This helped promote the number and was a useful telephone accessory that most people actually used.

Develop a Logo and Name for your Department

Image is an important part of communicating and your department's name and logo will help you build that image internally. A commercial property management company or FM service provider would already have its company name, logo and special branding on their communications. If you are managing an FM department that's part of your organization, you can borrow the same principles and apply them within your department since in effect, you are a service provider and the rest of the organization is your customer.

"Plant Services," for instance, is a common name for FM departments in institutions based on the old image of FM, where the focus was managing the physical infrastructure and most of the people involved had technical backgrounds.

The changing role and the change in the types of resources now involved in a full FM service means Plant Services is no longer a meaningful title. This is why many departments are changing their department names from Plant Services or

Physical Plant, to something like Facilities Services. The goal is to adopt a title that reflects the much broader scope and responsibilities your department has.

Where possible, a change in departmental name should be accompanied by a change in titles. Again, you want to use words that reflect the real value and function.

Similarly, departments once called Office Services are changing their names because they are actually responsible for much more, including leasing, build-outs, managing owned properties and more. A switch to the more relevant Facilities Services reflects the true role and responsibilities and aligns it more closely with the name of the profession.

When you change a department's name, you should also develop an identifiable logo or image. Create an internal logo to represent your facilities departments, or develop a variation of your organization's logo if permitted.

To develop this logo, hire a logo designer or hold a logo design competition for your staff or their families, for instance. You may find out that you have a talented artist in your group. If there are great ideas but no artists, their sketch can be used by a graphic designer and it will be cheaper. This also gets your staff engaged and involved.

Examples

Here is an example of a facility department's logo. This provides a branding opportunity and makes it clear to all occupants that anything with this logo is related to facilities.

As you can see, the logo itself doesn't need to be elaborate, nor does it have to be a version of the overall organization's logos. Like any logo, however, it does have to be distinctive and it to be used consistently.

Other organizations develop their logos by adapting the overall organization's logo. For internal use, this isn't necessary. Moreover, the organization's marketing department may not allow an adaptation.

The examples below are from Bristol Myers Squibb's facilities department in France, where they developed not only a logo for their department, but a series of icons they use to brand specific services. This approach increases the visibility of their FM department while clearly identifying communications and information related to various services.

Facility department logo. The French translation actually means "general services."	This is their logo for the maintenance function. Similar images were developed for parking, reprographics, cafeteria services, etc.

With an internal logo, you can then brand all your communications so it's clear that they are facilities related. This is a good way to increase FM visibility and improve your ability to communicate with occupants.

Move Your Offices

While you are at it, consider your office location. Few organizations give the facilities department prime space, particularly if they own their own facilities. Traditionally, the facility manager feels obligated to give the better and more visible space to the other departments. Indeed, as a service department, FM often moves frequently to make space available, or takes the least-attractive space in the basement or service building.

For organizations that own their space and provide maintenance of the mechanical and electrical systems, this seems to be related to the "Plant Services" issues mentioned above. That is, the people running the physical plant should be close to the plant, which is likely housed in the basement or mechanical rooms.

But ask yourselves if other service departments get the same treatment. Is the IT department hidden away? Does Finance and Human Resources get sub-standard space? If they don't, there isn't a good reason for FM to get sub-standard space either. In fact, by taking sub-standard space, FM reduces the opportunities it has to be recognized as an important part of the company. This location also makes it more difficult for FM mangers to interact with the decision makers and customers within the organization and it short-changes FM staff by giving them less desirable space.

In one example, an entire FM department was relocated to basement space and because of the lack of windows, large flat screen TVs were installed and connected to video cameras to give the employees an outside view. While it made the environment a little better, it was still the basement.

When you are involved in making space and move decisions, don't put yourself in the basement; treat your department and your staff the same as all other support groups. This improves the visibility of FM and ensures better access to decision makers in your organization.

Switch from Tactical to Strategic

In addition to the specific actions outlined above, think about ways to improve your FM group's image and get better results by a shift in the FM mindset. While specific strategic management options are discussed in the *Strategic Management* section, I want you to start thinking about new ways to approach and define your management and leadership roles. Instead of fighting fires, I want you to think about ways to prevent those fires from happening!

The need to shift from tactical to strategic management is rooted in a typical problem faced by facility managers and it's partly based on the nature of building management itself. It is, by definition, the FM professional's job to manage the "current issue." That means you must be responsive to the day-to-day needs of the organization and the building occupants. Most individuals working in FM take professional pride in getting things done. From their point of view, any time spent thinking and planning keeps them away from the jobs they are paid to do. Their roles as fixers and doers is the crux of their contribution to the organization.

This is short-sighted. Since FM is also about the strategic use of resources, this day-to-day focus is detrimental to overall services and long-term results. It often prevents FM managers from adequately assessing, analyzing and developing improved (and leader-like) approaches to service delivery, systems, procedures, service contracts, space utilization and more.

As an FM professional, it's your responsibility to develop strategies and planning that adds value to your organization, not just deliver tactical day-to-day services.

To do it effectively, you need uninterrupted time to think. Think about it: constant phone calls, emails or people entering your office negatively affect your ability to develop strategies. As planning also needs involvement from others in your organization, be sure to involve them in the strategic process, which is discussed later in the book.

Consider This

Since it's very hard to mix day-to-day activity with strategic planning, you need to get off the treadmill once in a while and spend the time developing and implementing plans. You can make time by staying out of the office and working from home, or spending time in a coffee shop or even the cafeteria to give yourself some think time and develop strategic plans. The key is to stop fighting fires and lead the solutions instead of chasing them. This also means delegating and prioritizing.

Demonstrating Value

In addition to drawing more attention to what your FM department does, or to your role in FM, look for ways to demonstrate that value. The demands of the FM job are intense, the stakes high and the credit often elusive. But FM professionals know how important the job is and as the cost of doing business increases in terms of real estate and operations, including human resources, quality FM gets even more critical. Recognition for the FM role, however, is not likely to increase unless the FM industry is prepared to speak up.

To make that happen, FM professionals need to strategically remind their organizations of the impact of what you do and why it matters. But don't promote your industry's value in isolation. Join an association where you can learn about ways to implement leading practices. Talk to others about how they sell FM innovations to their organizations. Read magazines that profile FM success stories and study how others are bringing projects to fruition. Mine your organization's own help-desk data for problem areas and new ideas. Network with colleagues and share approaches. Learn about the latest hot-button issues and find ways to put a proverbial wedge in the C-Suite door by developing solutions to timely, critical issues they are concerned about.

As organizations develop an increased awareness of the costs, risks and opportunities inherent in owning or leasing facilities, FM professionals have an unequalled opportunity to shift their job descriptions every time they demonstrate their ability to deliver a strategically-important solution to one of the organization's problems.

By pushing your role past operations and maintenance, FM mangers can move from caretakers to influencers. Again, success is contingent on communicating strategic plans that clarify your value to the organization. This is not just about what you can do, but what you *say* and *prove* you can do.

Many FM contributions are tied up in day-to-day delivery of services. So look at those services and learn to see them as accomplishments. Talk about costs savings, cost avoidance, risk mitigation and service excellence. Acknowledge how sustainability and energy conservation initiatives impact economics and enhance corporate image. Don't be shy to promote what you do, why you do it and why it matters to the larger organization.

Facilities represent a large part of any company's assets and expenses, yet don't usually receive the same attention that other parts of the organization receive. Having an FM professional like you provide strategic direction and stewardship is critical to getting results, lowering costs and minimizing risk.

The bottom line is that while FM is a recognized profession supported by a growing number of college and university programs, many companies do not yet recognize its strategic value. Executives can talk about the costs, risks and opportunities inherent in owning or leasing facilities, but haven't yet made the connection to strategic FM management as an important professional role.

If you are working within an organization that hasn't yet made this strategic shift, here are nine good reasons it should. Read them carefully and look for ways to include these ideas in your communications approach:

1. Facilities are one of your company's largest assets and a represent a significant cost of doing business. An FM professional has the knowledge to maximize value and minimize costs, adding directly to the bottom line.

2. Facilities and the built environment interface with employees, processes and systems to have a large impact on productivity. A FM professional understands the company's business and the interaction with the facility necessary to maximize productivity.

3. Facility accommodations, whether in growth mode or not, require strategic planning to minimize costs and maximize value. A FM professional provides strategic direction and development or leasing guidance to achieve the results the company needs.

4. Sustainability is critical to the environment for the company and its employees as well as corporate image. A FM professional provides the stewardship required to maintain leadership on the environment.

5. The environmental and legislative complexity of owning or leasing facilities represents a huge risk to the company. A FM professional navigates the requirements and mitigates the risk.

6. Facilities require an entire team of generalists and specialists to provide services. A FM professional understands how to make these resources work together to maximize value, reduce risk and minimize costs.

7. The facilities that house your business can absorb considerable effort to manage effectively. A FM professional takes on this burden and frees up other resources to fully focus on what makes the company successful in delivering its core business and generating bottom-line results.

8. Managing facilities with an administrative resource or line manager means it won't get the attention it deserves and may put the organization at risk. A FM professional has training, background and experience in all

areas of the complex issues and services required to provide safe, effective stewardship to the organization's facility assets.

9. A FM professional has the experience and overall oversight for facilities issues, enabling them to see patterns, track changes and identify risks that may have a future negative impact. Their knowledge enables them to take corrective action now to reduce your risk and costs.

These reasons should be compelling to your organization, but it's your job to promote yourself and your group's value within your organization.

Quick Summary

Key Points	➡ Facilities costs are a large part of the company costs.
	➡ A FM professional with experience, training and involvement with the industry is best suited to manage those costs.
Executive Tips	➡ Communicate success relentlessly.
	➡ Work with colleagues and department heads to demonstrate value.
Traps to Avoid	➡ Continuing to be the service that isn't seen.
	➡ Failing to see, and promote, the value you add to the company.
	➡ Maintaining an internal focus instead of getting involved with the industry, colleagues in competing corporations, etc.

4

Leadership for Facility Managers

Leadership isn't reserved for the CEO of your company.

"Management is doing things right; leadership is doing the right things." - Peter F. Drucker, American Management Guru

As a facility manager, you are in a leadership role. To exercise that leadership role as effectively as possible, you must approach all aspects of facility services from that leadership perspective, whether it's a current matter or a long-range issue.

In FM, there is a great deal of focus on the technical knowledge and skills required in many aspects of the job. These are certainly important for success, but without effective management and leadership, you may not be able to leverage your skills as effectively as possible and you certainly won't be able to rise above the noise of the daily job and leverage your skills and those of your staff.

While interest in FM as a profession is growing with new post-secondary programs, many FM professionals still struggle with the difference between effective leadership versus effective management. By understanding the difference and why your role is not just management, it's leadership, you will develop your career and serve your organization better.

Manage or Lead?

The difference between management and leadership is essentially the difference between timelines and resources. Management is a here and now activity that uses process and resources to efficiently achieve a specific outcome. Leadership, on the other hand, is a forward-looking activity in which a future goal is identified and people are inspired to move towards it. In fact, leadership leverages the value of effective management.

Jim Clemmer, a leadership training and consulting company, says that leaders, "show the way by going in advance. To lead is to guide or direct a course of action. To lead is to influence the behavior or opinion of others. We all need to be leaders, regardless of our formal title or role."

That wisdom applies to the modern FM professional, where the role has transformed from a technical, tactical function to an important leadership role within their organization. The increasing awareness by executives about how important facilities and the work environment are to the productivity and success of every organization's employees and processes has transformed the profession.

Leadership in FM

FM is a complex profession that impacts an organization at many different levels. As a result, the leadership skills you apply must be multi-directional. To achieve this, you must first be able to provide leadership to your staff and contractors towards specific goals and objectives. You must also provide the ground-level management of resources and issues that it takes to get the job done.

You must also provide leadership sideways to your colleagues and other business owners within the company. Here, leadership influences and guides the decisions and strategies others will take in relation to the facility's resources and services.

You must also provide leadership upwards, all the way to the CEO, on facilities issues that affect the decisions of the company as a whole. This includes, among other things, financial and environmental leadership, as well as an increasing emphasis on security issues.

By looking past the day-to-day management of issues that come your way, and making the time to address and provide leadership over issues that are on the horizon, you will add value to your organization, enhance your career prospects, and increase the profile and status of facilities management.

Developing Leadership

Very few facility managers have had specific leadership or management training as part of their formal education. That's unfortunate, given that the ability to lead and manage people effectively is as important as having technical knowledge.

This can be changed. Regardless of where you are in your career or your position within your organization, you should seek out and take opportunities to learn and apply leadership.

If you've already received leadership training or are an experienced leader, consider providing the opportunity to your staff. At all levels, these skills will improve their ability to get results, support the facilities department and support your organization's core business if they have these types of skills in addition to their specialized or technical skills.

Leadership Training

While it isn't always obvious, your organization may have leadership and management training available to you. Check with your boss or HR department and ask how you can access the training. Be sure to bring it up during your quarterly or annual performance review. Many good companies will help you with professional development. Skilled and motivated staff may also be able to access training funds or programs. Take advantage of this commitment to advance your skills and career. Where programs are not available, make sure your manager knows about outside training you could access.

Those who show interest in professional development, especially when they can demonstrate a program's value to the company, are more likely to earn the support of managers. While many still find it easier to support technical training, those who seek to develop their management and leadership skills will find support (and further their own careers) when they show initiative and can demonstrate a link to improved performance on the FM front.

If your company doesn't have internal training programs available, look for programs at local colleges or universities that provide you with leadership training. Approach your managers and HR departments with information about the curriculum, benefits to the company and the cost. If you are investing your own time during evenings or weekends to take the courses, you'll demonstrate your commitment and will have a better chance to get the costs reimbursed. Again, these are skills that will benefit you and your team.

Leadership Books

One easy way to improve your management and leadership skills is to read books on the subject and apply what you learn. Even if you don't see a directly-applicable use for what you read, you will absorb ideas and techniques that eventually you will be able to use.

The books you read should include management-related topics and leadership books. Even if you don't see your current position as a leadership role, the leadership techniques and skills are valuable for any facility manager.

If you feel your learning style depends on the hands-on training that classroom-based courses provide, round out your training with books, which go into much more depth and cover a much broader range of topics.

Consider This

Look for business books that are well-written and offer real-world examples that will have you nodding your head in agreement while you read. Keep in mind that it's unrealistic to expect to absorb everything from a book. Instead, expect to take away a few very specific points. If you use that data effectively to make a difference in your job and improve your career options, the book will have been a success for you.

You can also refer to them whenever you need and they are much less expensive, thereby representing a more efficient investment of time and money. Another advantage is that by nature, they provide self-paced learning that is ideal for the busy facility manager.

While you will find some ideas put forward in the books you read are refreshingly new, you may also use the information to formalize techniques and approaches you already use or are thinking about adopting. The end result is a much broader set of tools at your disposal.

Selecting books to read can be a daunting task. There are literally thousands of books related to management and leadership in print, covering a wide variety of topics.

Your local bookstore will probably have a modest section devoted to management and leadership, and the internet can provide even more options for you to choose from, with the added benefit of "top ten lists,", online reviews and synopsis of the books. Use those tools to make your selection even easier. Then order the book online, or ask your local bookstore to order it for you.

Here are some tips for getting the most from your books, including this one:

- ✓ Buy them and keep them.
- ✓ Keep a highlighter and small pad of post-it-notes with you while you read. Don't be afraid to highlight key information or use post-it notes to mark pages and add your own notes.
- ✓ Re-read interesting or pertinent sections after you have finished the book. This repetition will help you remember important points.
- ✓ Make your own quick notes about key parts of the book for future reference.
- ✓ After reading your books, keep them within reach for inspiration or reference.
- ✓ Don't be in a hurry to finish a book. Maintain an even pace and absorb what you read.
- ✓ Consider using audio books if you have a long commute.

Quick Summary

Key Points

➡ Leadership is required at all levels.

➡ You need to take time from day-to-day activities to focus on professional development, including your long-term leadership skills.

Executive Tips

➡ Leadership isn't about communicating "down" to staff or suppliers. Effective leadership values communcation with staff, colleagues and higher-ups.

➡ Develop your own leadership skills and help your staff develop theirs.

Traps to Avoid

➡ Don't use workload as a reason to not practice your leadership skills.

➡ Don't assume that leadership isn't required for Facility Managers.

5

Facility Managers Don't Have All The Answers.

But you should know where to go to get the answers

"Coming together is a beginning. Keeping together is progress, Working together is success." – Henry Ford

FM is a complex, issues-based role. The reality is that nobody in the industry knows it all, and the best way to be successful is to leverage the knowledge and great ideas of others, including your staff, colleagues, suppliers and customers.

The most successful FM managers realize they can't possibly know everything. They have a broad base of knowledge and an overview of all areas, including how they link together, but rely on experts in specific areas. The ability to know when to tap into other experts and resources, as well as knowing where to go for the information and how to verify and interpret it, are key skills for the FM professional.

While managing by committee never works, a skilled facility manager does seek input from various resources before deciding on a course of action. They recognize that ideas, information and expertise from a wider range of individuals will improve decision making and results. This includes working with your own staff, colleagues in the industry and service providers.

The best way to be successful is to recognize your own limitations and surround yourself with skilled and knowledgeable staff that complement you, not mirror you. This diversity, if you manage it properly, will be a significant driver in your success within your organization and for your career.

Networking

Networking is a valuable way to gain new knowledge and ideas. First, you need to recognize that there are many good ideas you can borrow from around the world, both within your specific sector or facility type and from other facility types. Rather than limiting yourself, extend your reach and learn from other sectors. The reality is that regardless of the organization and facility type, they likely have the same issues you do and over 90% of managing facilities is the same, no matter what type of facility you manage.

Membership in an association and attending association-sponsored conferences are useful ways to network. The skilled manager knows you can also network without leaving your office or taking up too much of your time.

Associations like the International Facility Management Association (IFMA) have online forums where members post questions, ask about resources and provide solutions and ideas based on their experience. This links you with a large number of fellow professionals and gives you access to ideas and solutions you wouldn't otherwise be able to access.

You can also network through the business-based social networking site LinkedIn (www.linkedin.com). It lets you link with others in the industry to provide and receive updates from each other. A valuable networking tool is LinkedIn's Groups. These Groups extend the value of networking by providing an opportunity to ask questions, start a discussion, get input and announce news to group members. There are many facilities and property management related groups including groups associated with some of the major facilities and property management associations. Once you set up your profile, you can upload your current contact list and see who you already know who is a member on LinkedIn and link with them. Your next step should be to go to the Groups section and search for groups related to facilities management. They range from general to specific areas such as corporate real estate, CMMS, maintenance, environment, energy conservation, HVAC, janitorial and more. Finally, be sure to link with me by using the email address at the back of the book.

Getting Value from Teamwork

One compelling example of the value of teamwork comes from an exercise by a company called Human Synergistics. The exercise involved a situation where individuals face a problem and then work as a group to arrive at a solution.

One of their exercises is called the Subarctic Survival Situation®. If surviving the cold doesn't interest you, they have one set in the desert, as well as several others in similarly interesting situations.

In the subarctic exercise, individuals have crash landed in Northern Canada. Each individual has 15 items that were salvaged before the airplane sank and they rank the items individually in order of importance to their survival. The group then works together to collectively rank the same 15 items and both individual and group rankings are scored against rankings from experts.

After the team works together to rank the importance of the 15 items, their collective score, based on a comparison with experts, is calculated. The lower the score, the better they did. Many individuals are surprised to see that the best individual score is typically much worse than the team score. When I did this exercise a long time ago with a group, my individual score was 42. The lowest individual score was only 40 and the average was 49. Working as a group, our score was reduced to only 18. The end result is that participants can see how teamwork improves our ability to analyze important issues.

While fostering teamwork with your team is important, always make sure the exercise is appropriate to the team. Some of your staff may not respond well to, or appreciate, the "touchy feely" exercises favored by some team builders. Others may take issue with exercises they deem childish.

In one example, an HR department put on some customer service training for the field staff. The session and content was developed by head-office with an emphasis on soft issues and fun exercises. The field staff, however, were mostly highly-experienced people in very serious technical roles. The end result was disastrous. First, the information was delivered at such a low-level that participants assumed head office didn't think they knew much about serving the customer. As the exercises were also childish and didn't seem to have a direct connection to the work participants did, the exercise was not a very good match.

The key lesson is that you need to consider the audience. If you don't adapt the lesson to their sensitivities, the initiative won't be successful, no matter how fun and engaging the exercises may be to another group.

Also remember that if your goal is change on-the-job behavior, the exercises must be relevant to what's needed on a particular job. Ideally, the exercises and team sessions will be reinforced by senior management who already walk the talk or support the need for changed behavior and are willing to put new approaches in action. Once again, consistent communication is essential to reinforce the message and the behavior. Without reinforcement and follow-through, change will be superficial and unsustainable, lacking positive impact and potentially even contributing to negative changes.

Leveraging Others

Translating this to the FM professional, it's clear that your success isn't based on what you know, it's based on how well you combine what you know with the expertise and knowledge of those around you. Using this strategy, which is clearly a management / leadership skill that all facility managers need, you will be in a better position to develop solutions and initiatives that improve services, enhance efficiency and reduce total costs for your facilities.

Let's face it, you are only as successful as your team, so if you want to be successful, you need to help your team be successful first. Here are three basic techniques you should use to help them be successful:

1. Hire people who know what they are doing (and know more than you do about their specialty) and give them guidance and support to help them be successful. Insulate them from distractions to the best of your ability and give them the tools and resources they need to do their job. That's the best way for both you and your staff to succeed.

2. Have your staff focus on the things they are good at. Get them support for things they don't do well or give that task to someone else. A sure way for everyone to fail is forcing someone to spend time trying to do

what they aren't good at while the things they are good at go neglected. They'll be happier and more productive.

3. Don't treat everyone the same. We are all different and need different things, are motivated differently, have different strengths, etc. Understand and adapt to your staff to get the best out of them.

Getting Involved with an Associations

Building a career means more than simply doing a good job for your employer. It also means getting involved in associations that represent your industry. These associations can bring a great deal of value to your career and your job, ultimately benefiting your employer at the same time.

Since most associations exist to further the industry and benefit their members, they usually have resources to expand your knowledge in the field beyond the scope and experiences of your current role. This benefits you by introducing you to the skills and issues of a larger team of FM professionals and it benefits your employer every time you bring new ideas and technologies to the work environment of your current job.

Associations make a wealth of information available to their members. These include books, reading lists, research reports, seminars, industry councils, annual conferences and association publications such as newsletters and magazines. In addition, the association gives you many opportunities to network with other professionals and solution providers within your industry. These resources give you a wider perspective on the issues and solutions that impact your profession.

There are three key things that professional association memberships provide for you and your organization.

Your Network

Networking is more important than many facility managers think. If you're not interested in socializing or looking for another job, you don't need to network, right? Wrong. By actively networking with others in your field, the FM professional gets to know the people and technologies he will need to solve future problems and find appropriate (and sometimes highly-specialized) resources. People in a successful professional network often play a mentorship role and can give advice about how they handled something successfully. By expanding the number of people you know and vice versa, you are building a future in FM. Here are a few basic benefits to networking:

- ✓ Making contacts with peers & suppliers.
- ✓ Sharing resources & solutions.
- ✓ Accessing the FM community.
- ✓ Learning about opportunities.

Your Profession

Once you start thinking of FM as a profession more than a job, you realize there are many opportunities to grow and develop your professional qualifications while also benefiting your company. Learning from others through training, conferences and other forms of education, both formal and informal, will increase the status of the profession with others in your company as well. Here some of the benefits to continuous education:

- ✓ Earn professional designations.
- ✓ Advance your career through visibility.
- ✓ Stay current with leading practices.
- ✓ Access professional development training & learning.

Your Facilities

Your role in a company exists to manage the buildings or facilities for your organization. By enhancing your professional status, getting involved, getting a professional designation, accessing training and resources and networking, you can fulfill your role to a higher level and contribute even more to your organization. Here are the main benefits to developing your professional involvement in the industry:

- ✓ Ensuring a productive environment.
- ✓ Taking care of assets.
- ✓ Maintaining standards.
- ✓ Finding Solutions to Problems.

Deciding which association is the best fit for your current role and your career aspirations is important. There are a variety of associations that cater to similar professions and each one has a particular emphasis or focus. Often, membership in more than one association is ideal, since you are exposed to a broader range of fellow professionals, resources, industry experts and experiences. Some associations also have industry-recognized certification or designation programs that help demonstrate your base of knowledge to current and future employers.

While it may be tempting to only join an association that focuses specifically on your type of facility, such as education, recreation, government, religious, hospital, commercial, etc., this will narrow the experiences and expertise at your disposal.

While each facility type has its own unique requirements and issues, the majority of what facility and property managers do is common across all building-use types and opening yourself to other broader associations, through membership or professional development programs, will broaden the resources and solutions you bring to your own work environment and resume.

To optimize an association membership, do more than sign up and pay your dues. Resolve to be an active member by becoming involved in the association as a volunteer in some capacity.

Being involved in the association itself can be quite rewarding, whether you hold a formal position or become part of a committee. Committees usually cover a wide range of functions, provide lots of opportunities and certainly welcome volunteers. By volunteering for a committee, you will get exposure to the association, increase your networking opportunities and give something back to the association. Committee work, which often focuses on a certain issue or event, can help you decide whether you want to pursue a formal position in the association.

Why Become a Member?

Regardless of where you are in your career, you will benefit from becoming a member in a professional association. It will expose you to others who can help you find resources, solve problems, share successes, support initiatives and open career paths. You can also share your experience and skills with others to help them implement ideas and solutions that improve facilities.

If you already oversee the entire FM group within your organization or you've become the senior resource in one of the many specialties in FM, you can still benefit from the networking and educational resources and learn about other resources you may want to call upon or hire in the future. You also have a great opportunity to share your experience with others who are just starting out or building their career in the profession. Participation in a professional organization allows you to:

- ✓ Share your expertise in your industry and solidify your reputation.
- ✓ Learn about opportunities where you can make a difference.
- ✓ Network to discover resources you can bring into your organization.
- ✓ Find out about solutions and leading practices to get results for your organization.
- ✓ Solidify your credibility by contributing to the industry and gaining certification.

You may have a number of years experience in the industry and be gradually developing your experience and making your mark in the industry. Involvement with an association will be very valuable to your career as you move into different roles or take on more scope. This is where you can:

- ✓ Connect with colleagues to expand your visibility.
- ✓ Contribute to the industry and build your reputation.
- ✓ Expand and increase your knowledge with access to research and specialized training.
- ✓ Learn about solutions you can use directly from industry suppliers in a non-sales environment.
- ✓ Build your credibility with industry-recognized designations.

If you are just starting your career, whether you've finished a formal program in school or have moved into it from a different role in the company, you will benefit by learning even more from others on a very practical level.

   ✓ Connect with established facility managers.

   ✓ Find out about resources, tools and solutions.

   ✓ Network with industry leaders for future career opportunities.

   ✓ Learn how to sell your profession and your benefits to the organization.

   ✓ Begin the process to get your industry-recognized designation.

What's the Business Case?

Unfortunately, many facility managers don't get much support from their organizations to join associations or even to attend training and conferences. This is especially true in organizations where facility and property management are not recognized as a profession with strategic importance to an organization. While they may well recognize professionals in many other fields and support their memberships and ongoing certification requirements, FM has not attained this same level of professional recognition.

That lack of recognition is one of the reasons it makes sense for FM professionals to get involved with FM organizations. When you demonstrate your commitment to continual FM improvement, you make a strategic business case for why your employer should support your membership costs, the costs associated with attending local events and seminars and the cost of the time you will need to invest in being involved in the organization. Here are a few points you can use to support your membership and ongoing involvement:

   ✓ You will learn about leading practices that drive improvement and reduce costs for your employer through networking with other professionals.

   ✓ You will access professional development to ensure your career and organization aren't left behind.

   ✓ You will access research, benchmarking, publications and other resources to guide initiatives that improve service and save costs.

   ✓ You will stay current on the hot topics that impact your organization, such as pandemics, health & safety, environmental issues, energy conservation, green power and more.

A list of mostly national and international associations is included in the *Reference* section at the end of this book. Many associations have regional or local chapters and there are also many good associations that are only regionally or locally focused. To find out about them, ask others in your network.

Attend Trade Shows and Conferences

Attending facility or property management-related trade shows and conferences is a great way to keep up with the industry, network with colleagues and discover solutions and products that will benefit your company. Sometimes, you will find solutions to facilities problems you didn't know you had.

Some are free to attend if you register in advance, with a pay-as-you-go approach for individual seminars. Others have a conference fee that enables you to attend all the educational sessions and many events.

Trade shows and conferences give you access to educational sessions, many of which apply towards maintenance credits for professional designations. You also get to look, touch and feel new and improved products and to talk to the sales folks.

There are general property and facility management conferences as well annual conferences that are part of national or international associations.

To avoid unwelcome sales calls, collect the vendor's information but don't give them your card or let them scan your badge. Do take the opportunity to talk to sales people, however. You will get insight into your industry while you hear about their product or service but most won't use a hard sales pitch at these kinds of events. To get even more value, ask questions about issues that relate to their company's expertise.

Review the program to watch for free seminars on the trade floor and to make note of interesting keynote speakers. Both can provide important information and motivation to help you in your job. Also look beyond the traditional vendors for those offering innovative services and solutions. You may find a solution to a problem you currently have, or make a valuable contact for information you'll need down the road.

Think of conferences and tradeshows as professional development and an investment in your career. If a trade show or conference is local, you don't have much reason not to go. If they are out-of-town or have a steep registration fee, you need to make the case to your boss.

For links to associations, many of whom hold trade shows and conferences and post links to events staged by related organizations, check out the *References* section at the end of the book

Consider This

Make your own professional development a career priority. If you're switching jobs, negotiate association membership fees as well as conference or tradeshow fees and attendance costs into your employment agreement.

What's the Business Case

While some organizations are more enlightened about the need to attend professional conferences, others misunderstand the value by defining the request only in terms of fiscal expense or the days out of the office. There are a few things you can do to build your business case and convince your organization.

To make the case for attending a conference or other educational event, you need to put it in terms of the benefits to your organization and your function in managing facilities. The information must be presented as a working trip where you get industry information, education and solutions to bring back and benefit your organization immediately or down the road.

The money and time you spend must be shown to be reasonable in the overall context of your role. Moreover, you must make the case that the time out of the office is productive and that there are clear benefits for you to attend. Here are a few points you can use:

- ✓ Identify specific seminars that are directly applicable to your role and issues you are currently facing. Review how they will help you deliver better service to your organization.
- ✓ List some of the key vendors and exhibitors who have products or technical solutions that could be a benefit. Highlight opportunities to

improve efficiency, reduce risk and lower costs. Identify what and how you are going to learn from the vendor.

✓ Pick specific issues you want to benchmark to see where you can improve. Through networking, seminars or vendors, you will be able to explore those issues and understand where your organization is relative to leading practices.

✓ Outline how you will bring what you learn back to your own operation. Share that knowledge through a report you will prepare, or a seminar you will deliver to your staff using the material and information you collected at the conference.

If you've been networking, check to see who else is attending. Use that fact to support your need to attend and the fact that other organizations see the value. If it's a large conference, get an idea of the numbers of attendees. Attendance shows that it's a well-respected conference and makes the case that your attendance keeps your organization at the forefront of FM practices and knowledge.

Learn from Industry Magazines

It's not always easy to find the time to read magazines, but the reality is that you don't have to read them from cover-to-cover. Magazines are an excellent source of information and leading practices you can use. Subscribing to a magazine and sharing it (or particular articles) with your staff or colleagues is a productive way to gain from the knowledge of other FM experts.

Some magazines are free for qualified industry professionals and others have a subscription fee. The cost of an annual subscription is very minor when you compare it to other professional development costs, including training seminars, for instance.

Keep back issues of these magazines in a file. This builds an office reference library you can use for guidance as new issues arise. The key is to be selective in your reading and not be afraid to pass over other articles that aren't relevant.

You could also have an assistant file articles about specific topics in a binder for future reference.

Instead of getting several of the same magazines in your group, get only one and then circulate it. Different articles will interest different individuals with different roles.

Consider This

If you don't have the time to read the whole magazine, scan it and choose one or two articles that are relevant to your position or your issues. Then schedule the time to read those articles over the next month. This is time well spent and focusing on particular articles ensures you will learn something specific that benefits you or your organization.

A comprehensive listing of magazines, many with online content, is included in the *Reference* section at the end of this book.

Learn from the FM Outsourcing Industry

FM outsourcing companies manage a huge amount of real estate on behalf of their customer Introduction of the largest corporations, government and institutions. Th space or space management is increasing, so they must be doing something righ – Preparation

Their success Regulation's influence that are hard to reproduce in sn on Environment / Climate ou can't learn from an outsourcing Change ng. Here's a review of some key pra on to improve your service delivery,

Performance Management

Outsourcing con on the client's priorities and resources. An effective performance fra which can also be applied to use delivery or subcontracted ser

First, establish your corporation's primary objectives and design performance measurements (Key Performance Indicators) to support those objectives. Translate these to the activities and services you deliver and establish measures, targets, reports and review processes. Use the results to spot trends or missed performance and implement changes to address problems with staff or subcontractors. Build these measures into your next round of procurement.

Quality Assurance (QA)

While some outsourcing companies are ISO certified, you don't need certification to apply the principles of QA to your internal services or subcontractors. Start by learning the basis of QA, which includes documenting processes and procedures, identifying inputs and outputs, key process elements, tracking and reporting, adherence to procedures and auditing. Apply these principles to your staff and subcontractors for improved results.

QA itself doesn't ensure you are doing the right things, but once you establish leading practices, it ensures they are followed. The best QA implementations enable innovation by your staff and promote continuous improvement of your processes.

Customer Service and Satisfaction

Another benefit to outsourcing involves new and stronger supplier/customer relationships to replace an internal culture not usually focused on customer satisfaction. The satisfaction of internal business units and occupants is important to ensure they are efficiently and effectively contributing to your company's core business.

To change internal culture, implement change management with your staff. Educate them on the importance and reasons for customer satisfaction, train them in techniques, provide them with tools and processes to deal with customer issues and measure customer satisfaction results with the purpose of introducing improvements. Maintain this focus as a constant initiative to ensure it won't fade away.

Policies and Procedures

Outsourcing companies use policies and procedures to reduce management and administrative costs while focusing on higher-value initiatives. This isn't simply about documenting what you do, it's assessing all aspects of the service delivery and developing procedures, tools and even systems that support efficiency, consistency and quality.

Since outsourcers operate large portfolios, this is critical to their success. To achieve these benefits, look closely at what you do and make changes, implement processes, add tools and train your staff.

Systems

Outsourcing firms have an economy of scale you can't match. But you can prioritize and address key systems for more effective management of your services and assets. Implement a single solution or individual modules for work order tracking, space management, lease administration, preventive maintenance, capital planning, etc. Research implementation and ongoing maintenance costs and then establish priorities to keep costs down. Web-based applications, reducing IT support and hardware costs, may be one solution.

Centralized Services / Specialized Expertise

Outsourcing companies have the volume for centralized services and expertise. They hire subject matter experts who provide assistance and guidance to field staff who can then focus on their direct service delivery requirements. This includes energy, environment, project delivery, systems, call centers, quality assurance, compliance and health and safety, for instance. Your corporation may have expertise in some areas, but they are usually focused on the core business, not FM-related issues and requirements.

Apply the principles creatively. For small organizations, identify existing individuals with the right background or aptitude and train them in the specialty. Keep them current and backfill a portion of their existing responsibilities. Tap into existing specialty consultants or companies with standing offers and retainers or join forces with colleagues at other organizations to share specialized expertise.

Strategic procurement

Saving money and improving services through procurement is something almost any organization can do. Strategically procure services in larger volume packages to benefit from economies of scale. Bundle different services together to increase the volume in combinations the market will respond to.

This saves resources needed to procure and manage the contracts while reducing your provider's costs, which are passed on to you. You also get more consistency and improved services when combined with performance management, QA and effective contract management.

Quick Summary

Key Points	➡ Build and lead a *team* of experts. Teamwork can get better results for you and your organization
	➡ Join FM associations and subscribe to FM-related publications that will benefit your organization and aid your professional development.
	➡ Learn and implement some of the practices that make outsourcing companies so efficient and effective.
Executive Tips	➡ Rely on your team, suppliers and resources to make better decisions and solve problems.
	➡ Negotiate professional memberships and conference/tradeshow attendance into your job description.
	➡ Learn and implement some of the practices that make outsourcing companies so efficient and effective.
Traps to Avoid	➡ Not admitting you don't know something is risky. You aren't expected to know everything there is to know.
	➡ Doing things like you have always done them.

Your Strategic Plan

Based on this section, what strategic initiatives do you plan to implement that will help you manage your assets better and when do you expect to accomplish them?

What are you going to do?	When

Notes

_____

_____

_____

_____

_____

_____

_____

_____

_____

_____

_____

_____

Strategies, approaches
and leading practices

Strategic Management

Introduction

If you don't have a strategy for what you do, you are probably just fighting fires and keeping the status quo.

Develop a strategy for the next year at least, and even for the next few years. It doesn't need to be a 100-page document. The trick is to keep it simple, even a few pages to start. Focus on what's important to your organization's success. Promote it to your leadership and get buy-in based on improved results.

Think into the corners to discover things you can do to improve results. Eliminate filters and abandon the "not invented here" or "it's the way we've always done it" attitude from your team. Look outside your organization to understand how others are doing it.

Improve your visibility. You may be considered a cost centre, so turn that around and promote yourself as a saving centre. You can reduce costs, whether it's operation costs, project costs or lease/portfolio costs. Align those initiatives with the important sustainability issues to get attention.

Strategic Planning

Develop Strategic Plans for improvement

"Plans are of little importance, but planning is essential."
– Sir Winston Churchill

Strategic Planning is simply having a goal and thinking ahead about how to achieve it. While day-to-operations are paramount, strategic planning enables you to be more successful in the long run.

Long-term success, both for your organization and your career, depends on strategic planning that moves your department forward along with key issues that enable you to provide an effective and efficient environment for occupants, tenants and even production equipment. Strategic plans are the tool you need to use to develop, sell and subsequently implement your initiatives.

Strategic plans generally consist of a goal or objective along with the main activities and requirements to achieve that objective. The plans are usually developed to proactively make changes that improve results and reduce costs through an organized and goal-driven, planned approach. The plans may guide your entire department, target a key responsibility, or focus on a specific issue or element of your role.

Consider This

Strategic planning works. If you're not in a position to implement a department-wide plan, look at ways to do just one part of it better. Design a plan of action, put it in place-and take credit for its success.

There are some very important reasons for putting in the time and effort to develop strategic plans for your department and your responsibilities. These include the following. A plan:

- ✓ Clearly identifies your goals and objectives and how they align with your organization.
- ✓ Requires you to examine the issues, hurdles and resources you have to deal with.
- ✓ Helps you determine how to solve the issues and hurdles.
- ✓ Provides a commmunication tool for you to use with your stakeholders.
- ✓ Establishes the basis for your implementation plan or plans.

What is Strategic Planning?

As noted in the introduction, a strategic plan is a tool you use to develop, sell and implement your initiatives. But don't get hung up on the word "strategic," or to think the plan needs to be long, detailed and complicated to be effective.

It also doesn't need to be a "brick" in terms of how it impacts your job responsibilities and your work environment. In fact, you are more likely to develop and implement your strategic plan if you keep it to a manageable size and focus on specific things instead of creating a plan that attempts to cover everything at once. When it comes to strategic plans, focus is more important than breadth. Indeed, a one-page document that provides guidance and takes you in the direction you need to move to achieve a specific goal is an effective strategic plan.

Of course, a strategic plan can be much longer and more detailed, providing context, historical perspective, details and evidence that supports your plan. It can even include elements like benchmark data or cost analysis data that is essential to form part of a business case. If that's the route you take, try to keep this background material separate from the plan itself. In other words, don't let your data and argument get in the way of showing why your plan will be effective and efficient to implement. This tendency to think that a long, detailed strategic plan is required is based in the fact that some organizations seem to value volume over substance. That said, strategic plans that require a long and tedious process to develop may never see the light of day.

Getting Started

To develop a strategic plan and keep it manageable, keep asking:

- ✓ Where
- ✓ Why?
- ✓ What?
- ✓ When?

Then, after you've answered these questions, your implementation plan will deal with the more detailed question:

- ✓ How?

If it makes sense to develop a detailed strategic plan that can be used to support a business case for specific innovations, remember to keep the "implementation" side of the plan separate. Your strategic plan provides direction and rationale, your implementation plan will extend that plan into the activities and steps you take to make it happen. When you keep these separate, your strategic plans will be more manageable (and your implementation plans more specific).

Link your Strategic Plan to your Organization's own Goals & Plans

Your strategic plan should be closely linked with your own organization's plans, since your department exists to support their core business, whether you are a commercial property manager, residential manager, institutional organization, non-profit, corporate or government. Each of these types of organizations has a reason for existing and you are there to support them. With a strong link to their strategic planning and goals, you are also more likely to get support for your own related initiatives.

Part of your role is to recognize issues and factors that will influence the facilities and real estate needs of your organization and anticipate the changes needed to meet them.

Don't spend too much time trying to decide what a short-, medium- or long-range strategic plan is. You should focus instead on the timeframe that makes sense to you and your organization. Generally speaking, the FM strategic plan needs to tie into the organization's overall strategic plan. That said, your implementation timeframe will often be relatively short. For example, you and your organization may both value energy efficiency in the long-term, but your department may have specific targets for the next six months. As always, ask your clients what their needs are before you start your strategic plan.

According to IFMA's latest Facility Management Forecast, the top five strategic issues for FM are:

1. Linking facility management to strategy.

2. Emergency preparedness.

3. Change management.

4. Sustainability.

5. Emerging technology.

Since the top issue in the list is about linking FM to strategy (your organization's strategy), it's clear that developing your facilities' strategic plans are important, but you can't do them independently. FM always exists within a larger organization. If you want others to recognize FM's importance, you must always value FM as part of the whole.

How does Strategy Differ from Implementation?

The difference between a strategic plan and an implementation/delivery plan is all in the details.

Think of the strategic plan is your itinerary and your implementation plan as your roadmap, complete with all the logistical data and resources necessary to get you to your destination. Whereas the strategic plan says where you are and where you're headed, the implementation plan covers everything from route to fuel, food and rest stops along the way.

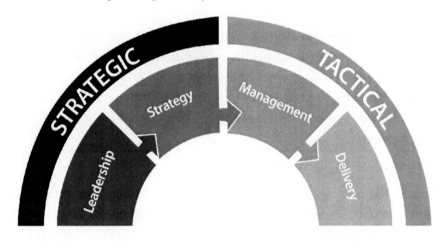

In the FM environment, your strategic plan may say that in order to implement a new FM software system, you need to gain approval for purchasing the system and for adding a resource to manage it. Your strategic plan may also talk about the need to make some organizational changes in order to accommodate the new system. The implementation plan expands on the strategic plan and provides the details necessary to actually execute each of those strategic steps.

Why Strategic Planning Benefits FM

While the value of strategic planning is not in dispute, some organizations only apply the principles of strategic planning to "problems" like space occupancy requirements.

That's unfortunate. But when faced with day-to-day FM issues and pressures, many facility managers won't spend time on something that provides a future benefit. Successful facility managers must challenge the idea that strategic planning is nonproductive. In fact, successful facility managers take the time to sit down and plan all areas of their responsibilities. While they may get a great deal of satisfaction from the hands-on responsibilities of handling day-to-day issues and problems, they must learn to recognize strategic planning as a way to add value to their role within the larger organization. Anything less short changes your organization and your career.

Consider This

As discussed in the section *Leadership for Facility Managers*, facility managers must take a leadership approach to their roles–especially if they want to be seen as leaders in the organization they serve. When you develop strategic plans, you exercise management and leadership skills. A plan's success is your success.

Ultimately, the time spent on strategic plans will be the most productive time you ever spend because it will have a positive impact on the future results you achieve and the increase the benefits you provide your organization as a steward of the physical environment.

Strategic Planning as Investment

All organizations are dealing with powerful changes such as globalization, economic pressures, environmental issues, diverse workforces and aging infrastructure. When you make strategic planning an FM priority, you invest in your FM environment and career by giving yourself and the organization you serve a chance to get ahead of the issues.

The increasingly complex role of the facility manager requires that kind of planning more than ever, and to promote the value of the profession, you need to compete with your non-facilities colleagues to make sure that your value to your organization is recognized.

It's likely that your colleagues in other departments within your organization have strategic plans related to their department or their responsibilities. For you to compete with them for attention and resources to achieve your overall goals, you need to have a documented approach to achieving those goals so you can communicate your plans and secure the resources you need.

A strategic plan is also an excellent opportunity to help focus you and your team on longer-range initiatives and ensure that while you go about your day-to-day activities, you are always working towards the ultimate goal. It's a way to help you switch from being only reactive to also being proactive while providing key benefits such as:

- ✓ Leadership and direction for your staff.
- ✓ Improved processes and systems.
- ✓ Forward-looking initiatives.
- ✓ Reduce fire fighting and improve prevention.

I've already talked about bringing the FM profession's profile to a higher level within your organization. Strategic planning is one of the steps you can take to promote your value and demonstrate that FM is a profession, not just a job. In a way, it's about demonstrating the following:

- ✓ Facility management isn't just about dealing with day-to-day occupancy issues.
- ✓ Space use and cost are important drivers to the organization.
- ✓ Your needs for funding, resources and support are just as valid as other departments needs.
- ✓ With the right tools, you can save costs or mitigate expenses for the company.

Choose the issues you need to deal with based on your own benchmarking or by using the Health Check exercises described later in this section. Then, using your goals and objectives, tightly linked with your organization's goals to establish a plan for the issues, focus first on the ones with the highest risk and/or highest benefit. If you've been networking with other facility managers, attending conferences and learning from related magazines, you may have discovered initiatives, solutions and other areas where you are lagging behind. Those are good areas around which to develop a plan.

When deciding what to focus on, consider the following five areas, which cross most of your functional responsibilities:

- ✓ Assets (capital, buildings, furniture, etc.)
- ✓ Occupancy (space utilization and moves)
- ✓ Services (work orders, conference rooms, mail, furniture, etc.)
- ✓ Systems (processes or software to improve results)
- ✓ People (organization, staffing, etc.).

As mentioned, strategic plans can be developed for highly-specific issues or for your overall department. Here are a few of the more common areas where strategic plans are developed:

- ✓ Implementing a new FM system to gather information, improve service delivery processes and track results.
- ✓ Making organizational changes to address your organization's growth or changes and to improve results.
- ✓ Developing space use/leasing plans to consolidate and reduce space, eliminate leases and save costs.
- ✓ Developing an overall procurement approach to consolidate contracts or bundle services for cost savings and improved service management.
- ✓ Developing a capital plan for next year's budget process.
- ✓ Implementing energy management or envrionmental conservation related initiatives.
- ✓ Implementing new processes or policies.

Know what Makes a Strategic Plan Work

We've all heard about strategic plans that failed. They were too big, too small, too expensive or too cheap to make a difference. Push the excuses aside and aim to succeed. Most strategic plans fail because of poor implementation. That means you can improve your chance of success by paying attention to the links between strategy and implementation.

The key is to target success and build on that success for each new initiative. Don't bite off too much or try to be too ambitious. Consider these tips when you begin to develop your plans:

- ✓ Take your time and keep it manageable.
- ✓ Link your plan to your company's strategy.
- ✓ Justify your initiative and get buy-in and support.
- ✓ Don't re-invent, rebuild.
- ✓ Go slow, manage change.
- ✓ Set aside time from your operational responsibilities to make it happen.

To develop your strategic plan, you need information, analysis, research and involvement from others. It may be the only way you know where you should be going. One of the best ways to start is to develop your Mission, Vision and Values (MVV) statement. MVV statements will help drive individual goals and objectives. Their development also helps you make good use of your own staff to identify areas, concerns and opportunities to make changes that will benefit your department.

Hold planning sessions to get everyone's input. Make sure these sessions are well structured and are designed to result in recommendations and agreement about the directions you should take. Don't just involve your direct reports or senior staff–everyone in your organization can contribute.

Conduct a benchmarking exercise to decide where you should focus attention and resist the temptation to only use high-level numbers or to target areas with widespread agreement. While benchmark data will point you in the right direction, you should engage your colleagues and your network to learn what others are doing. Be prepared to compare your practices, resources, tools and operational approaches directly to understand where you should improve.

Combine this with the *Conducting a Health Check* section that follows to focus on specific areas and to help you pinpoint the goals you put in place and develop the strategic plans that will help you achieve them.

When you've collected enough information and know what your goal or goals are, it's time to start the development of your plan. Don't make it into a business case. It should simply be your plan. You can develop your business case to sell the plan after you've established your plan. By keeping them separate, you'll be more likely to succeed.

Start by keeping it very simple and documenting it using this 3-Step Strategic Planning Tool:

The 3- Step Strategic Planning Tool

Most strategic plans never get written or aren't followed because they are too involved and complex. Keep them simple and use these three basic steps as your core approach:

Steps	Planning Notes
What is your goal?	
Why do you need to do it?	
What are the things you need to do to achieve your goal	

By following the three steps above and writing them down, you will have the outline of your strategic plan.

Once your outline is complete, you can expand the information where needed to assure approvals and communication. That will also help you develop your implementation plan.

Part of the process in writing a strategic plan involves identifying the options you have to achieve your goals. With each option identified, you can better quantify the timelines, costs and resources involved in each option and settle on the best course of action.

Consider This

There will be times when it looks like there is only one real option. Always explore the alternatives and include them in your business case for implementing a chosen option in your strategic plan. This shows your organization that you've considered options. It also provides a valuable contrast between your choice and the alternatives. Never assume that others will give you the benefit of the doubt–make your own case convincingly.

Implementing Your Strategic Plan

Once you have established your strategic plan using the three-step process and then expanded it as necessary, you need to develop your implementation plan. By making this a separate endeavor, you can focus on your strategy without letting implementation issues negatively influence your strategic plans. If, down the road, it turns out that your strategy cannot be implemented, use that knowledge to create Plan B. But don't settle for Plan B in the first place.

The implementation phase includes getting approval and resources and defining the steps you need to take to achieve your strategic objective. Often, the implementation plan is iterative. That is, you come up with a plan, then verify it with others involved before adjusting it based on their input.

Start your implementation plan using this simple planning tool:

5-Step Implementation Plan

Use this form to start your implementation planning and expand as necessary once you've documented the key elements of your plan.

Planning	Main Points
What are the roadblocks	
How can you overcome the roadblocks?	
What resources do you need?	
What are your timelines?	
How can you get approval?	
What are the main steps to implement your strategic plan?	

Why Strategic Plans Fail

Strategic plans often fail. Sometimes they're never actually written and other times they're so complex and ambitious that it's impossible to implement successfully. That's why you should develop simple plans that focus on specific items you can successfully implement one by one. To keep your implementation plan on track, you can follow some simple advice. First and foremost, split a department-wide or highly-detailed plan into separate plans that you can individually implement to achieve the overall goals.

Some of the other main reasons for failure include:

- ✓ No support
- ✓ Lack of involvement by stakeholders
- ✓ Poor processes
- ✓ Wrong focus
- ✓ Lack of resources
- ✓ Ineffective implementation.

Selling your Strategic Plan

Your strategic plan won't sell itself, no matter how compelling it is to you. Your supervisors often don't have a facilities background and don't have the same objectives as you do, even though your objectives may be supporting your overall organization.

To get approval for implementation, actively sell it by including the resources, budget and internal support you need to show it will work.

Use some of the approaches identified in the *Communicating to Influence* section to foster internal support, establish the drivers that will support your initiative and then develop a business case as described later in this book to sell your strategic plan. Keep your strategic plan and the business case separate.

If you can't quite sell your full strategic plan, instead of the final destination, select some major milestones or initiatives that can be used as stepping stones towards your ultimate plan. Here is an example of how you would structure your overall plan:

Itinerary (Strategic Plans)	Road Map (Implementation)
6 months Goals	Implementation Details
12 Months Goals	Implementation Details
24 Months Goals	Implementation Details

By doing things incrementally, you can often get approvals for each of the incremental changes easier than trying to get approval for your ultimate destination. With the interim steps approved, implemented and successful, it will be easier for you to get approval for the rest of your plan.

Quick Summary

Key Points
- ➡ Keep your strategic plans focused, short and concise.
- ➡ Strategic plans will help you switch from reactive to proactive.

Executive Tips
- ➡ Link your strategic plan to your organization's goals and plans.
- ➡ Take time from your operational responsibilities.

Traps to Avoid
- ➡ Don't re-invent the wheel.
- ➡ Don't make it too comprehensive or complex.
- ➡ Don't confuse your implementation plan with your strategic plan.

7

Developing Mission, Vision & Value Statements

Start your strategic planning while providing direction and guidance to your staff.

"A Vision is something to be pursued;
A Mission is something to be accomplished."

Mission, Vision and Value (MVV) statements can be a powerful tool to provide guidance and direction to your organization if they are carefully developed and follow some basic concepts.

MVV Statements can be used to motivate staff, guide decisions and frame your strategic plans. They should be linked to your organization's MVV and serve as a tool for internal use by you and your staff, not as a message to the rest of your organization.

Developing your own MVV will take some time and effort, but if you integrate it into your overall strategic planning and management processes, it will help you get better results.

While some facilities-specific MVV samples are provided later in this section, we use a more generic example to demonstrate a good approach to the importance of MVV statements.

What is a Mission Statement?

A mission statement is concrete and tangible. It inspires and focuses efforts towards a single purpose.

It describes **what** you do, **who** you do it for and **why** you do it. Basically, it sums up why the organization exists.

Why have one?

The mission statement guides everyone in their day-to-day activities and keeps the goals front and centre for decision making and initiatives.

Example: *BizAir improves the productivity of business customers by getting them to their destination on-time while they enjoy amenities that let them get work done while flying.*

What is a Vision Statement?

A vision statement illustrates the future of the organization or the ultimate goals of the Mission. It defines **what** will happen as a result of your Mission.

The vision statement focuses on tomorrow. It is inspirational, timeless and provides clear decision-making criteria.

Why have one?

The vision statement tells you where you should be heading and what the outcome of your mission should be. It will inspire while guiding long-term decisions.

Example: | *BizAir and its people will be regarded as the best and most sought after business airline in North America.*

What is a Value Statement?

A value statement identifies the beliefs and behaviors that are reflected in all activities. It also defines how you carry out the mission.

The value statement can be a short paragraph accompanied by a list of values.

Why have one?

Stating your values provides more guidance for decision making and day-to-day work activities. These statements set the standard and expectations for everyone in the organization.

Example: | *BizAir cares about our customers and our people. We have values that attract and retain customers to our airline and employees to our business. Our values are:*

> *Integrity: Practices that are fair and transparent.*
>
> *Responsiveness: Customers and employees are paramount.*
>
> *Efficiency: Increase value and lower costs.*
>
> *Fun : Our employees want to come to work.*

What are good MVV statements?

MVV statements are not something you memorize and repeat by rote. They must be so meaningful that you can describe it easily without repeating it word for word. An MVV presents a statement that is:

- ✓ Clear and un-ambiguous
- ✓ Paints a vivid picture
- ✓ Realistic and concrete
- ✓ Short and to the point
- ✓ Easily interpreted and acted upon.

Developing MVV Statements

MVV statements should be developed with involvement from your staff and other stakeholders. The best way to gain understanding and buy-in is through involvement.

Involve your Staff

Conduct a session with your staff about the FM department's mission, vision and values and then combine the key elements of those sessions into short, focused statements. If you have a large number of staff, split them up and do several sessions with various groups, mixing staff from different groups or shifts as necessary. Include management and non-management in your sessions, but hold a separate session for senior management personnel or include them in groups where their own direct reports aren't present to facilitate their full involvement. Understand that staff may be more reserved and self-conscious if their supervisors are present.

Take them through a series of questions that gather key information and their thoughts on issues that are relevant to your FM mission, vision and values.

The following exercise includes a list of questions that will solicit staff contribution and provide you with material you can use for the final statements. Use this as presented, or augment as necessary.

Document all the answers on a pad board and if necessary, prioritize or group answers to make the information more manageable, particularly if you hold more than one session.

Mission Statement

These questions will help you develop your mission statement:

What are the key phrases, words and themes from our organization's mission statement?	While you are developing your mission statements specifically for your facilities responsibilities, you should tie into your organization's statements if possible – after all, you are supporting them in their mission.
What do we actually do?	When you ask this question, try to get at the root of the services you deliver. Simply listing things like maintenance, janitorial, grounds, projects and work orders for instance, isn't enough.
Who are our customers?	While it may seem obvious, often it is more complex and each customer or stakeholder has different needs. This may need to be reflected in your statements.
Why is it important to our customers?	This is where you try to understand why what you do matters to your customers. How does it help them achieve their own objectives? How does failure on your part to deliver impact them?
Words, Phrases & Themes	Ask them to identify words, phrases and themes that should be part of the mission statement. One way is to simply go around the group and ask everyone to say what they feel should be in the mission statement.
Finish this sentence : "Our mission is to..."	Finally, ask the group to finish this sentence. This could be a first draft or concept you will use for the final mission statement. Give them 10 or 15 minutes to write something down, then ask each one in the group to share what they wrote. Collect the phrases at the end.

Vision Statement

These questions will help you develop your vision statement:

What are the key phrases, words and themes from our organization's vision statement?	Like with the Mission statement, you should tie into your organization's statements if possible since you're supporting them in their mission.
How do you want to be seen by others?	By discussing how you want to be seen by others and defining how you want to be perceived, it will help you develop your mission statement.
What is the ultimate goal of the department?	Since a vision statement is about an ultimate objective, asking this question specifically about your department separately from your organization will help you understand your vision.
Where do you think the department should be in 10 years or more	This is another way to understand your goals so you can develop them into a vision statement. It makes it more concrete for your team.
Words, Phrases & Themes	Ask them to identify words, phrases and themes that should be part of the vision statement, similar to what you did for the mission statement.
Finish this sentence: "Our vision is..."	Similar to the mission statement exercise, ask the group to finish this sentence.

Value Statement

These questions will help you develop your value statement:

What are our department's values?	Ask them to identify values, usually single words, that they feel should be formally identified as your department's values. It's important to determine whether these are values they feel currently exist, or that need to be achieved. Give them some time to write down the values and then go around the group to write them down. Identify how often each one is listed.

If your group is having a hard time listing values, you can throw out some of these to start the process and give them examples they can relate to.

- o Accountability
- o Commitment
- o Competence
- o Consistency
- o Continuous Learning
- o Efficiency
- o Generosity
- o Independence
- o Innovation
- o Integrity
- o Leadership
- o Perseverance
- o Quality
- o Respect
- o Responsibility
- o Responsiveness
- o Teamwork
- o Tolerance
- o Trust

Involve your Stakeholders

The MVV statements you develop for your FM department should be used internally to guide your staff. But you do need input from your stakeholders, whether they are customers or occupants. This will add to the information you gather from your own team and provide additional perspective about your services, what they mean in your organization and what matters most. This gives you information that will shape your MVV statements.

Depending on your organization, you can do this one-on-one with your key stakeholders, with a facilitated session or through a simple survey. Either way, here are some questions you should get answers to:

For you to be successful, what do you need from the FM Department? Please rank them for us.

Service Quality	1	2	3	4
Quick Service				
Flexibility				
Additional Services				
Low Cost				
Other (enter other item)				

What Values do you currently see in the FM Department and how important are they?

Values	1	2	3	4
Professionalism				
Integrity				
Quality				
Reliability				
Respectful of Others				
Responsiveness				
Accountability				
Consistency				
Innovation				
Teamwork (with other departments)				
Other (enter other item)				

What additional values do you believe the FM Department should adhere to?

If you were to prioritize the responsibilities of the Facilities Department, what would be the relative importance of each one?

Responsibilities	1	2	3	4
Grounds (landscaping & snow removal)				
Maintenance (plumbing, electrical, walls, etc.)				
Renovations (office relocations and remodeling, built-in cabinets, walls, etc.)				
Custodial				
Miscellaneous requests (keys, signs, electrical outlets, painting, etc.)				
Other (enter other items)				

Please indicate why the services provided by the Facility Management Department are important to you specifically (leave space for text).

Case Study Example:

Brock University, St. Catharines, Ontario, Canada

In addition to changing the name of their department from "Plant Services" to "Facilities Management" to evolve the department as part of a customer service initiative into a more responsible, accountable and responsible stakeholder, Brock University developed MVV statements as part of its strategic planning process.

They involved all their staff from senior managers to custodial workers to create statements that were meaningful to them instead of developing them using a top-down process. They also gathered input from senior decision makers within the university and linked it to the MVV of the overall institution where possible.

In addition to displaying it on their website, they developed a folded card with the MVV statements on them so they could be distributed to their staff.

Here is the front and back of the card:

Vision

Our Vision is to be a leading professional Facilities Management team that is widely recognized for the creation and maintenance of exceptional and innovative learning environments.

Brock
University

FACILITIES MANAGEMENT

Mission

Our Mission is to provide a safe, clean, productive and well-maintained physical environment for the University community by planning and delivering professional services that are sustainable and supportive of Academic excellence, now and into the future.

Facilities Management Values

Respect To respect individual personal and professional needs by encouraging communication and an understanding of each others' needs.

Integrity To use ethical behavior, transparency and fairness in all of our dealings.

Excellence To strive for quality and excellence throughout our activities and in the delivery of our services.

Accountability To be responsible for the quality, results, professionalism, and costs of the services that we provide.

Cooperation To use teamwork within the Facilities Management Department and cooperation with stakeholders in order to work together for mutual benefit and success.

Responsiveness To meet the University community's needs and expectations in a timely and reliable manner so as to provide them with the services that they need to be successful.

Efficiency To strive to identify and implement efficiencies which create the best value.

Innovation By valuing knowledge and supporting creativity, we encourage innovation by our staff to provide the best services and highest level of stewardship.

Look at the development of MVV statements as a strategic tool meant to provide direction and guidance to your group. Be sure to write them in plain, direct language instead of trying to use fancier corporate language. Really good MVV statements won't need to be memorized since they are easy to understand and relate to.

Quick Summary

Key Points

➡ MVV statements can help your staff, but only if they understand them and are involved in their development.

Executive Tips

➡ Get your staff involved in developing the statements for better results.

➡ Ensure everyone understands how this ties in to your overall strategic plans.

Traps to Avoid

➡ Don't create them in isolation.

➡ Don't create statements that are long and complex

➡ Don't expect people to memorize them by rote — it's better if they understand the intent.

8

Conducting a Health Check

A health check is critical to your success.

"You may never know what results come of your action, but if you do nothing there will be no result." – Mahatma Gandhi

A Health Check is a valuable tool that helps you look critically at your department and identify whether your FM operations are as efficient and effective as possible and identifies things you can do to enable you to serve your corporation's core needs better.

This is especially the case if your FM department is part of a larger organization whose core business isn't FM. Managing the facility department of a large organization puts you at a disadvantage over an organization whose sole business is FM, but a Health Check can put you on an even footing.

As the FM department of an organization, you have less opportunity for exposure to other methods, procedures and latest practices in FM since you don't have peers in your organization to interact with and learn from. Moreover, the supervisors and other senior members of your organization may not have relevant knowledge and experience in the FM profession, so won't be sources of guidance. Here, you are the sole champion and sole knowledge source for FM in your organization

What is a Health Check?

A Health Check tells you whether your organization is efficiently and effectively delivering the services and results your organization needs for its core business success. You can use it to compare how you are doing against benchmarks that include leading practices.

A Health Check should be objective and measureable. It provides you with a non-judgmental comparison of your specific organization's structure, systems, access to expertise, service delivery models, practices and procedures, systems, information and functionality.

A Health Check comparison is typically applied to practices used by leading organizations. It gives you the information to assess whether your practices match your organization's requirements and priorities, or whether other practices should be carefully assessed and considered for implementation.

A key element of a Health Check is to take into account the specific needs and objectives of your organization. After all, a leading practice used by one organization may not be appropriate or suitable for your organization.

It should deliver clear, easily actionable information you can use to identify and prioritize strategies for your operational delivery of facility or property management services. You can do a Health Check regardless of the size of your organization or your responsibilities and scope.

How can I do A Health Check?

Conducting a Health Check on your operations involves a number of different components. It's important to go beyond a superficial assessment that may lead you towards initiatives that don't match your company's strategic objectives. Implementing leading practices just because someone else is, or making changes because basic benchmarking indicates you should, can be counter-productive.

This is the main problem most facility managers face. To know whether you are doing the right things, you need to know what your corporation's core business requires and then compare how you deliver it with others. Comparing is not easy. It takes time and must be done carefully to avoid incorrect comparisons that lead you to conclusions that are not right for your organization.

For your Health Check, here are five key steps:

Step 1: Establish Core Business Requirements

Regardless of whether your organization rents or owns its properties and regardless of your industry, it has requirements that if met, will improve its chance of success in the competitive marketplace.

The FM department supports these requirements and helps the company be successful in its core business.

Establish a clear understanding of your impact and importance to the organization's core business and use that information to help you evaluate and then prioritize your initiatives.

Step 2: Benchmarking

Benchmarking is the most fundamental form of comparison. It is a great starting point, but always use benchmarking along with other techniques to understand and identify what changes you need to make.

Benchmarking requires a cautious approach because accurate comparison is not as easy as it seems and using averages provided in published benchmarks can result in wrong decisions. You may end up comparing things that are completely different.

If possible, dig deeper with specific organizations to learn how they achieve their results. High-level benchmarking might not provide the information you need to make changes, but it may point you in the right direction.

Consider This

Detailed benchmarking exercises must begin with assessments of things that are the *same*. You may even need to make adjustments to ensure an equal comparison. Once you have relevant benchmarking information, you have the starting point for your Health Check evaluation.

Step 3: Leading Practices Checklist

A leading practices checklist provides a short, fact-based review against an extensive list of practices in major groupings, along with a short summary for each of the groups.

The following checklist includes leading practices from some of the largest FM organizations. It identifies areas where your current practices match leading practices and identifies where gaps exist in your current organization or operational models. Use it to assess the high-level aspects of your operations from a process and procedures perspective and to identify areas where you may be lagging and should focus your attention.

Checklist Assessment

Use this checklist to identify areas where you should focus your attention. This checklist identifies where your current practices match leading practices and identifies where gaps exist in your current organization or operational models.

Practice	Expectation	
Asset Management	You regularly review property condition using formal processes. You integrate results from this and your FM system into your capital and maintenance plans.	☐
Communications	You use newsletters, emails, meetings, etc. in a planned and controlled way to communicate with occupants	☐
Customer Service	You have policies and procedures in place to deal with customer / occupant communications and issues. You measure satisfaction, develop and implement corrective plans. You have telephone and internet based coverage 24/7 for emergencies and requests.	☐
Emergency Management	You have written plans for dealing with emergencies and issues, including disasters, accidents and business recovery.	☐
Energy Management	You actively manage energy with formal initiatives, including communications, projects, studies, project standards, etc.	☐
Environmental Management	You have written plans that for all environmental issues such as CFC's, hazardous waste, spills, etc. to reduce impacts.	☐
General Management	You develop annual plans to address issues, set initiatives and targets, including facility plans, asset and capital plans, staff training & communications	☐
Lease Management	You have formal processes and resources to scrutinize lease charges from landlords and property tax.	☐
Maintenance Management	You have a computerized system that tracks assets, plans preventive maintenance, tracks corrective maintenance and demand work orders and provides reporting for management, compliance and performance.	☐
Occupancy Management	You have systems to track, analyze and report usage to provide management and strategic information for cost containment and planning to drive behaviors and reduce total cost of ownership/occupancy.	☐
Performance Management	You have quantifiable measurements of key deliverables and processes for suppliers and in-house staff. You have a formal process and measurement framework that drives improvements.	☐
Quality Assurance	You have a formal quality assurance process in place that ensures consistent processes and procedures, results are monitored and compliance audits performed. Mechanisms are in place for continuous improvement.	☐
Staff Development	You annually review, recommend and implement training for your team to stay current and develop your staff. You participate in associations and subscribe to related publications to stay current in the industry.	☐
Standards	You have standards to minimize costs and ensure consistencyc for space layouts, furniture, fit-up and capital or base-building projects.	☐
	Total	
	Your score = Total divided by 14 * 100	

Step 4: Detailed Evaluation

The advantage of this process is that the first, simpler steps enable you to quickly identify areas where you should focus your attention for the best results.

The next step is a full evaluation of the key areas identified in the checklist. But checking off an item doesn't mean it shouldn't still be evaluated. This simply provides some direction on priorities.

Once you have identified areas that need your attention, do a detailed evaluation of these items to determine what you are doing. Then compare this with other organizations, including your peers, and identify processes, procedures, techniques and systems they are using that you aren't and should adopt. Look at resources, systems and processes. When doing this evaluation, consider your organization's needs and priorities as a starting point for change.

Consider This

When doing an evaluation assessment, remember that a leading practice used by one company may not be the best practice for yours. It depends on many factors including the size of your organization and your responsibilities. For instance, not every organization requires a full systems approach with full-scale integrated or enterprise FM systems. Your solution needs to be scaled to your size and needs. If you manage a large portfolio, a full system may be required. If you manage a small portfolio, smaller systems, web-based applications or even databases or spreadsheets may provide some of your requirements.

The existing issues and corporate priorities should also influence which areas you evaluate, so start your evaluation with areas that involve your corporate priorities and the areas where the checklist identifies gaps.

The review must include an assessment of the current organization's staffing, procedures, policies, systems and support structure. This review should be based on your organization's needs and current leading practices.

This involves on-site interviews with staff, customers/occupants and senior management in addition to a review of documents, processes, procedures and systems used to deliver services.

Use industry-leading practices as a baseline, but make sure the analysis reflects the realities your organization faces and practices that are relevant and achievable for your organization.

After your evaluation, develop an action plan for change, including business cases to implement changes or new systems. The initiatives must be prioritized to ensure successful implementation.

Knowledge is King

Your assessment must include a careful assessment of your own operations within the context of industry practices.

Build your network.

The first place to learn about initiatives and leading practices is from other members of the FM community, either by direct interaction and networking, or through involvement on associations. Talking with other FM professionals to discuss your issues and learn what others do is the best way to clearly identify what you can do to improve your operations.

Other industry experiences can also help you develop business cases to convince your organization to support you and approve changes like implement new systems, policies, staffing changes and more to make your organization more effective.

Conferences and seminars are another means to gain information. Quite often the courses or seminars are short and won't be filled with a great deal of detail but they are a great starting point. Often you can get some time to speak with the seminar leader to learn more.

Effective networking can also provide the knowledge you need. Associations provide this networking as long as you take advantage of them and initiate contact with your peers. There are global associations that cover the entire range of facility and property management organization covering general FM or specialties such as health care, recreational facilities, commercial buildings and more.

Read those magazines.

Knowledge is also available in trade magazines. By keeping on top of the issues and reading about initiatives and solutions implemented by others, usually leaders in the industry, you can make an objective assessment of your own operation.

You have a wide variety of magazines available, covering all areas of facility and property management, including leasing, project management, interior design, relocations, cleaning, maintenance and more. Some require a subscription while others are free for qualified professionals. Get them and share with your staff

What areas should I look at?

Doing a Health Check involves looking at each of the main functional areas, but for each of those, you need to review the three main components that impact efficient and effective operations. They are:

- ✓ Procedures
- ✓ Systems
- ✓ Resources.

Do a careful analysis of whether the responsibilities you have in your FM department are the correct ones for your organization.

The size of your organization and what other departments exist will greatly influence the kind of thing that your organization should be doing. Your assessment should include the hierarchy within your organization and look at who supports you and who you interface with. Looking at how well others support your requirements is critical. Once you identify areas where change may be needed, you need to know who is going support or detract from your success.

Procedures tie everything together

Processes and procedures involve more than FM functions. HR processes, communications, quality assurance programs and other extra-FM functions can also impact the success of your FM services. Ignore these connections at your peril.

Take a look at everything, ranging from your work order process to your procurement process, training policies and processes, moves, adds and changes, maintenance, environmental, safety and security, capital planning and more.

Your procedures need to cover the fundamental requirements, track and maintain information you can use to make decisions and provide suitable guidance while enabling staff and contractors to deliver in a flexible way.

Systems support your procedures

Having quality procedures in place is never enough. Make sure your processes are used and that they add value, not rigidity.

When assessing their value, look at whether the systems you use support your procedures and enable your resources to be employed effectively and efficiently. Processes should also provide you with the information you need to make decisions that improve your results and support your company's core business.

Not every organization requires a full systems approach with full-scale integrated or enterprise systems. Your solution needs to be scaled to your size and needs. If you manage a large portfolio, a full system may be required. If you manage a small portfolio, then smaller systems, web-based applications or even databases or spreadsheets may provide some of your requirements.

While integration can be critical to some organizations, integration for integration's sake can be a drain on your resources and detract from the implementation of a successful strategic plan. Focus on what needs to be integrated; consider volumes and determine whether you need consistency or shared data. If that is important, look at why and how often. Do you need to share data live, daily, or as-needed?

Data in and of itself isn't useful. You need information that gives you the knowledge to make good decisions. Systems should manage the information you need to make those specific decisions, foster organizational change or implement new initiatives. If your current systems don't give you good decision-making information, focus on that key area.

You also need to be able to support your procedures and the key activities you provide to your company so they can be successful.

Take a look at your systems and identify critical areas and then assess whether you have what you need. Again, look at what should be integrated and what doesn't need to be integrated. Assess what is available to meet your particular needs and scale and develop the business cases to implement.

Resources make the systems and procedures work

When you address the resources you need to make management systems and procedures work, always consider human resources and communications technology. For human resources, look at whether you have the right number of staff and the right *kind* of staff t o do the things you need to do.

A good example is project management, which requires a very specific set of skills and knowledge. The wrong fit, combined with poor processes and systems, has a negative impact on success.

Assess what individual members of your team spend their time doing. While you don't need to do a detailed time-in-motion study, do a broad-based assessment of their functions and the time they spend doing tasks, managing contractors, doing administrative work, attending meetings and even traveling. You can use a questionnaire format that has them estimate their time spent on key functions.

Then look at the job descriptions and whether they still match actual work done with the organization's needs. Review the resumes and background of the individuals doing that work and see whether they match. You can also interview the staff to learn more about how they assess their work and the organization's needs. This is an important opportunity to identify areas where training is required or responsibilities should be shifted. Your goal is to find ways to help individuals do a better job.

Step 5: Take Action

Use the results from your FM Health Check to develop a strategic plan and an implementation strategy. Break the plan into manageable parts and implement the necessary changes or, if necessary, develop compelling business cases to sell your changes within the organization.

Your senior management should be aware of your initiative, and expect changes to be recommended to them for approval. Don't be shy to identify things that need improvement. You are showcasing leadership as well as good ideas. Some FM professionals may be reluctant to champion change in case senior management sees it as a critique of the status quo. Push past that attitude. Standing still is a sure way to fail, and not admitting you can improve your organization is the same as standing still.

Prepare your organization for the possible outcome, which may include organization changes, business cases for new systems or developing/implementing new processes or activities. These things take resources, so be ready to develop a strong business case and sell your change.

Consider This

Making changes takes effort. Plans aren't worth anything unless you implement them, so be proactive and push for changes and take action. With change, you will get results, get attention and get ahead.

Summary - 5 Steps for Better Health

In summary, you can use the following five key steps to assess and improve your FM organization's effectiveness and success:

1. Core Business: identify how you contribute to your company's core business and use this knowledge in your assessment

2. Benchmarking: use this to identify areas to focus on. Even if you exceed the averages, you need to assess them unless you are the leader.

3. Checklist Assessment: start with a quick checklist to identify areas where you don't have leading practices and use this information along with the core business and benchmarking results to focus your assessment efforts.

4. Evaluation: do an evaluation of the processes, systems and resources involved in the areas which you identified as priorities. The results should include recommendations on things that need improvement.

5. Take action: don't wait, develop a strategy and business case, sell the changes to your senior management and implement for better results.

Quick Summary

Key Points

➡ The only way to improve results is to take a look at what you are doing to achieve those results.

➡ A formal process to review, assess and change is part of a facility manager's strategic responsibility.

Executive Tips

➡ Prepare your organization for change before you have to make it.

➡ If you don't change and improve something each year, you aren't managing effectively.

Traps to Avoid

➡ Don't use a review to justify the status quo.

➡ Don't just benchmark with numbers - dig deep and assess operational procedures, resources and systems.

Using Information for Decisions

You can't make good decisions without Information.

"Making good decisions is a crucial skill at every level."
– Peter Drucker

In the facility and property management profession, an important ingredient that is often missing from many organizations is good information.

If you are like most property and facility managers, you are inundated with data and information on a daily basis, yet not much of it helps you make decisions.

You (hopefully) have lots of data available to you about your operation, but often it's raw data. You need to turn it into information and knowledge you can use to make decisions that improve results or save money. Albert Einstein once said, "We do things, but we do not know why we do them." That same problem is at work here. Information lets you focus your activities and your initiatives based on facts. It helps you know *why* you do things and makes it more likely you can do the right things.

If you have a help desk and a work order management system, you likely have the information you need to make strategic decisions. But are you collecting, analyzing and the data to your benefit, or assuming that the systems alone give you better performance?

Make no mistake. There is real long-term value in the information these systems provide. If they are not already in place, you need to implement them and make them part of your strategic plan. Here are some ideas about how you can put specific information to work.

Condition Information

Information about the condition of your facilities will improve your capital planning and help you justify projects and activities. Collecting and assessing the data formally each year will highlight changes that need action. For leased buildings, you can use the information (along with help desk information) as leverage during negotiations.

Customer Service

Is the customer satisfaction information you collect designed to gather information you can analyze to improve performance, including management of subcontractors? Look carefully at your process and your questions. Do they deliver valuable information? Are you analyzing and creating action plans based on the data? Do you communicate back to the tenants/occupants? All of this can help you improve results.

Reporting Systems

What do you do with the information reported by your systems? Ask yourself whether the information adds value to your decision-making process. Could you show that value to other stakeholders in your organization? If not, put something useful in place that gives you information you can use to make decision. Are your subcontractors required to provide reports? Is the information useful? Establish viable report requirements and make sure you're not just getting lists. You want information you can analyze to guide and measure operational improvements.

Consider This

Your suppliers and contractors are supposed to be experts in their areas, so leverage their knowledge to your advantage. If the reporting they currently provide under their contract does not provide the information you need, work with them to improve what you get. Use that experience to modify existing and future contracts. Contracts can be changed or eliminated to meet your needs.

Focus on Results

If you are serious about improving performance by implementing strategic management practices in all aspects of your responsibilities, focus on getting the results you want.

All too often, property and facility managers spend most of their time managing the day-to-day issues and focusing on the tactical services on which their customers rely. You need to change this dynamic. Getting better results means carving out some time to think ahead, develop ideas and sell both the ideas and the implementation to senior management.

Aim to leverage the fundamentals you already know and implement practical tools and techniques that maximize value. Use these techniques to drive performance from yourself and the staff, systems, suppliers and contractors who deliver services and manage your facilities or buildings.

Start by looking at your organization's own strategy and goals. What do you need to do to support them? What are you missing that will help you achieve results? Do you have the right staffing, skill sets, systems, internal support and information to get results?

While a Mission, Vision and Values (MVV) statement is often seen as a head office issue, it can serve a very important purpose if developed properly from the ground up for your team instead of in a corporate boardroom. Developing an MVV statement with your staff can foster useful discussion, focus attention on what matters and guide decisions.

It can also be a launching board for developing a strategic plan, which is an important way to set your direction and identify what you need to implement or change to improve your operations.

Visibility into your Operations

There is a trend with senior facility and property professionals about their processes and systems. The trend is a lack of visibility into crucial aspects of their costs and activities.

While they may have implemented systems and processes for managing their facilities, visibility into their operational decisions is often lacking. Visibility (in the form of management information, not just data), would enable facility and property managers to take the next step towards improving their operations.

Aberdeen Group, a leading provider of research into supply chain and other business processes, reports that real estate and facility management costs represent over 30% of non-payroll costs, yet 40% of managers say they have poor or no visibility into the costs of this important function.

Few FM professionals also have visibility into key processes, work loading, work order activity, maintenance activity, moves, projects, etc. That's a problem, since this strategic information can be used to build business cases with senior management and make strategic decisions related to process, resourcing and subcontracts.

To change that around, facility and property managers need to focus on one area at a time and gather only the data and information they need to make decisions. Too often, initiatives and systems are implemented which overwhelm facility and property managers with excessive process, time requirements, integration and excess data. The end result is more information, but less meaningful information on which to make decisions.

To avoid that, decide why you need the information and what decisions you expect to make from that information, and then implement only the processes and systems that give you what you need.

The Value of Information

While the example isn't directly related to FM, Wal-Mart's approach to information-based decision making success is something that facility managers can learn from. Wal-Mart is the largest retailer in the world and one of the key things that made them successful is their information systems. These systems come very close to delivering to management real-time information about their business. Not next month, not next week, not tomorrow - today. This involves lots of data that includes reporting/analysis to make it meaningful.

There is a lot of value in having information and many drawbacks from not having it. Consider what it would be like to have all work order information from a large portfolio at your fingertips, where you can review the information by city, technician, supplier, completion, etc. and drill down to the comments. Without that information, it's challenging to see what is happening and nearly impossible to identify things that need to be fixed.

If all you have is a monthly list of call information and possibly the results of an annual customer satisfaction survey, but no detail or close-out information, you still should make the best of it until you get better information. In a bid to leverage the data so it helps suppliers make better decisions, too, Wal-Mart actually shares the data it collects with key suppliers. You should do the same to help them understand what they need to do better.

It's surprising when companies don't understand the value of information. Some large companies don't have good facilities-related information and don't understand why it's important. They probably have great data and information on their core business and probably for other support services, but don't support the facility manager to implement systems.

Many other organizations don't have any information available to FM decision makers, or collect data from a computerized system (such as CMMS or CAFM), but do not use that data effectively. This is a lost opportunity, since the information they can get from the systems could enable them to make decisions that save operating costs.

If you don't have the information you need to manage your facilities or property responsibilities, how can you be effective? Start now and get the information you need to make decisions that improve results and reduce costs.

You need Information, not Data

One of the most fundamental problem we all face involves having too much data (because we know that's a good thing), yet not being able to use that data to make effective decisions. Often, the data can't help because it's not the right kind of data or it isn't properly compiled and analyzed to give you information you can make decisions with.

Let's say a facility manager has been getting reports from their subcontractors that were intended to be used to better manage the facilities. The reports were simply lists of help desk calls and copies of work orders filled in by the technicians and this data comes with a monthly tally of total calls and work orders completed. Even worse, the reports represented a considerable volume of paper because the portfolio itself is large. Here, the issue is too much data and no information. The facility manager simply doesn't have time to read through the reports and analyze the content so he better understands what is happening in the portfolio. There may be issues to address, but these are disguised behind numbers.

Generally speaking, the subcontractor may well be delivering what's expected in terms of raw data. Contractual obligations aside, the FM professional is a long way from getting what he needs.

To fix the situation, the call data should be in a database that enables trending and tracking of calls as well as comparisons to previous periods, comparisons between buildings and performance information such as closed calls, calls that resulted in work orders, etc. The work orders should have to be in a database that enables tracking of repeat maintenance, for instance, to help with capital planning. The subcontractor providing the maintenance services should also be required to provide analysis and advice based on their knowledge and expertise. That kind of information would help the facility manager make decisions about preventive maintenance, replacement, risk and tracking performance.

While this example is based on a subcontracted service, many in-house services face the same issue. They have lots of data, but lack real information.

Converting Data to Information

Understanding the difference between data and information is an important step towards improving your operations and your decision making. The easy-to-collect data should be addressed first, since it's either meaningless as-is, or yields such volume you don't have time to study and use it. Printouts of calls and photocopies of work orders are great examples of meaningless data that's often delivered in great volume.

Information, on the other hand, is data that has been processed so that patterns and trends are visible. Information enables you to apply your knowledge to make decisions. It is also more compact and accessible than data, which tends to be raw and unprocessed.

The easiest example of unprocessed data comes from the data generated by the list of calls to your help desk. The data is a list of calls along with the time, date, caller, topic, issue, resolution and completion date, for instance. This kind of data is readily tracked and available in modern FM systems.

It isn't information until you process it, however. This could be as simple as converting it to a chart that shows the percentage of calls by topic, such as hot/cold, cleaning complaint, burnt light, move request, etc. Unfortunately, this isn't very helpful either, because it lacks context.

Context is where you get the best information. By tracking and comparing the percentage of calls each month, you will have context. Comparing them by building, department or other characteristic provides even more context.

As an example, you could look at the trend of burnt lights and combine this with the floor or building data. If the number of lights burning out is increasing and the area is an older renovation, you can decide whether to do a relamping. If it's a newly-renovated area, you can explore other reasons for the burnt lights, including power quality, faulty ballasts or other issues.

This kind of *information*, puts you in a position to make decisions and take proactive steps instead of simply continuing to react to the same problems over and over again. Of course, information is also useful when managing the performance of your in-house or subcontracted services, as discussed in the *Getting Performance* section of this book.

Consider This

The next time you look at implementing a process, system, reporting, survey or other means to gather and track data or information, take a step back and ask the fundamental question: Will this data or information help me make decisions that will improve services and reduce costs? When you understand the answer to that question, you will be in a better position to get the information you need to make decisions.

Successful facility managers understand this issue and focus only on information they need to make decisions. Eliminate the clutter and improve your decision making.

Quick Summary

| **Key Points** | ➡ The most successful corporations use information to get results. |
| | ➡ Without information, you can't make good decisions. |

| **Executive Tips** | ➡ Focus your attention on information you need to make decisions and improve results. |

| **Traps to Avoid** | ➡ Don't collect information just for the sake of collecting information. |
| | ➡ Raw data is not information. Analysis and assessment are required. |

10

Getting Information

To make good decisions, you need good information.

"Information is a source of learning. But unless it is organized, processed, and available to the right people in a format for decision making, it is a burden, not a benefit." – William Pollard

Developing strategy and making decisions takes information, not just data. Data is simply a series of facts while information gives meaning to the data and provides the knowledge necessary to make decisions that improve results.

A good example is measuring performance. A performance dashboard that shows results at a point in time is just data. A 12-month trend graph of the same data provides information.

Also, don't focus as much attention on what is going well; focus on the results that are outside of the norm. This takes less time and gives you the best value. If you have call centre information, filter out the so-called normal results and dig into the issues and problems to find root causes and correct problems or adopt solutions. For instance, an unusually low number of janitorial calls in one building or area may mean someone is bypassing the system, not that there are fewer problems. Comparing those results to satisfaction survey results, for instance, can reveal the truth.

You can leverage existing systems and processes to get the information you need or plan changes or new systems to give you what you need. Often, corporate systems are not designed to give you the information you need, so you must seek other ways to get the information or implement your own facility/property systems.

Better Results through Data

Improving results requires information and information takes data. Getting the data is an important process and if you have systems and processes that provide it, you need to leverage them. If you don't have data, the best way to improve results is to implement ways to get it. Let's look at some of the most common ways to collect data.

Computerized FM Systems

This includes the full range of FM systems, including project management, lease administration, maintenance and space management.

For instance, having a Computerized Maintenance Management System (CMMS) enables you to schedule regular preventive maintenance routines, track failures in service or equipment, document corrective action and manage service requests, including things like moves. By tracking work against equipment, space or departments and where possible, identifying the resources, time and cost of the work, you can use the information as part of your capital replacement programs, service management, customer satisfaction, supplier assessment and future business cases, both for projects and resources.

It helps you make decisions on what equipment should be replaced and contributes to the justification you need for funding. It also helps support environmental and energy projects, a key area for getting results.

An example is an organization that had its subcontracted maintenance contractor on a work order system, but not their in-house staff activities. After adding the in-house staff to the same system, they discovered patterns that allowed them to redirect in-house staff to higher value work and reduce overall costs. That's an example of using a maintenance management system to provide information that gets you results.

A well-implemented system includes collecting information about equipment, including age. Once you are using your system, you should also track failures, repairs and where possible, predictive measurements that indicate imminent failure or the condition of the equipment. With this information, you can develop an effective capital renewal/replacement plan that you can defend to your organization based on facts and information, not just theoretical life cycle limits.

Tracking and managing space through a Computer Aided Facility Management system (CAFM) enables you to gather the data you need to make strategic decisions about space and its related cost. Track space use, density and vacant space by department to identify groups that should be re-arranged to free up space or who are occupying more space than your standards suggest they should. This lets you investigate and plan for reductions. When you need to implement a move, the data and related information help you decide where they will fit best and where space can be found. Blocking and stacking diagrams along with department affinity planning will improve the efficiency of your organization and you can even track space costs against departments to foster accountability.

Call Tracking

Understanding what is happening in your buildings or portfolios is important. Tracking calls from occupants and categorizing them can provide you with information you need to assess subcontractors, identify trends that need to be corrected, support capital planning and business cases.

While a formal call centre is ideal, smaller portfolios or buildings may use a simplified system, such as an Excel spreadsheet, to provide you with the data you need as you track all calls and requests. This includes all sources, including your suppliers, technicians, security staff, and calls you field yourself. In one example, tracking the number and type of problems related to elevators, which were often made to the security guard in the lobby, helped support an elevator modernization project. A building with similar elevator problems that was managed by a different property manager wasn't tracking the problems and couldn't justify their own elevator project, since they didn't have any information to back-up their business case.

Be sure to track the data in a way that you can analyze and turn into information you can make decisions with. Categorize the calls and record the date in a format that can be sorted and analyzed.

Customer Satisfaction Surveys

Feedback is an important part of any efforts to improve results and service and the best way to get that feedback is to ask your customers. Use several techniques. While you may already visit your occupants and ask them how satisfied they are with services, this is often only with the tenant or occupant representative and misses information from everyone else. As well, it isn't in a format you can use to compare trends or analyze results.

Develop customer/occupant satisfaction processes and programs that enable you to effectively measure results and act upon the information to make improvements instead of simply benchmarking satisfaction results. Don't just use an annual survey. Implement a transaction survey to follow-up on their satisfaction with specific issues they have called about and work performed on a monthly basis.

Ask a modest number of questions and make sure you can act on the questions. Try to track the location of the response, for instance by building, floor, tenant or occupant. Keep the same questions each time you do the survey to enable comparisons over time. If you ask for comments, don't leave it open. Be specific and you are more likely to get responses.

Enter the information into a spreadsheet or other system so you can do comparisons and get information that you can use. Different results for cleaning on different floors may be related to the janitorial staff themselves, for instance, and are easily corrected. Temperature problems with one tenant may indicate problems with the system. Concerns about response time to issues may prompt you to re-examine your process and improve it.

Performance Management

Performance management is often seen simply as measures in the form of Key Performance Indicators (KPIs)

There is much more to it, however, and by using the techniques as part of a larger process instead of simply a way of measuring and penalizing poor performance, you can get better results from your staff and suppliers.

First, the very nature of measurements looks backwards at past results, not forward. Expand it out by using historical and trending techniques with the data and create information you can use to manage performance going forward by preventing problems before they result in failed service.

While measuring key results (i.e., KPIs) is important, you should also look at the underlying processes that create those results and measure them as well. Use the data to develop information that you use constructively with your staff or suppliers to analyze and solve problems rather than waiting for failure.

Include costing information in your performance measurements. In corporate facilities, this would include cost per square foot, real estate cost per Full Time Equivalent Employee (FTE), cost per move/add/change, etc. For commercial property management, this also includes cost per-square-foot and the cost of delivering work order services, maintenance, etc.

Have a formal process with your staff or suppliers. This gives them a chance to see the results on an ongoing basis and to identify solutions and changes that will have a positive impact. Sometimes their suggestions will be outside their area of control, but if they identify them, you can take action and improve results.

By looking strategically at what you do and trying to improve results using performance-based approaches, you will make it easier to make decisions and manage your operations. That will get the results that get attention and foster support for your corporation's goals, thus increasing the visibility of your role in the organization.

Suppliers & Subcontractors

Suppliers and subcontractors present another critical source of data. If you subcontract some or all of your facility functions to others, they should be your source for information. When developing your scope and specifications to procure the services, include a requirement to provide you with the information you need.

By including it in the contract, you ensure you get the information and the supplier understands their responsibilities when they price the work.

Don't just ask for reports, copies of work orders and data. Expect your subcontractors to provide you with analysis and information you can use to make decisions. Have them tap into their expertise and experience so you benefit and are better equipped to make decisions.

Quick Summary

Key Points	➡ Data is not the same thing as information.
	➡ You need information, not just data, to make decisions.
Executive Tips	➡ Design your data collection so that it delivers information you can use to make decisions.
	➡ Get your suppliers and subcontractors to give you information and analysis, not just data and reports.
Traps to Avoid	➡ Don't collect so much data that you are overwhelmed and can't use it effectively.
	➡ Don't confuse data with information.

11

Intelligent Benchmarking & Beyond

Measuring is the best way to improve what you are doing. Doing it right is the trick.

"What gets copied is symptoms of success, not the cause."
– Dr. Ed Baker, Ford (on benchmarking)

Benchmarking is a form of measurement – where you measure against something else to see where you are lagging, identify the areas and take corrective action. This is the essence of benchmarking. Incorporate this as part of your Health Check, as discussed earlier.

Even if you think you are doing everything right, how do you know unless you compare? No organization is the best at everything and the same is true for yours.

Measuring results is the best way to improve what you are doing. This is the core of almost all quality management systems and benchmarking is a form of measurement. This is where you measure against something else to see where you are lagging, identify weaker areas and take corrective action.

Benchmarking should be a learning process, however, not just a measurement exercise. It's a starting point for continuous improvement.

Consider This

Even if you think you are doing everything right, how do you know unless you compare? If you aren't benchmarking, you can't possibly be doing everything you should be doing. Benchmarking is essential to continuous improvement.

Pick Your Battles

You have limited time and energy, so focus your benchmarking initiative on key areas that will have a large impact rather than on everything you do. You can always go back to the other areas later.

You can also start with a quick exercise that covers most areas and use that to focus your efforts on more in-depth issues or areas of importance to your organization. If you already have an idea of where you are lagging, focus on that area and then use that success to build on future success.

Intelligent Benchmarking

Published benchmarking results are a good start to identify areas for further study, but even at a high-level, you need to use them carefully. Review the methodology and look at the sample size, number of participants, facility types and volumes, if applicable. You will probably need to make adjustments to the information based on your specific situation, geography and other factors that are unique to you to ensure an equal comparison.

Many benchmarking results use averages, which can be very misleading, driving you to the wrong conclusion and decisions. That's why you need to dig deep and fully understand what you are comparing. Averages can include a wide sampling of comparisons, not all of which will be relevant.

Be sure they include the same information you include and adjust as necessary. For costs, make sure they include the same type of sub-accounts. For staffing levels, assess the functions and titles and be sure of the work activity, roles and responsibilities that are included.

Not comparing apples to oranges is important, but the bigger risk is the more subtle differences between apples. Accurate comparison is not as easy as it seems, and using averages provided in published benchmarks can result in wrong decisions. You don't want to compare apples to oranges for sure, but you also don't want to compare a Golden Delicious with a Macintosh. To get a proper comparison, assess each component and compare things that are the same, making adjustments as necessary to ensure an equal comparison.

If you do your own survey to gather information, whether internal or external, be clear about what information you are looking for and focus on data that will be meaningful. Ask the right questions and build-in the ability to identify unique issues that will affect your comparisons.

While you are at it, expand your survey beyond numbers and include information on process, systems and resourcing, which will tell you more than numbers, giving you more information to analyze and assess.

Misleading Benchmarking Information

Since raw benchmarking results can be deceptive, it can be easy to justify the status quo with benchmarking. Unfortunately, this is not what benchmarking is meant to do.

As the first step, you need to understand how the benchmarking results you are using have been compiled. To perform an effective comparison, consider the sample size, the type of facilities, location, services, etc. As an example, one major benchmarking report had a category for buildings over 1-million square feet. They separated the results by region and one region had just over 7-million square feet in total in the sample. One company who participated in the benchmarking study submitted three of their buildings, totaling over 3-million square feet. As a result, just under 50% of the sample was from a single company.

Clearly, this wasn't a representative benchmark, but other organizations wouldn't have known this fact unless they studied the information very carefully.

In an example of benchmarking being used ineffectively, a senior facility manager was satisfied that his facility fell in the middle range of benchmarking results for his category. Realistically, it's too bad he was satisfied with being average. Then again, his category of facilities wasn't known for leading the industry.

Only a Starting Point

In any case, benchmarking should be a starting point, not an ending point. If you use generic benchmarking results from associations or private organizations, they should simply point you to areas that you will study in more depth. Always take care when comparing benchmarking results to your buildings and make suitable adjustments before making any decisions.

The most effective benchmarking is between selected facilities with similar characteristics as yours where the differences are understood and are adjusted for up-front. This provides you with a real comparison. Then the next step is to understand why you are under (or over) performing in certain areas. Armed with that knowledge, you can take action.

Beyond Benchmarking

Benchmarking is just part of a longer process. Once you have gone through the traditional benchmarking exercise, you can move from comparing numbers to assessing procedures, systems and resources. This gives you real information about what needs to change to improve your results.

Traditional benchmarking simply compares numbers, which can be a good starting point if you are comparing the right things. You need to go beyond traditional benchmarking to look at resources, procedures and systems to find out why you are performing well. More importantly, you should use that information to keep doing the things that are going well - and to change the things that are not working.

Compare how you operate with processes, people and systems against other high-performing organizations and understand what they do differently. Then, assess whether you can emulate what they do to be successful and implement it. No matter what you think you are doing well, and sometimes even when the benchmarking results indicate you are above average, it's a mistake to assume you are doing everything you should be doing if you want to promote continuous improvement.

Consider This

There will always be someone else doing something better. Learn from them. Look at how a change in resources, new training, revised proceedures, new initiatives and expertise, technology or systems can help you improve your results. To figure out what you should change, use benchmarking information, reports, studies, surveys and your own networking to find out how others are doing things.

An important caveat is that the leading practices used by one organization may not be the best for yours. Your organization's size, priorities, resources and other factors need to be taken into account and your initiative should be customized.

Why go Beyond Benchmarking?

Going beyond benchmarking and evaluating your operations is critical to your success. It tells you whether your FM operations are as efficient and effective as possible and identifies things you can do to enable you to serve your corporation's core needs better.

This is especially the case if your FM department is part of a larger organization whose core business isn't FM. Managing the facility department of a large organization puts you at a disadvantage over an organization whose sole business is FM and going beyond benchmarking can put you on an even footing.

As the FM department of a organization, you have less opportunity for exposure to other methods, procedures and latest practices in FM since you don't have peers in your organization to interact with and learn from. Also, your supervisors and other senior members of your organization don't have knowledge and experience in your profession they can share with you or provide guidance for. This makes you the sole champion and sole knowledge source for FM in your organization

As a result, you need to compare yourself with other FM organizations and departments, not only through traditional benchmarking of numbers, but by comparing your performance against leading practices.

The comparison is typically with practices used by leading organizations and gives you the information to assess whether your practices match your organization's requirements and priorities, or whether other practices should be carefully assess and considered for implementation.

A key element of this next step is to take into account the specific needs and objectives of your organization. After all, a leading practice used by one organization may not be appropriate or suitable for your organization.

It should deliver clear, easily actionable information you can use to identify and prioritize strategies for your operational delivery of facility or property management services. You can do this operational benchmarking regardless of the size of your organization or your responsibilities and scope.

What is Benchmarking Not?

Benchmarking isn't just about numbers. That is, you don't just compare numbers and, if your results are average or better, keep on doing what you've always been doing.

More than anything, benchmarking should be a learning process, not just a measurement exercise. You should effectively compare the results and then dig deep to understand what you can do differently.

Consider several runners who ran a race and finished with the same time. Let's say all of the runners had excellent technique except for Runner #2. If you were benchmarking their times, you would say the second runner did well and that would be that. In fact, you shouldn't be satisfied with how the numbers look. By focusing on more than just their time, you can see the real benchmark was technique and with improvement in technique, Runner #2 could easily win next time.

Remember, benchmarking goes past the numbers, it's about learning and improving.

Things You Need To Know

Benchmarking can be a great tool for organizational improvement, but it must be used properly and carefully to avoid the many traps you can fall into. Use benchmarking as a basis for improvement and be careful to avoid the traps.

Understanding Why

The first step when benchmarking is to be clear on why you are doing it and what you will use the results for. That will dictate how your benchmarking exercise should be structured and managed for the best results.

Decide on your goal and what decisions you will make before you start, and what next steps you will take to investigate the cause of the results and recommendations for change. If you don't think you can make changes or influence your results, then rethink the priorities or find ways to make it happen. Use the results to push change and make your business case within the organization.

Comparing Effectively

Accurately comparing results and measurements is not as easy as it seems, and using averages can sometimes result in wrong decisions.

Since you have decided to benchmark and clearly understand why, you can focus your attention on the areas that are most important and understand how to do the comparisons so they are meaningful and lead you to more detailed information you can use to make good decisions.

For any detailed benchmarking exercise, assess each component or measurement and compare the situations, then make adjustments to ensure an equal comparison. The similarity is important, since many factors influence costs and results.

Some of the things that you need to adjust for include:

Sample Size

- ✓ Total Numbers (locations, area, etc.)
- ✓ Size / Use
- ✓ Distribution
- ✓ Type of locations.

Characteristics

- ✓ Geography
- ✓ Size
- ✓ # Buildings
- ✓ Age
- ✓ Type
- ✓ Staffing (union/non union)
- ✓ Volumes
- ✓ Related benchmarks (churn vs. resources).

Methodology

- ✓ Number of results
- ✓ Definitions (i.e. what's included)
- ✓ How are outliers dealt with.

Calculations

You need to know how the results are calculated in addition to understanding how to compare and adjust. The technique used can influence the number you are trying to compare against and not yield accurate comparisons.

When comparing to calculated benchmarks, be very careful since they can be misleading. That's why you need to dig deep and fully understand what you are comparing.

Here are the typical ways that benchmarking results are calculated.

Average / Mean

The average and mean are the same thing. You simply add each number together and divide by the number of results you have.

$9.26 / 4 = $2.32 per Sq. Ft.

Unfortunately, this can easily misrepresent information. Since it doesn't take into account the relative sizes of the numbers, it can be influenced by a small number of high or low numbers. If the sample has an unreasonably high or low number, they should be removed from the sample, but not all benchmarking does this. It's important to know how these statistical "outliers" are dealt with.

Cost PSF	# Results
$1.87	1
$2.12	1
$2.25	1
$3.02	1
$9.26	4

Weighted Average

An improvement on the average calculation, the weighted average takes into account the simple fact that the numbers in any benchmark study have different impacts on the total. In the case of costs per square feet, the size of the facility is an important factor. The weighted average adjusts for this.

In this example, the high result of $3.02 is for a small 10,000 sq. ft. building while another 100,000 sq. ft. building has a $2.12 cost.

In the table, the same four cost PSF results are shown, however the related building size is also included.

Cost PSF	Sq. Ft.	Total Cost
$1.87	75,000	$140,250
$2.12	100,000	$212,000
$2.25	50,000	$112,500
$3.02	10,000	$30,200
$9.26	235,000	$494,950

To find the weighted average, we multiply the cost PSF by the sq. ft. to get the total cost for each result. The total cost is divided by the total sq. ft. to arrive at the weighted average.

$494,950 / 235,000 = $2.11 per sq. ft.

You can see that the difference between the average and the weighted average is $0.22, or around a 10% difference.

If you don't know what the areas are for the buildings included in the benchmark study, you don't know what impact each one has and you won't be able to easily relate it to your own facility costs.

Median

The median is simply the middle number in a list. Half the results are above and half the results are below. Again, like the average, this can be misleading. The two tables below show two different ranges of numbers that result in the same median, but very different averages.

Cost PSF	
$1.87	
$1.96	
$2.12	
$2.13	
$2.25	Median
$2.34	
$2.36	
$2.57	
$2.61	
$2.13	Average

Cost PSF	
$2.05	
$2.11	
$2.12	
$2.13	
$2.25	Median
$2.67	
$3.36	
$3.67	
$3.81	
$2.69	Average

Distribution matters

These examples show that the distribution of the benchmarking numbers are very important and can easily skew the results. As a result, you need to know more about the numbers involved in the benchmarking exercise before you use them. Even then, you must adjust the results or use them carefully.

Continuous Process

Benchmarking isn't just an exercise you do once and forget about it. Continue to measure internally and compare your new results with the benchmark results as well as your own historical results to see how you are trending and to identify and take action if you start to slip.

Periodically re-assess your resources, processes and systems to make sure they are still delivering the best results. Drill down again to see what else to change that will improve results. As necessary, focus on a new area and repeat the process.

Be prepared to change

Your goal is to find things to improve or change that achieve better results, so expect to implement changes before you even begin. Prepare your organization for the possible outcome, which may include organizational changes, business cases for new systems or developing/implementing new processes or activities. These changes often take resources to plan and implement properly, so be ready to develop a strong business case and sell your recommended changes. Your benchmarking and further analysis provide you with the evidence you need.

- ✓ If you are benchmarking, hopefully it's to find things you need to improve or change, so be prepared to implement changes before you even begin.
- ✓ Don't be shy to identify things that need improvement; it's more a statement on your leadership than trying to sell the status-quo as the best it can get.
- ✓ Prepare your organization for the possible outcome, including organization changes, business cases for new systems or developing / implementing new processes or activities. These things take resources, so be ready to develop a strong business case and sell your change.

Intelligent Benchmarking Process

Intelligent benchmarking isn't just about comparing benchmarking numbers, it's about a process to target problem areas, identify solutions and implement changes that will get better results. Benchmarking is part of the process, including general benchmarking as well as detailed, focused benchmarking that compares processes, resources and systems rather than just numbers. These 10 steps will help guide you to better results:

Step 1: Identify and Rank Critical Success Areas

Before you begin, you need to know what is important to your organization. You support your core business and the things you do will have an impact. Establish the ones with the biggest impact that you have influence over.

Step 2: Select Areas to Improve

Once you have identified the critical success areas, select the ones you can improve. Target a couple at first and make sure they are in a high-impact area where you can make changes. For the first round, don't waste your time on things you will have a hard time changing or influencing.

Step 3: Compare Results using Benchmarks

Use general benchmarking information to compare results in the area you have selected. Benchmarking can be from industry sources, studies and reports, colleagues and internal comparisons.

Step 4: Choose Results that are not Superior

Carefully assess the results and choose the benchmarked results where your performance is either equal or below the benchmarks. Leave the ones that perform better for later, but you will be able to find improvements in those areas, too.

Step 5: Isolate supporting processes, resources and systems

In areas where the results aren't better than the benchmarks, dig deep to identify the processes, resources (including staff, supplies, subcontractors, etc.) and systems that are used or required to get results. These would all support the areas you are focusing on and should be things you can influence or change.

Step 6: Analyze each process, resource and system for impacts

One by one, analyze each of the processes, resources and systems to see where there are bottlenecks, performance problems and other issues that prevent results. Compare what you do to others, ask your staff and suppliers and investigate all possibilities.

Step 7: Focus on problems

The problem areas will become evident and you can then focus on those areas, gathering more information and going into more details as required.

Step 8: Test your practices against leading practices

Collect information, understand what is happening and seek out other direct benchmarking information to compare your practices with. This shouldn't be simple number comparisons, it should include how you are organized, the type of systems you have in place, training you provide and procedures you employ.

Step 9: Adopt leading practices and change existing practices

When you have identified leading practices that are better than yours, develop a plan to adopt them in your organization and create an implementation strategy.

Step 10: Repeat for other Areas

Now that you have found and fixed one critical success area, start again and improve the next critical success area you identified in Step 1.

Summary Process

The 10 steps identified above can be summarized into a shorter five-step process that is very similar to other quality assurance processes. The diagram illustrates the five steps.

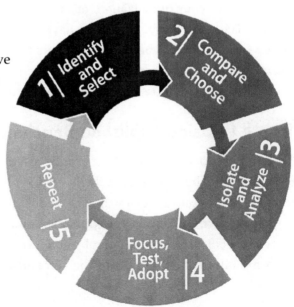

Avoid the Benchmarking Traps

Benchmarking is a valuable tool for business improvement, but there are many traps you can fall into. We've listed seven key traps you should avoid.

Trap #1 - It's all about numbers

Benchmarking isn't about comparing numbers, it's a process of identifying where you can improve and learning new approaches, processes and techniques used by other leading organizations that you can apply to improve results. Comparing your results with a benchmark number is only the starting point for benchmarking.

Trap #2 - There isn't anything else to learn

If you think you know all there is to know already, you won't do what it takes to benchmark effectively. Admitting that you can't possibly know it all and that others may be doing some things better is critical to moving benchmarking from a numbers exercise to a process that adds value to your organization.

Trap #3 - Using your Shotgun

You have limited time and energy, so focus your benchmarking on key areas that will have a large impact. You can always go back to the other areas later. You can start with a quick exercise that covers most areas and use that to identify areas of importance to your organization, or areas you are already lagging in, and then focus in-depth on those. Once you have gone through the first benchmarking exercise, moving from comparing numbers to assessing procedures, systems and resources and then implementing change, you can move to other areas and apply what you learned to those areas and continue to improve.

Trap #4 - Using Published Benchmarking As-Is

Generic published benchmarking results are a good start to identify areas for further study, but even at a high-level, you need to be careful with the comparisons. Carefully review the methodology and look at the sample size and participant profiles. You may need to make adjustments to the information based on your specific situation, geography and more. For costing, be sure they include the same information you do in the comparisons and adjust as necessary. For staffing levels, assess the functions and titles and be sure of the roles and responsibilities.

Look closely at the sample sizes, number of participants and volumes if applicable. These can be misleading and not provide suitable comparisons. If you do your own surveys, be clear about what information you are looking for. Ask the right questions and build in the ability to identify unique issues that will affect your comparisons. While you are at it, expand your survey beyond simple costing numbers and include process, systems and resourcing when possible. Alternately, this type of information can be in a follow-up survey or direct discussion with organizations who appear to be the best match.

Trap #5 - Justifying the Status Quo

Some people use benchmarking results to justify the status quo. Since raw benchmarking results can be deceptive, this is easy to accomplish. You need to understand how the results have been compiled, the sample size, the type of facilities, location, services and more to do an effective comparison. You must benchmark with the intent to improve, not to justify the status quo. Just because you are within the average of published benchmarks is no reason to be complacent. Do you want to be average, or do you want to be a leader? Learn from what the others are doing and implement change in any areas where you don't lead.

Trap #6 - One-Time Effort

Benchmarking isn't just an exercise to do once and forget about it. Once you benchmark, you should continue to measure internally and compare your new results with the benchmark results and your own historical results to see how you are trending and to identify and take action if you start to slip. Periodically, drill down again to look at procedures, processes and resources for key benchmarks to see whether there are more changes you can make to improve results. As necessary, focus on a new area.

Trap #7 - Comparing Apples to Apples

Everybody talks about not comparing apples to oranges, but the bigger risk is the more subtle differences between apples. Accurate comparison is not as easy as it seems, and using averages provided in published benchmarks can result in wrong decisions. As noted before, you don't want to compare one type of apple with another. You need to compare things that really are the same. You may even need to make adjustments to ensure an equal comparison. The similarity of comparisons is important, since there are many factors at play.

Quick Summary

| **Key Points** | ➡ Benchmarking is the first step to improvement. |
| | ➡ Never use benchmarking results on their own. |

| **Executive Tips** | ➡ Know what you will do with the results before you start. |
| | ➡ Promote the exercise upwards and use the results to drive decisions and support for business cases. |

| **Traps to Avoid** | ➡ Don't just compare numbers. |
| | ➡ Adjust comparisons to reflect your specific situation |

12

Thinking Into The Corners™

Successfully developing and fostering ideas from your team improves your success.

> *"Knowing a great deal is not the same as being smart;*
> *intelligence is not information alone but also judgment, the*
> *manner in which information is collected and used."*
> *– Carl Sagan*

One of the biggest challenges facility managers face is developing new great ideas. Usually, people tell you to "'think outside the box" as a way to generate creativity and develop new ideas. Unfortunately, access to such a wide open canvas to create ideas on makes it hard for participants to develop concrete, useable, implementable ideas. It also misses an important point: we all have limits that constrict our options and our ideas.

Thinking Into The Corners™ acknowledges this original limitation and focuses on how we all think in our own comfortable zone and don't always "stretch" to come up with the ideas and solutions that work the best.

Like all good concepts, Thinking Into The Corners™ isn't difficult; it simply sets the stage to get the best results from your team. It actually relies on existing proven techniques for group discussion, problem solving and idea generation.

Thinking Into The Corners™ is the opposite of the old notion that you have to "think outside the box" to generate ideas and solutions. We all have limitations (boxes) we can't go outside of, so let's focus on solutions that are within the limitations we have to work with; limitations that are often outside of our control.

In fact, creativity within a framework is more effective for most of us, while abstract thinking is not a good way to get results. After all, great thinking isn't necessarily about a creative result, it's about a creative way to achieve the pre-defined result. For instance, give someone a coloring book with a picture of a cat and tell them they can color outside the lines and you may end up with a rabbit. That's ok, unless you really need a picture of a cat.

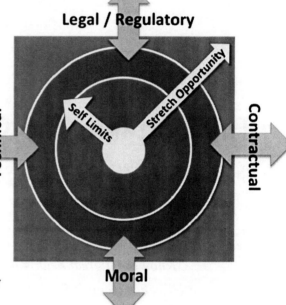

We all have Limits

Thinking Into The Corners™ recognizes that we all work with outside constraints (the box) which help us anchor our ideas. Moreover, we all have internal limits (the circle) that prevent us from stretching outside of our comfort zone.

When you combine the box and the circle, it becomes clear there are ideas hidden in the corners that we haven't reached yet. There's no need to try to go outside of the box to find and implement good ideas.

The process involves confirming the size of our box, including breaking down limits that are only in our minds and where possible, stretching the box to make it bigger. The reality is that there are always limits we simply can't do anything about. Spending time on ideas that can't be implemented is a waste of time and demoralizing to your team.

What we need are practical, achievable ideas – sometimes they just happen to look creative.

The Circle

Understanding the circle is important to help you and your staff break out of the self-limitations that exist when developing ideas for managing and delivering facilities services.

These limits affect the ability to create strategic plans, solve problems and even recognize issues and problems in the first place.

Quite simply, they keep us within a safe, comfortable range and mean we don't stretch to find new ideas that can be implemented.

They are a combination of many restrictions and internal limits we each have to one degree or another, although we all have different-sized circles.

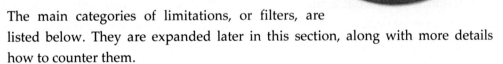

Even if we don't think we have these limitations, they will exist and impact us in some way. The limitations are sometimes obvious but they are usually subtle and are based on our own background, personal situation, comfort level and motivations.

The main categories of limitations, or filters, are listed below. They are expanded later in this section, along with more details how to counter them.

- ✓ Sunglasses – These are the simple filters usually based on experience and background.
- ✓ Time – These filters are related to the amount of effort it takes.
- ✓ Group think – These filters are created by a group envirienment
- ✓ Personal – these are personal filters based on the impact to ourselves.

The Box

While our own limitations illustrated by the circle have the biggest impact on our ability to be creative and develop new ideas, the box we work within has always been seen as a limit to overcome, particularly in the "Think Outside The Box: philosophy.

Since we all truly have a box in which we have to operate, it makes sense to define the outer limits of the box and then and anchor our creative process around those limits instead of wasting time on a process that leads us well beyond where we need to be, or in fact are able to be.

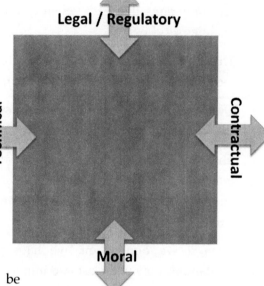

The box gives you the outside limits to use in your solution. The sides of your box are defined by legal, contractual, technical and moral limits.

Unlike the circle, everyone in an identical situation would have the same sized box. By the same token, individuals in identical situations may be able to change the size of that box. Your challenge when developing creative ideas is first to make sure the box is as large as possible, while still putting appropriate limits on the creative process.

For instance, while contractual limits are part of the box, there may be clauses built into those contracts that let you expand the box. When you start the process of expanding your circle and reaching into the corners of the box, you have to communicate the limits as you know them to the participants in the process.

The process of Thinking Into The Corners™ is flexible. As you are able to expand your box, your circle also needs to expand, enabling you to reach the corners where the best ideas are found.

Managing the Filters

We all develop filters that affect how we think, create and function. They are based on our experiences and internal factors such as our desire to maintain the status quo, stay safe and stay comfortable. Whether we recognize them or not, they act on all of us every day. We all have them, just to varying degrees, and they all contribute to how large our circle is and what our limits are for stretching beyond our comfort zone.

Recognizing the limits that affect you and your team's ability to creatively solve problems and implement new solutions is an important step to improving results. While they will affect us all in different ways, by understanding them, you can work to eliminate or minimize them for yourself and for your team, getting better results in the process.

Here are the key filters that affect us all to one degree or another:

Sunglasses

What the Filters Are

This is mostly our own internal filter. It includes being "set in our ways." We maintain the way it's always been done, don't try ideas that were tried before, hold onto our assumptions, fail to get new information and nurture our own bias towards experts, authorities and our boss's opinion.

How to Deal with Them

Structure your idea generation processes to avoid these issues. Make initial idea generation an anonymous activity so they aren't influenced by others. Establish that you are looking forward and foster a "green light" approach that looks at all ideas.

Time/effort

What the Filters Are

This is an external issue that dampens our creativity.

Anything that takes extra time, keeps us from our personal life and family and requires additional effort may stay in the back of your mind.

Type "A" personalities don't have this filter.

How to Deal with Them

It's easier to come up with an idea if you don't have to implement them

Better if the thinkers don't have to implement since we all limit our own ideas based on the level of effort it takes to accomplish them or our perception of the likelihood of success.

Dominant Player

What the Filters Are

When there is a dominant or aggressive member with strong opinions, many will filter their ideas if they think they'll have to argue with this person. Others will simply become weary of the process and stop contributing.

How to Deal with Them

Reign in the individual by speaking with them before the session or hold sessions without them present. During your session, be firm if necessary and ask them to hold back their opinions until the assessment phase of the idea-generation process.

Group Think

What the Filters Are

This filter is like abdicating your responsibility or your opinion to someone else. In society, it's when nobody calls to report a crime because they're sure someone else already has.

How to Deal with Them

Whenever everyone is thinking the same thing, or if one or two speak out and nobody else bothers to contribute, call on several individuals and challenge them to develop an alternate position or to be the "devil's advocate."

Saboteur

What the Filters Are

Someone who simply wants to sabotage the process is either adding a filter or strengthening others' filters. It's when instead of positive contribution, they always take a negative position and find the ways something can't work.

How to Deal with Them

This type of person will seriously dampen others' contributions. Don't invite them to the session or take a firm position with them and cut them off when they start to go in a negative or counter-productive direction. Knowing who they are in the first place will help you deal with them effectively.

Wallflowers

What the Filters Are

This filter is when participants don't bother to share their thoughts and ideas. It may be caused by other issues such as self-confidence or because other participants act as saboteur or dominant player.

How to Deal with Them

Reduce the impact of the other filters that cause this problem. If you know them to be quiet, speak with them in advance to encourage their participation. Manage the session so when they contribute, there is no negative responses and call upon them specifically for their thoughts rather than waiting for them to volunteer.

Risk Aversion

What the Filters Are

Risk is a powerful motivator and it impacts your filters as well. Whenever there is personal risk such as job security and income, it will create a strong filter that ranges from sabotage to a lack of participation.

How to Deal with Them

If the risks are only perceived, then re-assure the participants of your intent and that the risks they think are involved won't actually happen.

When there are real risks to their jobs, positions or income, be aware of the impact and plan your sessions carefully to avoid sabotage, whether intentional or not.

The Process - Thinking Into The Corners™

This important part of the process is about setting up your creative problem-solving exercise so that you can generate solutions and ideas that are practical and you can implement.

By setting up the environment first, based on the principles of Thinking Into The Corners™, you will get much more value out of the existing range of techniques and tools for generating ideas. Many of them are listed and discussed further below.

The process is mostly about communicating and understanding the limits of your box so you and your team can be focused and productive while also identifying and eliminating the things that create the circles that limit your reach.

Step	What to Do	How To Do It
1	Identify the problem	This has to be the root cause, not the result.
		Use a root cause analysis process with a fishbone diagram described below to identify the real problem you need to deal with. There may be more than one cause.
2	Identify the box limits as they relate to the problem and discuss ways to expand the box. Legal/regulatory Contractual Technical Moral	Once you know what the real problems are, you can frame your limits around them.
		Explore each of the areas to the left but don't just do it superficially: probe and explore each one to see if you can expand the box.
		For instance, if there is a contract limit, have it with you and explore all clauses to see where there may be flexibility.

Step	What to Do	How To Do It
3	Identify the circle limits and discuss to eliminate as many as possible. Sunglasses Time/effort Group dynamics Risk Aversion Etc.	Some of this you will want to do independent from the group. Consider the participants and pinpoint the possible limits each of them has. A good example is a group who already feels overworked and doesn't want something else to do, or long-term employees who thinks the way they've been doing it is good enough. Others may simply not like change. Once you identify the limits, consider how to deal with each one when you are in the facilitated session. This could be as simple as identifying an alternate resource who will run with the solution, or making the clear statement that we aren't looking backwards, only forwards. You won't be able to eliminate each one completely, but you can minimize them.
4	Use the problem solving tools below to develop ideas.	Each of the problem-solving methods below has its advantages and disadvantages, and you may even want to use more than one with your team. Do it in a structured, well-managed session that focuses on the problem and the need for a collaborative and concrete result that can be auctioned.
5	Prioritize/rank ideas	You are likely to come up with a number of ideas, solutions or approaches if you've looked at the problem carefully with your team and used all the tools at your disposal. Since you probably can't do everything, rank the ideas with the team so you can start with the highest impact ones that will take the least amount of work. Use a quadrant assessment like the one described below.

Step	What to Do	How To Do It
6	Select the highest-value ideas and test them against the limits	Once you've selected the best ideas or solutions, don't simply leave it at that. Take each one and test them against the original limits and explore the implementation issues in more details. This may result in changing the priorities or at least let you know the additional challenges you may face.
7	Re-do as necessary	If you have a large team and the time, you can duplicate the exercise with a different group and see whether the results are the same. Since the group will have different filters, they may see things differently and that's usually a good thing. If they aren't consistent, then you should explore why and re-assess. Even getting both teams together and discussing the differences may help with the decision.
8	Choose the idea(s) to implement	Once you finish the process, you will have a prioritized list of solutions or ideas. Select the ones you will tackle first based on the likelihood of success.

Consider This

A successful implementation demonstrates to your team and your boss that the process is valuable and that positive change is possible. With a success under your belt, you can tackle the harder issues.

Tools for Creative Ideas & Problem Solving

There are many very useful tools to generate and assess ideas and suggestions that work very well with the Thinking Into The Corners™ approach.

They are all tried and true techniques you will probably recognize, but they all work in different situations and for different types of problem solving, so use the ones that work best for your specific issues and group dynamics.

Facilitated Session

Teamwork and collaboration are proven ways to get better ideas from people instead of trying to work out solutions by yourself.

The problem is that just putting a bunch of people together and hoping for the best in a meeting won't work. You need a planned, structured approach that has a purpose, uses the right techniques and ends with a specific action plan.

While you should use the other tools listed further below to generate the ideas, you need to add the structure and framework by creating a formal session and facilitating it to keep it on-time and on-track as well as working to remove as many filters as you can in the idea creation process.

You can facilitate your team's session, but it is better to have someone not invested in the issue do the facilitation. If you bring in a facilitator from a different department such as human resources, or an external facilitator, you will be able to fully contribute to the session instead of having to manage it.

Facilitation includes establishing the goals and objectives, planning activities including the tools listed below, selecting the participants and doing some advance preparation to understand the participants, underlying group dynamics, potential trouble spots and both laying and policing the ground rules of the session.

Green Lighting (Brainstorming)

This is the best way to start developing ideas. After you provide the necessary introductions, frame the problem or issue, deal with the filters, limits and other preparation.

The idea is to get ideas on the table without discussing them. This way, all ideas are identified and they won't be suppressed by discussion, argument and dissent among the group.

Sometimes, this is very hard for the group to do, particularly if they are used to giving their opinion and have a strong background in the issues. Be sure to set the ground rules and be diligent in applying them. Whenever anyone starts to assess somebody else's idea, you simply ask them to reserve their comments for the follow-up process.

There are a several methods you can use to generate the ideas in a green lighting session.

Round Table

This is a simple approach and works with a smaller group. It forces everyone involved to be prepared and put out at least one solution when it's their turn. Just be sure to give them advance notice, otherwise the first participant you call on will be disadvantaged since they didn't have any time to think about it. You will need to acknowledge that the last ones to talk may not have anything to contribute that hasn't already been said. If you have people who are hesitant to contribute, this will force them to be involved, but be careful. Don't force shy or reserved participants to contribute, particularly if they may not be in a position to suggest solutions. If this appears to be the case, the facilitator can simply ask for volunteers to talk instead of going around the table, or use a different approach.

Break-Out Groups

With a large group, or when you have participants who are less likely to be able to contribute on their own, break-out groups are a great way to develop ideas. Break the entire group in groups of five to seven participants and give them time to collectively come up with their ideas and suggestions. Don't let the groups form on their own. Select participants for each group to get the best result. While the groups are working, you/the facilitator should circulate and ensure they are making progress and make sure everyone is contributing and someone isn't dominating the discussion. Once they are finished, they select a representative to go through their list of ideas.

Ballots

You can use this technique if you want the ideas to be anonymous or if you feel that a number of participants will hesitate to speak in front of the group. Give the participants time to think and to write down their ideas on pieces of paper that they can put inside a basket or box. Then pick the papers from the box and read them out without identifying the individual, unless he or she wants to talk about the idea. Have someone else write the ideas on a pad board. If ideas are contributed by more than one individual, combine them into one, but keep track of how many people came up with the idea.

...ons

...estions and probe deep enough to challenge ...wer to the issue, not just a superficial one.

...m these questions, you are really probing for ...answer. If you have a set of probing questions ...will get answers you can use on a more

...on. When you get the answer, ask another ...ariation on the fishbone technique often used ...en use it in your process to document the key ...the questions.

...y. Be sure to start on a large whiteboard or ...ou to expand it with more paper if necessary.

...ntial questions builds on previous answers to

...upant?

...important, why are they important?

...ortant, what is the risk of failure? What is

...ow can they be minimized or eliminated?

5. For each of the risk items, what do we do to minimize risk that benefits the occupant?

Often, the reasons for a problem are not readily apparent and unless you ask questions and dig deeper, you never find the real reason and therefore can't implement a solution that will work. Another application of the sequential question approach can also help you pinpoint the root cause of an issue.

Step	Question	Answer	
1	Why wasn't the work order completed on-time?	The technician had to go back a second time to finish the job.	
2	Why did he have to go back?	The tech didn't have the tools he needed.	
3	Why didn't he have the tools?	The work order didn't have the information the tech needed to select the right tools.	
4	Why didn't it have the information?	A	The help desk rep doesn't have the background needed to ask the right questions of the customer and write down the information.
		B	The technician didn't ask for more information or call the occupant.
A5	Why don't they have the background?	They were hired as administrative positions and then their role changed.	
A6	Why weren't they trained?	Nobody thought about training them since they were already part of the team.	
A7	How can we fix it?	Provide training.	
B5	Why didn't the technician get more information before going on site?	Most of the time they have the tools they need. Getting information on a work order is too hard to bother.	
B6	Why is it too hard to get information?	They are on the road and it's hard to get answers.	
B7	Why is it hard to get answers?	The help desk staff always have to call them back and they can't answer the phone when they are driving, causing a lot of telephone tag.	
B8	How can we fix it?	Add texting or email plans to the phones so the help desk can simply send them the information.	

Once you finish this exercise, you will have the information you need to develop a solution, whether it's details and examples, or a better overall understanding about the issues and requirements.

Fishbone Diagram

Sometimes, a diagram is the most effective way to illustrate and explore the results of the sequential questioning exercise described above. It's particularly useful when there are several answers or causes at various points, since tracking the separate paths of the questions starts to be very cumbersome compared to using other methods. The fishbone diagram enables you to follow many different paths of questions and answers using an illustration that is easy to visualize.

You can also get the same result with a flowchart as described below for some types of problems and issues. Nevertheless, a fishbone diagram is useful for following various paths until you get to the ones that you need to deal with – the root cause of the problem.

Consider This

A fishbone diagram is very easy to use, but be sure to start it on a large enough paper taped to the wall or on a large whiteboard.

The sample below is based on the earlier example. Here, the problem is shown in the box at the front of the diagram and whenever you arrive at the end of a particular path, usually with a solution or action item, you can add a circle to keep track. You'll notice that in this case, there are three solutions. In some cases, action is required on all three. Other times, one choice makes the others redundant. Keep an open mind because the best problem-solving action will depend on your specific situation.

To illustrate the technique, we simply identified that there may be other causes for the problem beyond the one we dealt with. In most cases, those other causes should also be explored.

To create your fishbone diagram, draw a line across the middle of a page or whiteboard and write down the problem in a box at the end.

Then, ask the first question and draw a line at an angle off the original line and write the short answer on the line. Ask another question, draw another line and write the short answer on that line. Ask more questions and continue to add the lines, with space between them, until your diagram looks like a fishbone.

Then, off each of the fishbones, draw horizontal lines and ask another question about the original answer and write it in on the line. Continue the process until you have probed enough and have all the information you need to find a solution.

Your diagram will eventually look similar to the example shown here:

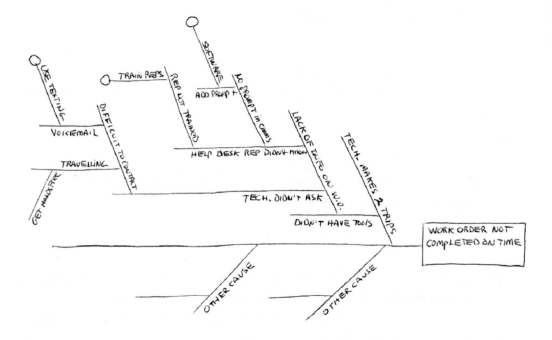

Flowcharts

Whenever you are looking at processes and interfaces, the best way to understand what's happening today and probe for the problem areas, roadblocks and pressure points, is to use a simple flowchart diagram. A visual representation of the problem always helps with the understanding and may reveal where the solution is needed.

The flowchart doesn't have to be complicated. Start with a simple one that covers the main processes and steps. Then, where needed, break them down into sub-processes on a different whiteboard or paper instead of creating a large, unmanageable flowchart.

If you create the flowcharts in a group setting, you may also find that there is some confusion about the process and the interfaces. Even if you don't do it in a group, have the group follow the process from start to finish to get agreement about the flow. This will help identify areas of the process that are not being done the way everyone believes they are and gives you a great start to improving the processes.

SWOT Analysis

Strength, Weakness, Opportunity, Threat (SWOT) analysis is a common tool for business planning and you can use a modified version to help develop your own strategic plan and explore ideas and solutions to problems.

Instead of considering the SWOT from a larger perspective, focus it directly on an issue you need to deal with and consider each of the strengths, weaknesses, opportunities and threats from that context.

The outcome of a SWOT analysis should support the specific problem, issue or strategic plan you are working on. It's the only reason you're doing it, so keep the end goal in mind throughout the process. If you start to look at things in your SWOT analysis that are outside your original goal, park those issues for a future session. While it's always tempting to expand the SWOT session beyond your intended goal, be prepared to manage your time and the involvement of the participants.

Strength

Strengths are related to the solution, problem or issue you are working on. Focus on them and develop clear, honest strengths on which you can focus. Depending on what you are working on, the strength may be the benefit or advantage of a particular solution or approach. When you look at strengths, they should be directly related to your needs. Ideally, they will also be quantifiable, if not immediately, then with time and study.

If you and your group have a hard time establishing a strength, first go through the attributes of the solution or approach and determine whether they are strengths or not. Focus on the strengths and park anything that will be included in the other three parts of the SWOT analysis.

Weakness

Use the same list of attributes from the strengths and look at each one carefully to find weaknesses. These may be cost, time, risk, or any of the traditional characteristics you would use for decision making.

Once you've identified weaknesses, address them immediately, which may result in them being removed from the weakness list, or list them and go back later to assess whether they can be overcome.

Whenever possible, quantify the weakness and identify their importance and impact on the idea's success.

Consider This

Where immediate action on a SWOT item can yield immediate results - take it. If possible, track improvements to make a business case for your leadership skills. Even small changes should be recognized for their incremental value.

Opportunities

Identify the opportunities from the idea or solution you are dealing with in terms of the immediate issue and its spin-off benefits. Where benefits extend beyond the FM department, take credit for having a positive impact on your organization.

As with the weaknesses, quantify opportunities when possible, either during this process or after you've completed the SWOT analysis. These are some of the things you'll use for your business case to demonstrate its value and sell the initiative.

Threats

Threats are essentially risks and problems that could happen if you implement new initiatives, or fail to take action.

Being honest about the threats is important, since these have to be dealt with if you are going to have a successful implementation. You can also develop your response and mitigation to the threats and include them in your business case. Identifying threats and showing your solutions, gains credibility from the approval authority.

Exploration

This is essentially a "what if?" process to fully explore ideas and solutions and assess what the problems are and address them or abandon the solution if necessary before too much time is spent. You do this after you have arrived at one or more solutions that appear viable.

The opposite of a "green light" session, exploration works with participants to try and identify as many valid "red lights'"' as possible. Look for problems, issues, roadblocks and limitations that will affect the viability of the solution.

It is important to discuss how they can be solved. In the end, you want to have as few "red lights" as possible.

Some of the "red lights" may be easily solved through discussion. Others have to be explored outside of the discussion but once you've identified them you should also be on track to overcome them.

Quadrant Assessment

Whenever you are faced with several options, a quadrant assessment can help you either decide which action to take. It can also help you prioritize the options based on important characteristics.

In this quadrant diagram, the x axis represents the level of effort from low on the left to high on the right. The y axis represents value, from low on the bottom to high on the top. If your characteristics have a more graduated range, you can further subdivide each quadrant into quadrants and position your options

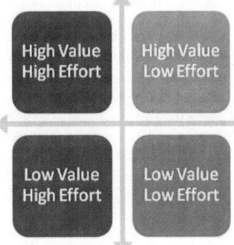

within each quadrant relative to each other to further refine the assessment.

After assessing your various options or solutions, the ones that end up in the top right quadrant are the most likely to implement first since they give you a high value with a low effort. It doesn't mean you wouldn't also implement something with a low value and low effort. The technique does ensure you base your decision on solid information.

While there may be more than just value and effort as important characteristics of the options, including cost or risk, for instance, you can start with whichever characteristics you feel are most important and then take the most likely options from the first quadrant assessment. By working them through again with different characteristics, you can move towards the best possible ones options.

Cross-Functional Groups

If managed properly, a cross-functional group will solve problems and develop ideas much better than a group consisting of the same types of functions or expertise. This approach helps to reduce some of the filters that come from being too close to the topic or issue. Staff from a different functional area may see issues and solutions that aren't seen by the people who've been doing the job for many years.

At the same time, there is a risk that some of the ideas are far off the mark because they don't have the knowledge level of those working in that area. This is a trade-off that's well worth it, but you do need to manage the process properly and prepare the group before you start. You do not want the functional experts, for example, to misunderstand the process or to dismiss or ridicule ideas coming from other staff members.

Combining this approach with some of the other tools will minimize the filtering and enable new ideas to be explored no matter how far off they seem to their colleagues. Sometimes even if the idea won't work as-is, concepts can be adjusted and applied with great success. They key is to develop an open mind within the group and minimize the filters.

Quick Summary

Key Points	➡ Don't try to think outside the box – boundaries help your creative process.
	➡ Everyone has filters that may suppress the best ideas.
	➡ You have to put the conditions in place for the best collaboration and teamwork.
Executive Tips	➡ Many existing tools can be used to help you generate ideas and solutions with your team.
	➡ Recognize the filters and work to counteract them.
Traps to Avoid	➡ Don't use the "blue-sky" approach to idea generation, it may waste time generating impractical ideas
	➡ Don't make groups from all the same people and experiences. Mixing it up will give you better results.

Your Strategic Plan

Based on this section, what strategic initiatives do you plan to implement that will help you manage your assets better and when do you expect to accomplish them?

What are you going to do?	When?

Notes

_____

_____

_____

_____

_____

_____

_____

_____

_____

_____

_____

_____

_____

Communicating to Influence

Introduction

Effective written communications is an important skill for facility managers, but is often under-appreciated in terms of being a skill that should be developed by the organization.

The reality is that no matter how good you are and how much you know, if you can't communicate effectively to convey your instructions or convince others of the need to take specific action, then you won't reach your full potential.

And communications goes far beyond internal communications, whether you manage your organization's own building or a commercial building with paying tenants. The image your communications present through memos, notices and postings in public areas affects your reputation as a professional organization.

13

Influence with Your Writing

If you can't get the message across, why bother?

*"Communicating without a strategy is like throwing darts
blindfolded, just less likely to hurt your audience."*
– Michel Theriault

*Facility managers write to influence others. You want them to agree to your
proposal, follow instructions or look favorably on you and your organization. Many
traditional ways of writing don't work when trying to influence someone in the
modern age.*

Effective FM is all about communications. Whether you are managing office
space, maintaining building systems, developing strategic asset plans or all of the
above, good communication skills are essential. Communications include written
material, presentations and even verbal discussions one-on-one and at meetings.
While each of these formats has its own challenges, the essence of good
communication is the same no matter which medium you use. The most
significant variables for good communications are the audience and the goal you
are trying to achieve. You need to zero in on what you want your message to
accomplish - and who will do the work.

Here are some of the typical types of communication tools used by facility managers and property managers:

- ✓ Letters to individual tenants / occupants
- ✓ Response to complaints
- ✓ Lease issues (including rent)
- ✓ Conveying information
- ✓ Memo's to occupants (general)
- ✓ Emails
- ✓ Newsletters
- ✓ Notices and posted items (in lobby's, washroom doors, construction, etc.)
- ✓ Policies, procedures and instructions
- ✓ Business cases/capital justifications
- ✓ Minutes/documenting issues and events.

Communicate to get Results

While it's easy to see why technical skills and knowledge are emphasized in FM, there is a growing awareness of the critical importance of softer skills such as communications.

And no wonder. With poor communications, memos and letters are easy to misunderstand or be dismissed as unconvincing, emails are ignored, procedures appear overly complex, building notices miss the point and look unprofessional, business cases aren't convincing, newsletters are deemed uninteresting and presentations fail to get the planned message across.

If you are not getting the results you need from your written communication, take a look at what you're doing and whether you're using modern techniques to communicate or following what you learned in high school English classes or your business communications course.

Accept that many of the traditional ways of writing simply don't work when you are trying to influence someone in the modern technological age. Moreover, way too many people write backwards by launching a message before they identify the message's purpose, assess their audience and develop a message that will focus on the critical issue.

Understand the Roadblocks

You are fighting against powerful forces that make it difficult to get your message across. Here is what you're up against:

Short attention spans

Get the point across quickly or you lose your audience's interest.

Information Overload

There is competition for their attention so your message must be uncluttered and dead simple to see, read and understand.

Very little time

Nobody has time to read everything that crosses their desk so you lose your audience quickly with long, tedious writing or presentations that don't immediately attract their attention.

Consider This

To earn success, be realistic about what you need to do to persuade your audience. Focus on content that hits the mark with structure that makes it easy to see and understand. If you're not sure your message works, test it with a trusted colleague. Where possible, engage input from someone else who is specifically impacted by the issue and wants to promote active change.

When all is said and done, there are only three reasons the FM professional needs to communicate. You communicate to:

- ✓ Get approval or buy-in.
- ✓ Have your instructions followed or your request obeyed.
- ✓ Build a positive reputation.

If you can make these three things happen with your writing and presentations, you will be more successful. Use any of these three reasons to communicate as the basis for your approach whenever you write or develop a presentation. They form the core of your strategy when developing communication tools.

Instead of worrying about spelling, fussing over grammar, trying to sound smart or following the same formats you see everyone else using, focus on what works and emphasize content that hits the mark with structure that makes it easy to see and understand. Then worry about spelling and grammar, or get someone else you trust to polish it up. (Even the best writers have an editor.)

Think Strategically

The key is to have a strategy before you start. Communicating without a strategy is like throwing darts blindfolded, just less likely to hurt your audience. You can improve your communications by following these key points:

- ✓ Be clear about your goal or message before you start to write.
- ✓ Provide information that is appropriate to the audience.
- ✓ Organize your information so it is easy to absorb.
- ✓ Be short and concise - don't make it longer than it needs to be and don't use long sentences or big words.
- ✓ Consider what the audience wants to hear about, not just what you want to say.
- ✓ Don't assume too much - spell it out if there is any doubt.

Avoiding some of the most common mistakes is also important if you want to gain influence and recognition through effective writing. Here are the 7 Deadly Sins of Writing.:

1. Writing without a plan.
2. Writing what you want to say, not what the reader wants to read.
3. Trying to sound smart.
4. Writing too much fluff.
5. Structure that is difficult to read.

6. Making your key message hard to find.

7. Leaving the good stuff for the end.

Keeping these in mind, I'll outline some of the most basic yet important steps to communicating effectively, whether in writing or a via an oral presentation.

Establish Your Purpose

Your message and goal must be integrated and guide your content and structure. Know what you want from the reader and make it clear. (e.g., I want you to understand x and do y.) For your newsletter, gain support for changes or show occupants how proactive you are. Your business case or proposal is selling your position to someone who can approve it. Your policy or building notice explains something in a way that ensures support and that instruction will be followed.

Assess and Target the Reader

Understanding and assessing the audience is critical. You can't influence someone unless you know what will influence them.

Even the best ideas fail unless you communicate with your audience in a way they understand. This is not an easy task, but by looking closely at what the audience wants or needs to hear, you can tailor your communications for maximum effectiveness. Consider how each element of your communication is received by the audience. This includes the level of detail, type of information, tone, wording and even the message. Keep in mind that your communications may span across different audiences with different needs.

Part of the planning includes understanding the audience's interest. For an article in a newsletter, the occupants need to know what it means to them. The reader of a business case will want to know what decision is necessary and what impact it will have. For a new policy, the audience needs to know why it is being implemented, exactly what is expected, and what the processes are.

Similarly, the content must support your purpose. Build your content with facts and examples that will be meaningful to the audience and support the purpose for your communications.

Where possible, consider possible objections and build those into your communications up front. Don't leave unanswered questions.

Speak the audience's language and address them directly. Focus on issues and information that will matter to them, not what you like and are comfortable with. Use examples they can relate to and avoid jargon they won't understand.

If you expect the audience or reader to take action, clearly outline what you expect from them and make it easy for them to take that action.

Prioritize Information

It's easy to pack lots of information into your communications, especially when you know the topic and are passionate about it. In the interest of keeping it simple and short, prioritize the information based on its potential influence and impact on the audience. Don't be afraid to throw out content that doesn't support your purpose.

Be sure that the information you use is important to the audience. You want them to be motivated by what they read.

Create a Structure

Great content is not enough to influence the audience if they don't bother to read it. Because of the audience's limited time, short attention span and information overload, your job is to structure the information to be compelling and easy to read.

Start with a compelling title and then hit them with a powerful first sentence or paragraph. Don't save the best content for the last paragraph, or they may never read it. The idea is to get them to keep reading by convincing them that they should. How you do this is part of understanding your audience.

Next, use lots of white space and visual cues such as headings, tables, diagrams and bullet lists to enhance concepts and relationships. Keep things short and to-the-point and only give people the information they need. Where appropriate, refer them to other sources, such as a web site or another document.

Your goal is to guide your reader to your message using visual cues and to focus their attention on what you want them to see. When possible, use side-bars, boxes and pull-out quotes to highlight information and give the audience a quick hit of important information.

Make your written material visually easy to read with short paragraphs, white space and simple language.

When writing reports, business cases or other long documents, use headings that are more descriptive instead of standard headings. For instance, use "Your Current Situation" instead of "Background," "Problems Being Solved" instead of "Objectives" and "Your Approval is Needed" instead of "Conclusion."

Use introductions and summaries in longer documents to help the reader know where they are and where they are going. Don't be afraid to repeat important content or messages.

Develop Format & Structure

The format and structure of your writing are an important part of persuading or informing the reader. Unless the reader is able to clearly see what you are saying, the efforts you put into your writing will be ineffective.

Why are Format and Structure so Important?

Your communication should lead the writer to the arguments and messages you are making in your writing, all in an effort to educate or convince the reader of something.

Structure is the visual representation of the information and includes headings, placement of graphics, and positioning of key information. It also includes how you organize your writing, including the type of information you provide and in what order.

Format is the size and font of your text, margins, headings and sub-headings. It's the indenting, bullets and other visual clues you provide to text and the overall document.

Structure and format provide the following benefits. Information that is visually easier-to-read:

- ✓ Helps retention
- ✓ Leads the reader to your message
- ✓ Focuses attention on what you want.

Overall Structure

The overall structure of your document and each separate section should be planned. This basic information structure can be repeated throughout your document. This includes the following elements:

- ✓ Lead-in
- ✓ Detail / facts / arguments
- ✓ Summary or conclusion.

Consider This

Mirror excellence. When you come across newsletter, trade articles or posted information you really like, study it and learn from it. What catches your eye? What sticks in your imagination? What makes you care? Imitation is the sincerest form of flattery.

Techniques

Being able to visibly separate out information to make it easier to read and easier to absorb the information, as well as relate it to the overall message, is one of the purposes of structure. Here are several techniques you should use in your proposal to achieve those goals:

Chunking

This involves pulling out key information from your main text and separating it. You can use a text box, an indented paragraph, separate graphic or a table. By using a text box, the main text can wrap around the box. Shading borders and bold titles will draw further attention to the call-out box. This is an excellent way to visibly highlight information. Use this technique to repeat material from your main text.

Get Attention
By using a text box, you can focus attention on a key point.

Bookends

Bookends are short statements at the beginning and end of your document or sections to get your message across quickly.

Depending on whether the bookends are used in a short or long document, the bookends may be your introduction and conclusion or be presented as a brief message that appears before the introduction and after the conclusion. To make bookends stand out, put them in a box or use other formatting such as italics or a larger font to separate the text and make it highly visible. Usually, these are short and sum up the key point or main message. Use different wording for each end of the bookends, but do make the same point. This reinforces your message through repetition and provides a short, simple, obvious message that the reader is more likely to read.

The advantage of using bookends is that they:

✓ Frame your point.
✓ Are the first and last paragraphs or statements, therefore are most likely to read and be remembered.
✓ Repeat your key message and arguments.

With bookends, you get your message across, reinforce it and ensure it's easy to see and likely to be read.

Signposts

Signposts are another visual reference. They point the reader to information you want them to see and provide a reference point for transitions. The most obvious examples of signposts are headings and sub-headings, but they do include other techniques identified below. All signposts break up the text and provide visual cues of a section's importance.

Visual Structure & White Space

By leaving enough white space and creating a pleasing visual structure to your written material, the text will be easier to read and absorb.

Headings

Make your headings meaningful where possible. Try not to use the same, boring headings in your documents.

Dull, Boring Headings	Relevant and Meaningful Headings
Purpose	Why This Policy will Keep you Safe
Benefits	How You Can Benefit
Responsibilities	Your Participation will Help Others

Pull Quotes / Info Boxes

Your word processing software makes it easy to add pull quotes or info boxes to your documents in many different formats and styles. You can position them anywhere within your text. The 'Consider This' boxes in this book are another example.

Important Info

Use pull quotes or information boxes to make interesting information stand out and be read.

Bullets

Bullets force you to organize information and distill it down to the core of the message. It's also much easier for the reader to see your message since it isn't buried in a long paragraph. Don't just use round bullets; other symbols can help convey your meaning, too.

➡ Bullets get attention.
✓ Bullets communicate your idea quickly.
☒ Bullets are easy to follow.

You can even use special icons or symbols that are easy to add with your word processor.

If you use Clipart for symbols, be careful to make it relevant and professional.

Bold text

Sometimes, you can highlight specific words, phrases or terms within your text to provide emphasis and make it stick out. **Use with caution**, however, since it can also be distracting and if you do too much of it, nothing looks important.

Tables (or table structure)

Some information is easily presented in a table format, which makes it clearer and more logical than writing several paragraphs. You can even nest tables within each other for more complex items.

Issue	Problem	Solution
Describe Issue #1	State the problem here	State the solution here
Describe Issue #2	Repeat as necessary	Repeat as necessary

Charts/diagrams/figures

If you are talking about numbers, process or anything that can be represented with a chart or diagram, make them simple and uncluttered to provide an easy visual reference.

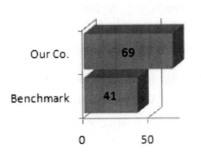

Churn Rate %

Boxing

Boxing involves separating information using a table structure that enables you to focus attention and organize the information so it is easy to see and follows a specific structure that makes it easier to comprehend.

Tables are easy to use and can be in-line with the text as shown below, or float with wraparound similar to the text box used in the chunking example above.

This is especially effective for policies, procedures and other instructional writing.

Visual	It structures the information visually, separating it from the main narrative.		
Easy to Find	Instead of being buried in the text, the information is easy to find.		
Organized Structure	The technique allows you to easily organize information you might have otherwise included in a hard to read paragraph.		
	Step 1	Decide how to structure your informatic
	Step 2	Create a table with the columns and ro
	Step 3	Enter your information.
	Step 4	Format the text and the table.

The Look and Feel of your Documents

For the look of your document, use lots of white space and visual cues such as headings, tables, diagrams and bullet lists described above to enhance concepts and relationships between information while making the entire document easier to read. Avoid long blocks of text, which are hard to read. Split them into shorter paragraphs or use sub-headings.

This highlights information and gives readers a quick hit of important information. While these are techniques you see more often in magazines and newspapers, they are powerful and can help you pull out important material from the main body of text.

Where possible, use color to provide some visual cues and make your proposal more interesting to look at. Don't overdo it, however as it can become a distraction.

Essentially, you are guiding the reader to your message with these visual cues and focusing their attention on what you want them to see. The white space and visual cues also require less effort to read and will create less fatigue for the evaluators and their eyes.

Writing

Don't try to impress with your writing; you are communicating useful information, not writing a novel. Using long sentences and fancy grammar detracts from your message and makes it less likely your audience will read or understand your message.

Shorten sentences and use more paragraphs for long documents. Simplify sentences with fewer words to convey the message and eliminate unnecessary language. Use active language when writing to show action. Active language conveys a more powerful, action-oriented impression of your message.

Keep it simple and eliminate extra words

Most people write like they speak. Often, this includes complicated phrases, long words and filler words. It's worse when the writer believes that fancy language conveys a sense of importance or intelligence. The editing process helps you eliminate these phrases and words, all of which make it harder to understand what you wrote. Some examples include:

Hard to absorb	Easy to absorb
In view of the fact that...	because
In the event that.....	if
Involves the use of.......	uses
Institute	begin / start
To this end, we want you to..	Please...
...so that you..	...so you....

Use Picture Language

Describing what you mean rather than using a single word is also much more powerful. It doesn't mean you should describe everything, but the more descriptive you are, the more interesting the text. Interesting text is easier to remember because it helps readers form mental pictures. When writing, using picture language will improve your communication. Remember:

- ✓ Non-technical language is easier to understand.
- ✓ Illustrating with picture language supports your message.
- ✓ It's easier to put it in the evaluator's perspective.
- ✓ You can include comparisons / examples the reader can imagine.

Short paragraphs, short sentences

When presented with information, the human mind benefits from "breaks" that help us absorb the information properly. Paragraphs are another tool you can use to break up a longer section into separate ideas or pieces of information that will be easier to see and read if there is a visible break in between. Improve it even more by adding headings.

Sentences should also be relatively short to help comprehension and make it less tiring to read. Don't make them too short and choppy, though, since that makes the flow of reading very difficult and the message won't be continuous.

Use active sentences

Avoid passive language, which typically uses more words and is harder to read and understand. Active language conveys a more powerful, action-oriented impression of your message. Active language is:

- ✓ Easier to read.
- ✓ Conveys a positive impression to the reader.
- ✓ Shows action and boosts confidence in what you say.

Passive Language	Active Language
We are looking forward to working with you and implementing the new policy.	We will implement the policy with you.
Our service will enable...	Our service enables...
Information is going to be provided in the meeting.	You will receive information at the meeting.
When required by the circumstances, we may provide ...	We provide prompt service
The air was tested by the specialist.	The specialist tested the air
Further to your drawings, specifications and details received, we would like to take this opportunity to advise that we approve the submitted drawings provided.	We approve the work based on the information submitted.
Upon approval of the business case, it would be our intent to commence working towards improvement of services right away.	With your approval, work to improve services can start immediately.

Use a Writing Process

The best way to write effectively is to use a process. A process introduces a structured approach and discipline into how you write and will produce more effective writing with less effort.

The following is a simple process you can use when writing almost anything, from short memos or notices to complicated business cases or procedures.

The POWER system for writing

Prepare

1. Establish the message.
2. Create your SOCO (Single Overriding Communication Objective).
3. Analyze the audience.
4. Decide on messaging, themes, hot buttons and solutions.
5. Collect your facts and supporting information, including images, samples, examples, etc.
6. Create compelling arguments.

Outline

1. Develop the overall structure and flow of your proposal response.
2. Define the headings and sub-headings that will cover all the information you need to include.
3. Identify the important information that needs to be highlighted.
4. Establish where tables, illustrations, bullet lists, etc., need to support your message.

Write/ Wait

1. Use the outline to start filling in the information and writing the material.
2. Don't initially self-edit. Get all your information down on paper.
3. Periodically go back and compare your material with the original message and your outline.
4. Wait or move on to another section, leaving at least a full day before coming back to edit what you've written.

Edit

1. Read your original writing from top to bottom.
2. Do a rough edit on content, structure and format. Be brutal. Don't be afraid to delete material that doesn't matter (do copy to another document just in case).
3. Do a final edit and then check style and spelling.
4. Have someone else review your text and give you feedback.
5. Edit again.

Review

1. Reread your newly-edited material. Be critical.
2. Compare your text with your message, SOCOs, themes, hot buttons and the evaluation criteria.
3. Edit again if necessary.

While technical skills and knowledge are critical to the FM professional, the soft skills separate the top performers from the good performers because top performers get results by influencing others.

Use a strategic approach to communicate and get your message across and you will contribute to your organization's success while enhancing your career. The best action is pro-active action.

- ✓ Always have a strategy / purpose.
- ✓ Only include content that meets your purpose.
- ✓ Focus on the audience.
- ✓ Keep it simple and it uncluttered.
- ✓ Use structure to highlight important info.
- ✓ Make your message stick.

Quick Summary

Key Points	➡ Communicate to get approval, buy-in, have instructions followed or to build a positive reputation.
Executive Tips	➡ Start with a purpose and a plan to influence with your words. ➡ Have strong content that gets your message across. ➡ Make it easy to see your key messages.
Traps to Avoid	➡ Don't try to sound smart by using long, complicated sentences ➡ Don't focus on spelling and grammar. Get someone else to proofread your writing. ➡ Don't create presentation slides as a crutch. They should only be your roadmap.

14

Influence with Your Presentations

Presentations are powerful unless used as a crutch.

"We communicate not by what we say, but by what the listener hears." - Waldo W. Braden

At some point, you will have to give a formal presentation. That usually includes presentation slides to convey information. How you develop these slides is important to the impact of your presentation and how you are perceived as a professional.

Presentations are recognized as an important business communication tool. They are delivered to get approval, get buy-in, motivate, inform, teach and sell. Whether you use them with your own staff, your occupants or your executive, they are a useful way to communicate your message and get results.

While Marshall McLuhan famously said, "the Medium is the Message," he did not mean your presentation slides should be the message. He did mean that the medium provides a good tool for message delivery and we should understand the tools we choose.

Developing Presentations

You can use many of the strategies and techniques explained in the previous section to develop your presentation material.

While many of the same principles apply, you must consider your oral delivery as well as the information you put on the slides. When it comes to delivery, show that you are the expert and use your nervous energy to your benefit; be passionate and animated; let yourself move as you speak.

Rules of Thumb

Before you start, review the following standard guidelines and my explanation.. They do not have to be followed exactly and in some cases, breaking the rule will be more effective. Much depends on the type of presentation, your audience and your objective. It's more important to consider what your objective is and focus your slides on meeting that objective than trying to fit your slides into a pre-defined mould, as long as what you do is effective.

"No more than 20 slides in your presentation"

The number of slides is actually irrelevant. It's the content, flow and pace that matters. You could have an hour-long presentation with a handful of slides where you talk for 10 minutes with each slide, or a presentation with 60 slides with a single point on them and spend a minute or less on each slide. Relevancy is more important than number.

"No more than five bullet points on each slide"

Generally speaking, the fewer bullet points the better. If the bullets prompt you to speak about specific points, have fewer on each slide and keep the presentation interesting by grouping points (perhaps by theme) on individual slides. Here, interest and relevancy trumps numbers.

If you are presenting a list of information you want the audience to read or if the presentation will be handed out for reference, you can introduce a slide with a long list of points, but not speak to the entire list. Do make sure the list is readable from the back of the room. This practical consideration will limit the information you put on a slide. If space is an issue, put it on a handout instead.

By getting creative, you could even have only one word on a slide along with an image to evoke a reaction and prompt you about what to talk about.

"No more than six words for each bullet point"

Again, it depends on the purpose, but shorter is always better if you are using the bullets as speaking points. In that case, even a single word will do. Where possible, bullet points should prompt you to talk about the topic, not spell it out completely.

Where you need to present more detail so the audience can read all of the information, use the extra words. make sure the points are readable from the back of the room and use these kinds of slides sparingly. No one wants to sit through a presentation filled with slides that carry entire blocks of text.

"2-3 minutes per slide"

This rule is deceptive since its application is only appropriate when you structure your slides and delivery approach to accommodate a two-to-three minute per-slide focus.

What's more important is that you create a good pace and keep the audience's interest. You can spend five or 10 minutes on some slides, just make sure you use that slide to discuss the issue, give examples and stories and solicit input and comment from the audience, etc. Similarly, you can spend 10 seconds on a slide that's used to illustrate a key point or give impact to your presentation.

Balance your Slides and Information

With any presentation, you need to balance what you put on your slides with the information you need to convey. An executive presentation is strategically different from a training presentation. Use slides to prompt and support what you say and don't use them to read verbatim information.

As readability is linked to understandability, keep the slides brief and uncluttered. Your delivery of information should be the real focus, not the text projected on the screen. If you need to provide more detail for the audience to take away with them, don't include it on your slides. Provide a separate handout or use the notes feature of your presentation software and print out pages for later reference. Use graphics whenever possible, but avoid using cheesy clipart. The graphics should support your message, not detract from it.

Use short bullets and single words when possible to make powerful statements. Eliminate dense slides. Deviate from the template when it's the right thing to do and mix it up a bit to keep it interesting.

Keep Slides Simple

Slides should be simple and easy-to-read without distracting the audience. They should have their attention on you and should not be trying to read the slide while you talk. If you know your material, you won't need all the details on the slide anyway. With adequate preparation, all you need are quick prompts to tell you what you should talk about.

Keep the following principles in mind when you develop your slides.

✓ Delivery and content are king.
✓ It's just a tool.
✓ Don't use it as a crutch.

Use the slides as a prompt for what you have to say and to reinforce your message with short, simple text.

Original Slide Text	Revised Slide Text
• Density occurs when there is too much text or too many thoughts on the same slides that force reading and bury the main points.	**Density** ✓ Too Much Stuff
• Eliminate density by focusing on the message and eliminating material that you will speak to anyway.	**Eliminate Density** ✓ Delete Stuff ✓ Speak to it

Slides that work

The speaker and his presentation are the most important part of a formal presentation, but slides run a close second in terms of their ability to support the speaker. Slides reinforce what you say and do need to be developed to deliver your message.

Regardless of whether your presentation's focus is on training or executive reporting, the most effective slide presentation will feature a single slide for each point or theme.

In fact, you can even do away with bullets if you use each point for a separate slide. This gives you more creativity and room to add visuals that illustrate the points.

Here are a few guidelines for developing your slides to support your presentation:

- ✓ Keep them simple
- ✓ One theme / one thought
- ✓ Large print
- ✓ Point form
- ✓ Images and illustrations
- ✓ Simple background.

Slide Examples

Here is an example of a slide that doesn't work. It has too much text and a cluttered background that makes it hard to read.

This next slide is an improved version. While it retains the cluttered background, the key concepts have been turned into three separate points. The graphic illustrates that there is a flow and the picture provides a relevant visual linkage to the theme. A cleaner background would improve it.

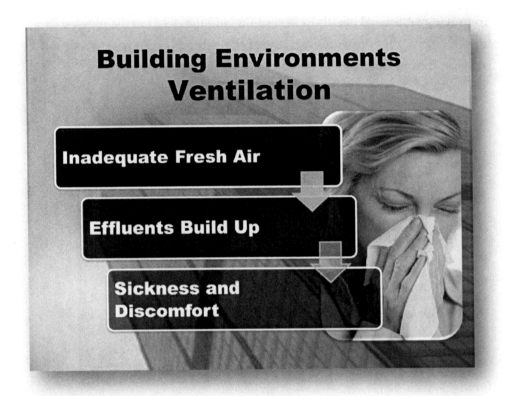

For an even better slide, eliminate the background so the message sticks out more. The facility manager who created this presentation clearly wanted to carry the theme of building environments through his slide presentation by including the building in the background. The end result is distracting. The audience would already be familiar with the context, so the image of the building isn't necessary.

To provide additional details in a handout, add the detail to the notes section of the slides and print the slides with the notes included. Your handouts would look like the one below:

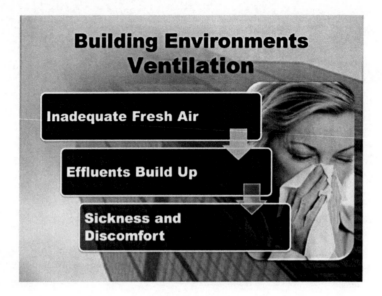

Ventilation

SBS apparently occurs most often in mechanically ventilated, air-conditioned buildings in which the amount or distribution of outdoor (fresh) air is inadequate.

In buildings lacking sufficient outdoor air supply, effluents from human occupants and their activities, as well as from building materials and other sources, can build up to levels where occupants may experience discomfort.

What follows is another example of a slide that is very cluttered. Unfortunately, many people opt for this approach because they wrongly believe it's better than too many slides.

As indicated earlier, it's not the number of slides that matters, it's how you organize your information and how you speak to the individual points that matters. It's more important to separate out the concepts and thoughts.

Think about it. You can spend the same amount of time presenting four slides as it takes to make one slide that conveys the same information.

Within The First Two Weeks

- Within Business Units, the manager should review details of the client contract paying particular attention to the impact the contract has on the new team member's role.

- Ensure that the Health and Safety modules from the online Health and Safety catalogue are completed.

- Explain the Performance Management and Bonus Program Process to the new team member. Advise them of timelines and when you will be conducting discussions and performance reviews.

- Review the appropriate Timesheet with the team member, explaining how and when vacation and sick leave are accrued and used, and recording of overtime, statutory holidays and training hours.

Here is one way to split up the four concepts from the previous slide and present them on four separate slides.

This also allows you to clearly list the separate points as bullets under each concept instead of burying them in a paragraph.

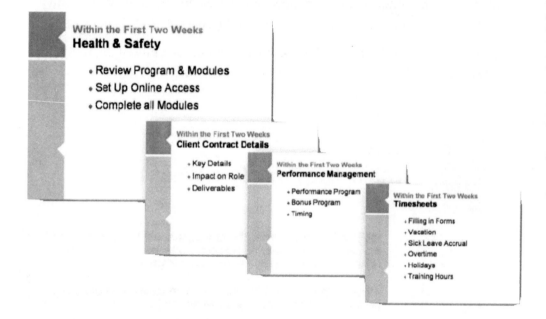

If there was enough information and discussion, you could even break up these slides into separate slides for each bullet point, depending on the purpose, audience and level of detail you are planning to cover.

If this is simply an overview, this level of detail is appropriate. If it's a training exercise, you can expand on them with more detail on additional slides so the slides become the reference material, or include the additional detail in the notes section in your slide software similar to the previous example. You can also develop separate training handouts that expand the material.

Delivery

While the slides themselves are important, your delivery is what really matters. After all, you could deliver your message without slides at all.

Combined with the slides, however, your delivery must get attention from your audience, keep their attention by making it interesting and memorable, and ensure that your message gets through. As always, your goal is to gain support for the outcome you want.

It's all about you

Besides the importance of the message you are trying to communicate, your image and professionalism will also influence the final result. If you are well prepared and deliver an interesting and compelling proposal, you are more likely to influence your audience. Some of the ways to do this include:

Use your own words

If you follow the advice above about developing slides, you won't be tempted to read them when you make your presentation. Instead, talk about them in your own words, making sure the focus is on what you're saying, not the slide.

Know your material

When you understand your material well enough, you can use the slides as a prompt. You should know what to say and how to get your message across. This comes with preparation of course, but if you are nervous about ad-libbing instead of reading from slides, you won't have a problem as long as you know your material. Just don't be thrown off if you forget to make a particular point or you say things slightly different from your rehearsals. Nobody but you will know the difference.

Use nervous energy

It's okay to be nervous. Some seasoned speakers still get butterflies before they start a presentation, but the energy and excitement soon overtake that feeling and that makes for a passionate presentation.

Be passionate

In most cases, passionate presenters are more interesting to listen to. A passionate delivery also shows you believe what you are saying and that lends credibility to your expertise.

Be mobile

Try not to stand behind a podium. If you can, use a wireless microphone and a wireless mouse to control the slides and get out in front of the audience and move around. This helps you channel your nervous energy and passion to illustrate your message.

Use your voice

Build on your passion and let your voice highlight and punctuate your message during your presentation. Don't maintain an even, monotonous tone. Speak fast, loudly and passionately where necessary and slow, low and seriously when relevant. These techniques are an effective way to keep the audience's attention and highlight your message in a way that will be more memorable. Vary your voice along with the slides and rhythm of the information.

Take pauses

Give the audience a chance to catch its breath while you catch yours. Pauses can be used for effect or to give the audience time to digest what you've said or to read something on the slide if that's part of your approach.

Make it personal

To maintain the audience's interest and attention, make your presentation personal. Include facts and information that relate to the audience. Tell stories and give examples that support your message and make what you're saying sound real and concrete, not theoretical.

It's all about your audience

While you are an important part of the presentation – much more important than the slides – the most important part is the audience. It's also the reason why a passive presentation won't be as effective. Unless you get the interest and attention of the audience, your goals for the presentation probably won't be met.

Understand your target

Knowing and understanding your audience will make your presentation more effective. If the audience will want lots of details and evidence, include it in your slides. If the audience prefers high-level information and concepts, keep it at that level. Presentation to your staff, peers or bosses will all be different, since each audience has its own specific needs and interests.

Engage the listeners

Sitting through a presentation can be a very boring and many people in your audience are apt to be distracted by busy schedules and the pile of work that's not getting done while they're at your presentation. Keeping them engaged in your presentation and getting them to forget about their distractions is one of your goals. Offer interesting and surprising information, have them read something interesting on a slide, ask them questions, and tell stories they relate to.

You can also make eye contact with members of the audience and since you are mobile, you can walk down an aisle or even walk near someone who doesn't look like they are giving you their attention.

Read and respond

Paying attention to the audience will help you adjust your delivery. If you see nodding, use it as a cue to ask if who agrees with your point or ask them if they can add anything. If someone looks doubtful, give them a chance to explain their concerns so you can address the issue. Similarly, if anyone looks confused or isn't following, backtrack and explain, or ask if there are questions. If the audience looks bored, pick up the pace or skip areas that may not be of interest and focus more discussion on the interesting parts.

Be sure to ask whether those in the back can hear you and periodically confirm that your audience understands your message and you aren't going too slow or fast.

Logistics

Preparation is critical to a good presentation. Be sure to practice and go through your presentation to identify key areas, points, information and stories you want to use. Print out a copy of your presentation and make short notes to remind you of things that aren't on the slides that you want to talk about. Don't constantly refer to it. Put it aside on a table and use it if you get off track or need a reminder.

Always bring a backup of your presentation on a CD or a memory stick and if you do bring your own laptop for the presentation, get there in advance to set it up and make sure it works. The same goes for any sound equipment and other items, such as pad boards, whiteboards or handouts you need for your presentation.

Handouts

If you provide handouts, carefully consider when to hand them out. If you are delivering training, handing it out at the beginning provides space for the participants to write notes about what you are saying. If you are giving an update, presenting a project or trying to sell an initiative, let your audience focus on your delivery, not on the papers in their hands.

In some cases, you may want to develop a separate handout that works with and supports your presentation. It can include more details or backup that support your slides and means you don't need to include it in the presentation itself. This is particularly useful if the information is detailed or isn't easily read on a slide.

Quick Summary

Key Points

➡ Your slides are a tool – but you should be the focus.

➡ Traditional rules of thumb should be used carefully.

➡ Develop your slides strategically and understand your audience, what you want from them and how to get it.

Executive Tips

➡ Your presentation should support your purpose and get the result you want.

➡ Make an impact in your organization with compelling presentations.

Traps to Avoid

➡ Don't use your slides as a crutch. They should guide and enhance the value of your presentation, not be the presentation.

➡ Don't hand out your presentation in advance. You want people focused on you, not the handout.

15

Getting Approval and Results with Business Cases

Your success depends on influencing others.

"The only people in the world who can change things are those who can sell ideas." - Lois Wyse, advertising executive

No matter what your role is, you will eventually have to write a business case to get approval, whether it's for funding, resources or executive support for an initiative.

If it's a formal structured business case you have to present, or an informal business case you can cover in an email, build on the techniques discussed earlier and incorporate these additional techniques to help win approval.

A business case is a very specific form of written communication where influence is the primary objective. Review the concepts and suggestions in the earlier parts of this section that deal with general written communication for ideas about how to structure and format your proposal for maximum impact.

Develop Your Strategy

While you may already have established your purpose for the business case, take it one step further and develop your strategy for getting approval. Simply putting words on paper isn't the best way to get your business case approved.

You should assess and target the individual empowered to give you approval before you start writing your business case. This helps you understand what their interests are, as discussed earlier. Once you understand their position and concerns, you can address them in your business case.

In addition to developing a strategy to get their approval, figure out what you will do if they don't give it. If you are not able to get your full request approved, perhaps you can get a part of it. A willingness to negotiate terms can eventually move you towards full approval.

Consider This

Avoid a win/lose approach to strategic plans that depend on someone else's approval. If you can negotiate key changes that were presented as part of a larger business case, it may be easier for you to advance the rest of the business case over time. Once people begin to adopt part of a plan, they are less likely to decide against future changes related to that first decision. In some cases, you may want to target an easy-to-approve concept and build on that.

What about the Stakeholders?

The individual who signs-off on the business case isn't usually the only one involved or affected. Instead of focusing only on the approval authority, assess who else has a stake in the approval or can influence the approval authority, and then work to build support from them.

These stakeholders include colleagues and other decision makers within your organization who will benefit from your initiative. Identify who they are and what their interest is relative to your initiative. Develop messages and arguments specifically related to them and meet with them to secure their advance support.

Where appropriate, go one step further and ask them for an endorsement and support influencing the decision.

This also applies to anyone who may oppose your business case. They can have an equal but opposite impact on your success so you should deal with them before you seek approval, not fight with them after. Figure out why they oppose your proposal and come up with a way to either appease them or to address their concerns. Where possible, address potential problems before you submit your business case. You can also address their concerns specifically within the business case. Either action shows leadership in problem-solving.

Solidify your Message

Your business case strategy should include key messages that gain support from the approval authority and any stakeholders.

The message is a specific, important item that addresses the key issues of the business case or the interests of the stakeholders. The message must be clear, concise and compelling and not be diluted with too many secondary messages. It should be a prominent part of the business case and be easy to identify within your document. Don't be afraid to repeat it to emphasize the point.

The message should also link your proposal with the interests of the approval authority or the stakeholders. If you've done the assessment, you know what matters and what doesn't, so omit what doesn't belong and focus your message on what matters to get approval. If you don't have a compelling message, your business case will seem weak and unimportant.

Depending on your business case, this will likely revolve around the key drivers in your organization, whether it's costs, risk, efficiency, reliability, etc.

Of course, your message may include things the stakeholders and approval authority don't realize are important. This is especially true when they don't understand facilities issues. Don't assume they will understand the basis of your message. Spell it out for them in language and terms they are likely to understand.

When developing your message, ensure it has these key attributes:

- ✓ It should have impact.
- ✓ It must be relevant .
- ✓ It must support your business case.

If your message doesn't have these key attributes, look for another message. It is possible to have more than one message in your business case, but make sure your key message is front and centre. If there are different stakeholders who must approve your business case, develop separate messages for each one and make sure they are each clearly and separately covered in your business case.

Hitting the Hot Buttons

Hot buttons are the most pressing and important issues facing the stakeholders or approval authority. In addition to the message, they would lend support to your business case and should have a specific impact to the approval authority.

While they may not be the key reason you think your business case should be approved, if you hit the hot buttons in addition to your message, you stand a better chance of getting approval.

Hot buttons are different from the message. Hot buttons are usually single-issue items that are dealt with in specific parts of the business case to support the overall initiative. They must have a high impact with the approval authority or stakeholders and while they may not be enough to carry an entire business case, they will get the attention of decision makers and decision influencers. That increases the likelihood they will consider the merits of the overall proposal. Where possible, use your proposal to try to solve these hot button issues or mitigate their impact.

When hot buttons are not obvious, you need to engage stakeholders and staff to learn more about the underlying issues. Use the information you collect to develop your business case and shed fresh light on the hot button topic.

Once you've identified the hot buttons and how you plan to address them within your business case, list them on a checklist to make sure you address all of them.

As with other important information within your business case, make sure that when you're addressing a hot button issue, your goals are obvious. Again, you want to be able to take credit for good ideas, not assume others will connect the dots.

Don't bury it with other material or hide it in long paragraphs. As discussed earlier in the section about using format and structure, use a heading, breakout box or other technique to direct the reader's attention to hot button topics and solutions.

Negate concerns

Another part of your strategy is to understand the approval authority's concerns and address them directly in your business case. Even if you will be presenting the business case and can deal with questions and concerns during the presentation, having your response to their concerns built-in to your business case is better. The biggest mistake you can make is pretending negative issues, or the concerns of the approval authority, don't exist.

Identifying potential concerns and dealing with them accomplishes two things. First, it moves your business case one step closer to approval and second, it boosts awareness of your leadership skills and gives the approval authority more confidence in your abilities. Some of these negative issues will come out of your analysis of the issue and discussions with the stakeholders. Others may be harder to find. Talk to your colleagues and your staff and run your initiative by them and ask them to play the devil's advocate and try to punch holes in your business case. Use this input and deal with the issues raised by incorporating them in your business case.

Making Your Message Stick

When writing the business case, you're trying to ensure the approval authority sees the messages and arguments you want them to see. You want them to remember what they've read and relate it to their criteria for approval, whether it's based on a tangible, measured result or not.

In the end, the best solution or initiative is worth little if you don't earn approval. As discussed earlier, you are competing for their attention with many other factors. You want the approval authority to easily see, remember and relate to your business case message and arguments.

To make that more likely, there are techniques to make sure your message sticks. Several of these techniques apply to written communications as well. They are:

Keep it simple

People remember simple things more easily than complicated, complex ideas and information. By keeping your language simple and using familiar terms, your message is easier to absorb. When writing business cases, many FM professionals use complex sentences, fancy language and long paragraphs because they believe their ideas need to sound formal and smart. In reality, readers understand and absorb less information when you present it this way. These are busy people with complex schedules and responsibilities. They do not, have the time or energy it may take to read and re-read complicated documents especially when they may present solutions to *your* problems, not theirs. Simple and clear messages will have more impact and influence.

Keep it real

It's tempting to use fancy language that's rich in concepts, promises and theoretical benefits. But a business case must be convincing. Even the busiest executive knows when something sounds too good to be true, If you lose credibility on one point, you risk losing it on your whole case. Real examples and situations will get the attention of the approval authority. Use your business case to present situations and demonstrate the merits of your innovation. Show clearly what the benefits will be to the organization.

Skip generalities and provide examples, facts and figures to make it more meaningful.

Keep it honest

No matter how much or how little the approval authority understands about specific FM issues, they are apt to be more aware of the underlying issues than you think. A weak business case won't stand up to the most cursory study.

Don't make promises you can't keep or statements that aren't backed by facts and evidence. Use this presentation as a way to build credibility in your FM leadership and management skills. Let them know that you know what you're talking about. This makes it easier for the approval authority to believe and support what you say. It also opens lines of communication for future discussions.

Make it relevant

What you say will have a greater impact and is more likely to be remembered if you back it up with relevant examples and stories that are directly linked to what you say in the business case.

Rather than describing benefits in general terms, find an example you can talk about. When you combine your statement with an experience, you build credibility and provide a relevant experience the approval authority can relate to when making its decision.

Where possible, share a story about the FM problems you are trying to address with your business case initiative. Be honest, but fair. By outlining the costs or risks related to the failure you describe, you give the approval authority a business case that is concrete and relevant, not theoretical.

Do use illustrations, diagrams, flowcharts and graphs to clearly illustrate your points. These should support what you write and not just be added for filler. Keep them simple and high-level. Get someone else to review them so they, convey the message you intend.

Mirroring

This is a very important technique to use when writing a business case. It helps the approval authority see, retain and use information they have read in your business case more clearly and that will impact their final decision.

Mirroring uses key phrases, terminology, issues and facts that are readily identifiable and already used by the approval authority. This approach helps them focus on the information you're providing by using the same terminology they know and understand. If the approval authority isn't experienced in FM issues, it's especially important to shift from FM-related terminology to more generally accepted terminology the reader is more likely to relate to and understand.

Consider This

Every industry has its jargon. When presenting a business case, avoid acronyms or terminology specific to FM unless you are sure the approval authority will understand your message. If you want to computerize a system, for example, zero in on what the change will mean. Your ability to track and compare BTUs or KWH may be meaningless to an individual who thinks in terms of cutting costs and earning tax credits for energy conservation initiatives.

As part of the mirroring process, take information and terminology from your discussions with the approval authority and from the stakeholders. Read your organization's MVV statements, policy documents and annual reports to identify terminology and hot buttons and messages you can use to strengthen your business case.

Bigger is Not Better

A long business case may look impressive, but it won't have the same impact as a short, concise business case with meaningful impact.

Striking the right balance depends on the amount of information you need to give to support your business case. How you structure your document can influence this. You also need to review and be clear about what the approval authority likes to see. Some will want a very concise document while others want to pore over the details and your supporting material. Save yourself valuable time by making sure you deliver the preferred approach. Anything less (or more) can prove problematic.

If you aren't sure which is better, write a short, concise business case with an appendix that has all the supporting material. Summarize supporting material in the main body and make it very easy for the approval authority to flip to the back and read the details as they go through the business case.

A Business Case Template

A well-structured business case conveys the important elements of your argument and leads the approval authority to the decisions you want them to make.

Before you begin with your business case, find out whether there is a standard template. If so, follow it, but be creative enough to deviate from the standard to better make your case. Sometimes corporate standards can actually be very restrictive when it comes to presenting information and making the point. The most important thing is to understand how the decisions are made and what will influence them. Whether it's a specific financial calculation or certain issues to address and satisfy, make sure you incorporate these data it into your business case in a way that makes it crystal clear that you met the criteria.

Regardless of how you're your specific business case influences the elements, or the constraints of your organization's standardized format, there are a few elements you should take care to include. The following section walks you through those suggestions and is followed by a simple template that can help you structure your business case so it is very easy to read and follow.

Business Case Headings

Notice that the headings suggested further below are not standard, ordinary headings you might see; they are more descriptive and unique, yet cover the same kind of material you expect to see. Modify them as required to suit your needs and add or subtract sections. Do include all the information you need to make a compelling business case that convinces the approval authority. The length and depth of detail will depend on the complexity of the issue – but your objective should always be shorter than longer.

Here are the recommended headings, along with a description of what should be included under the heading. They are worded in the form of questions as this tells them what you will answer in your text. It should cover all the questions they need answered before they approve the business case. It also makes the decision more personal to the approval authority, suggesting they are responsible to approve or reject proposed improvements and the related benefits, costs and risks associated with their decision. Adjust the headings as necessary to suit your business case and the related issues.

Why should you approve this business case?

This takes the place of a typical executive summary and you would provide similar information, including a short, concise outline of the problem, solution and request for approval. You should look at this as your main way to influence the approval authority, so put the best, most relevant information here. Be sure to keep it short and specifically ask for approval at the end.

Why does this need to be done?

This is the background that sets the stage for why your initiative must be approved. Describe what you know about the existing situation in a way that helps shape the solution and provide evidence about why the existing situation is not acceptable and needs to change.

Include the risks or negative consequences of not proceeding with the business case. This adds a sense of urgency and minimizes the possibility a business plan won't proceed.

Use sub-headings to expand on specific areas. Here are a few sample sub-headings.

Problem you are trying to solve (needs assessment)
Background related to the problem
Reasons it needs to be solved
Internal
External
Risks and costs with status quo
Who is impacted (stakeholders)

What are the options available?

Whenever there is a problem, there is often more than one solution. If you present only one solution, the approval authority will have questions about other options. Instead of letting those questions jeopardize your business case approval, establish the options in your business case and clearly explain the benefits and risks of each one. Show why your option is clearly the preferred solution.

It may make sense to position one of the options as the "second best" if your preferred option is not acceptable to the approval authority. In your approval section, enable them to choose.

Use sub-headings to expand on specific areas. Here are a few sample sub-headings.

> Options & Preferred Solutions
> Risks and costs
> Benefits (tangible and intangible)

Which option is the best one?

This is where you use the previous section to emphasize your preferred solution. You can provide a concise summary that includes a compelling argument for your preferred option. If you've presented a "second best" option, you can explain it here as well, thus positioning either option for approval.

Where necessary, repeat some of the information you presented above in your description of the various options, but don't repeat too much; keep it highly relevant and use only the information with the most impact.

How will we implement this initiative?

Now that you've convinced the approval authority that an initiative needs to be done, tell them how it will be implemented in a way that supports your request. A clear implementation plan which is highly likely to succeed will always support the decision. While you don't have to go into all the details, you should discuss the key areas that would be of interest to the approval authority and identify any potential roadblocks to success.

Also address potential objections up front. This shows that you've considered all the issues, including the difficult ones, and are committed to success.

If necessary, provide a summary schedule or work plan. The level of details will depend on your specific needs, but if it has to be detailed, summarize it here and include the details in the appendix.

Use sub-headings to expand on specific areas. Here are a few sample sub-headings:

> Assumptions & Constraints
> Timeline
> Budget
> Resources
> Reporting & Updates
> Communications
> Buy-in from Stakeholders
> Measuring Results

What are the results you will get?

While you discuss the results you expect in earlier sections, it's useful to target them in a separate section as well. Since results are a key part of business case approvals, make sure the approval authority knows what you are asking for and what you expect to gain. Re-iterate the risks and costs associated with not approving the business case.

Make this section concise. When possible, rely on graphs, charts and tables to clearly illustrate your points. The benefits and risks will vary depending on your organization and the specific business case. When establishing the benefits you should use to justify your business case, carefully consider everything that matters to the organization, both short- and long-range.

Use sub-headings to expand on specific areas. Here are a few sample sub-headings.

> Financial Benefits/Risks
> Efficiency Benefits/Risks
> Personnel / HR Benefits/Risks
> Intangible Benefits/Risks
> Perception and Public Relations Benefits/Risks
> Operational Risk Reduction/Risks
> Legislative Risk Mitigation/Risks

How can your approval help?

Before you ask for approval, clearly identify the benefits of proceeding and the risk of not proceeding.

This short summary should make the decision more personal for the approval authority. If necessary, you can also use this as an opportunity to qualify the results you can deliver if it isn't approved. Note real-world issues such as lower satisfaction rates, higher deferred maintenance, increased likelihood of system failure, etc.

How you word this section will depend on the culture of your organization and your relationship with the approval authority. Do suggest that the approval authority should take credit for the positive results you expect to achieve.

Your approval

Specifically ask for approval in your business case and if appropriate, include an approval page or signature block. If you have provided an alternative option, enable them to approve either one.

Appendix

Only include an appendix if the background and backup material is required as part of your business case submission. Instead of expanding the actual business case with this type of detail, include a summary in the body of your business case and provide the details in the appendix using an easy to use reference system, such as tabs. When business cases are read by several people, expect some to want more detail than others. Aim to support your business case without overloading it.

Business case Format

Content is a critical ingredient for your business case, but it's not much use if it's hard to read and follow. Start by following the concepts discussed earlier in this section and consider using a unique format that will get attention and stand out with the approval authority.

Here is a sample format you can use. It uses tables that are easily duplicated in your word processor. While this format may add a few pages to your overall document length, it makes for a clear, easy-to-follow document that has more impact.

Main Heading	**Brief, punchy summary for this heading. The main headings use a shaded box for emphasis and visual separation.**
Sub-heading	This is where you write your content for the sub-heading. Include text, graphics, tables, illustrations and formatted text, with sub-sub headings and bullets to make it easy-to-follow and see the key information. **Sub Heading** You can add sub-headings or nested tables to represent information in an easy to read tabular format instead of long paragraphs.
Sub Heading	This is a sample of a nested table. | Possible Options	Benefits	Risks
---	---	---
Option 1	Benefit 1 Benefit 2	Risk 1 Risk 1
Option 2	Benefit 1	Risk 1	
Main Heading	**Brief, punchy summary for this heading**
Sub Heading	Content

Quick Summary

Key Points	➡ Your ability to deliver an influential business case will improve your chances of implementing your ideas.
	➡ Use communication techniques to develop a business case with more impact.
	➡ Don't do it the same way everyone else does. Use a format that focuses attention on the information and stands out.
Executive Tips	➡ A business case is a sales tool that must focus on its single purpose: to get approval for an idea.
	➡ Know the audience and make sure you cover the issues and information they care about most.
Traps to Avoid	➡ Don't clutter your business case with information that the approval authority won't care about.
	➡ Don't use dull, boring headings. Make them meaningful.

16

Writing Facility Newsletters

Use newsletters to your advantage.

"Good communication is as stimulating as black coffee and just as hard to sleep after." - Anne Morrow Lindbergh

Let's face it, communicating with occupants is often at the bottom of a long list of priorities FM professionals deal with on a daily basis, yet effectively communicating with the people who use the buildings is critical. The newsletter is an often-overlooked and highly-underestimated tool for communicating.

If your newsletter is well laid-out and well-written, it informs the reader and delivers your message. It can be as simple as telling the occupant what you are doing for them – things they may take for granted – or reminding them about initiatives such as new security arrangements or new procedures for requesting services.

For commercial properties, excellent communications improves tenant retention and the newsletter is a simple, low-cost tool for this. By including information that is of interest to the tenants and delivering your message about the benefits of being a tenant at your building, you maintain and gain goodwill that improves your chances of tenant retention.

In corporate facilities, an FM newsletter promotes the FM function and helps educate the occupants about issues and procedures that can make your job easier. The information you include can prevent calls and complaints by informing the occupants about changes, issues and events before they happen.

While the underlying reason for using a newsletter may be different for commercial property management and corporate facilities management, the fundamentals are the same: you need to get your message across.

It's all About the Content

It often seems like the decision to start a newsletter is made without understanding how to use it as an advantage, and what the key messages will be. This results in a scramble for content and poorly-focused articles on items of little interest. This is a recipe for disaster as your audience won't read future copies of a newsletter they've already judged harshly.

To plan for success, determine your goals and actively seek articles that carry your message forward. Since the audience is both the occupant and your prime contacts, a careful balance is important. The content can be as simple as telling the reader what will be happening in the next few months, including window washing, construction and events. It can also remind readers what you have done for them over the last few months and educate them about issues and even their responsibilities regarding those issues.

Here are a few tips to consider:

1. It's a sales opportunity – You should use it to gently promote your FM team's accomplishments and benefits.

2. Write it for the audience – Don't use jargon, don't talk technical. Ask yourself "why should they care?" and write it with that question in mind. Your occupants care about different things than you do. Keep that in mind.

3. Use a catchy title – Use the examples of newspapers and magazines. If the title looks boring, they won't read anything else. Once you entice them with a catchy or thought-provoking title, the first sentence or

paragraph has to make them want to read the rest. Don't assume they want to read it just because it's from FM.

4. Use titles that are descriptive, like "How this affects you" or "What are your alternatives?"

5. Write tight, skip the fluff. Don't try to sound smart, your job is to communicate efficiently. Organize your information with headings and bullets instead of long paragraphs. Make sure the important information is easy to find.

Checklist

The most important part of a newsletter is content. Use this checklist as a guide to improve your content.

- ☐ Will your headline catch the readers' attention?
- ☐ Is the first sentence or paragraph of the article likely to entice the reader to continue reading?
- ☐ Does the article deliver your message?
- ☐ Is the article concise and to the point?
- ☐ Is your message repeated within the article and throughout the newsletter?
- ☐ Are you speaking to the reader directly and making the article personal instead of using general language?
- ☐ Do the photographs and graphics add to the article or are they filler?
- ☐ Does the article use active sentences instead of passive ones?
- ☐ Are you avoiding the technical terms and acronyms that readers won't understand?

Producing Your Newsletter

You can produce newsletters with high-end lay-out software such as Adobe PageMaker, word processing software or low-cost desktop publishing programs such as MS Publisher. For small newsletters, MS Publisher is ideal, since it is easy to use and has many templates that mean you don't have to worry about the creative part of the newsletter, just the content.

To decide on the size of your newsletter, take into account how much content you will have for each issue, and whether occupants will read more than a page or two. The format depends on how much content you have. For a one or two page newsletter, standard 8 ½" x 11" paper will do nicely. For a three to four page newsletter, consider an 11"x 17" sheet folded in two.

Keep your layout simple and professional, using "white space" to make it easy to read. A two or three column format provides flexibility and is also easy to read. Stick with standard fonts and use them consistently.

If you send it out in an email, avoid attachments or links as people seldom click on them. If you must, then include the headlines and first paragraph as a teaser, then provide a link for them to follow to your intranet or to download the PDF version. If you have an email with several long items, list the headings with the teaser paragraph and then include the full article further below.

The frequency of your newsletter is important. Don't plan a monthly newsletter if you can't fill it with useful content. When starting, avoid scheduling the newsletters; simply publish them when there is something to say, or for specific communication purposes.

If you distribute by email, consider sending shorter items more often versus following a quarterly format. Here, your subject line becomes your catchy heading.

Sample Newsletter

This sample illustrates an approach you can take. It was created with inexpensive layout software using a free template.

Distribution

You have several options for distribution, all of which will depend on your technology and your occupants. Paper distribution is easy, but is seen as being less than environmentally friendly. If you go this route, consider having the cleaning staff distribute the newsletter.

Electronic distribution can be through email or a web site. Software like MS Publisher gives you electronic options like converting your newsletter to a web page or a graphic file that can be attached to an email.

In both corporate and commercial buildings, it's important to consult with your prime contacts in the building before doing a mass distribution to the occupants. Your prime contacts may have a preferred approach to distributing information and not want you to send it directly to individuals. If this is the case, ensure it gets the distribution you expect.

Tips for Writing your Newsletter

Write a Catchy Heading

Use headings that actually say something and make the reader want to read more.

This catches your attention	This one doesn't
Better Heating This Winter	Capital Projects

Write a strong lead paragraph

Use a strong lead paragraph when writing about anything. The lead captures the readers' attention and gets them to read the rest of the article.

This makes you want to read	This doesn't make you want to read
This winter, your heating comfort will be vastly improved due to a project initiated by	The boiler project, which was started February 1st, was finally completed on March 4th, 2010 by John Q. Construction Inc. ...

Don't use terminology

Remember who your audience is. Use terminology they are likely to understand and explain quickly and briefly when necessary. Don't include information that doesn't matter to them, such as a contractor's name, etc.

This uses terminology	This doesn't use terminology
The coal fired low-pressure boilers were replaced with a high-efficiency gas boiler with a new GUI interface BAS system and remote access through dial-up remote from a handheld PDA.	The project includes a new boiler that supplies hot water to the radiators and a new system that separately controls each radiator to improve control over the temperature in each area.

Speak directly to the reader

Speak directly to the reader by avoiding general references.

This speaks to the reader	This doesn't
Your heating comfort will improve	Building comfort will improve

Show Action

The text must show action. Use active language instead of passive language.

This shows action	This one doesn't
We are replacing the boilers.....	We will be initiating a project that will replace the boilers.....

Frame your subject

The reason for the newsletter is to get a message across. Repeat your message at least twice, depending on the length of the newsletter item. Within reason, use the old adage "tell them what you are going to tell them, tell them, then tell them what you told them."

The first Sentence	The last Sentence
This winter, your heating comfort will be vastly improved due to a project we've initiated.	With the new system, we are confident you will be more comfortable this winter.

Tell the reader why it matters to them

You need to figure out why they should care about what you say and tell them why. Focus your writing on the impact to the reader and how it will improve things for them.

This example tells them why it matters	This example doesn't
Your comfort will improve now that we can separately control each radiator to set your area to just the right temperature.	The Controls project will improve our ability to separately control the radiators and regulate the temperature independently.

Quick Summary

Key Points	➡ Boring newsletters won't be read.
	➡ Create newsletters that interest your audience.
Executive Tips	➡ Use the newsletter to sell what you are doing for them.
	➡ Speak directly to the audience.
Traps to Avoid	➡ Keep it short, one or two pages are ideal.
	➡ Don't set regular dates until you are sure you can keep up the pace.

17

Communicating Green Initiatives

Developing buy-in and acceptance.

"Communication is the real work of leadership" – Nitin Nohria

Energy conservation and environmental responsibility are important topics to building owners and managers, yet the challenge of getting occupants to buy-in to your initiatives and actually change their behaviors remains difficult.

The occupants of our buildings are adopting an increasing number of environmental initiatives at home, yet they often have a difficult time linking these initiatives to actions they can do at work.

The only way to get most people to change the way they behave is to show them how it impacts them personally. At home, it's easy to do, since you conserve energy and pay less. At work, these incentives don't carry much weight, since the occupant is not affected by the costs of operating the buildings they work in.

This means the message and the communication methods must be directed to things that matter to your audience. Since the occupant isn't affected by costs, the environmental impacts provide the best motivation for change.

One of the best ways to communicate about the environmental impact is to give statistics and comparisons the average person can relate to.

A recent advertisement about a major city's Blue Box recycling program went beyond costs. It identified how many trees are saved, the reduction in the number of trucks hauling waste and the reduction in landfills. On the energy front, discussions of air emissions provide the best impact as people relate energy consumption to power plants and their emissions from burning fuel.

The Message and the Medium

All communications have to be built on both a message and the medium. The message is what you are trying to convince your occupants to do and it's designed in a way to interest the listener. The medium is the tool you use to convey the message, whether it is a newsletter, meeting, posters, etc. Use the mediums that work for your organization and the target audience. These include newsletters, memos, email notices, posters, information sessions and open houses. The message should be repeated frequently. In advertising, repetition of the same message is considered important to get the message across, so do use the same concept and provide multiple communications.

Your communication about environmental initiatives, whether for a commercial property or corporate facilities, must be directed at two different key targets, and each requires a different message.

The first target audience is decision makers, those who approve or support your initiatives. For commercial buildings, this is the key tenant representative, preferably the ones accountable for the rent they pay. In corporate facilities, this audience is the executive and department managers.

By communicating to these people first, you can get buy-in to the actual implementation, both financially and operationally. With implementation supported from above, you can then turn your attention to the occupants and design your communication to get their cooperation.

Decision Makers

Implementation may require investment and will certainly require buy-in from the occupants to get their passive or active participation, so you need support from the decision makers before you proceed.

The decision makers may be within your own organization, or within your tenant or client organization. Either way, their support improves the likelihood of your initiative's success.

Focus you communication with this group on the benefits they care about. Target financial issues as well as the opportunity to present the organization as a green organization and as a leader in environmental initiatives. You need to know the audience and emphasize the aspects that will be most important to them. Of course, if the decision rests on payback calculations, put them front and centre. But never exclude the other benefits, as they provide the icing on the cake.

Formal communications are usually necessary and should include a business case and presentation. Don't rely on formal channels, however. Take time to speak one-on-one with the decision makers in an informal setting first. This helps you gain buy-in and address any issues they may raise before the formal presentation.

Once you get buy-in, be sure to communicate your progress and if possible, send them copies of any communications you use with the occupants. If issues with implementation or acceptance arise, communicate your solution to them first, before anyone else can raise the issue.

Since the decision makers can help you with resistance to your initiative, it is important to maintain communications and the relationship so you can use their influence effectively.

Occupants

Communicating successfully with occupants when implementing initiatives should be done in all phases of your initiative, not just during implementation. The typical phases include Planning and Design, Implementation and Steady-State. Each requires a different communication mechanism.

If you are armed with support from the decision makers, you may be tempted to force implementation on the occupants. Acceptance of the initiative will be compromised where this top-down approach is used. Instead, use senior-level support as a launching point and build direct buy-in through communication, persuasion and good implementation.

Planning and Design

Once you have support, the first step is to communicate to the occupants during the planning stage in order to build buy-in and help work the bugs out of your implementation, ensuring it is workable and easy to accept by occupants.

In some situations, communication during this phase will need to go through tenant or department representatives. Where possible, go directly to the occupant to ensure the message gets through.

At this point, using a newsletter, even a single-page format, is an effective mechanism for communicating broadly. Personal letters directed to key managers, union representatives, committees or similar stakeholders should be part of your communication plan, too.

Open houses or information sessions should also be used to engage the occupants. With an open invitation, you attract both supporters and detractors. By identifying these people early, you can use them to your advantage. The supporters will help convey your message and the detractors are a good litmus test for your initiative. Listen carefully to both sides as they will help you identify the best way to gain buy-in.

Set up a committee to review and recommend the implementation mechanisms, including the communication and education tools you need for the next phases. Communicate the results, particularly when you change your implementation design based on occupant feedback. This tells everyone you are listening to their concerns.

Implementation

Successful start-up of a new initiative such as a new recycling process or a lighting control system relies on effective communication as much as a good design. There are many different communication tools, and the more you use, the better.

Continue with newsletters and memos, supplemented with emails, tent cards, instruction cards and posters. If the initiative is somewhat complex, such as a new recycling system that requires the occupant to separate their waste, simple instructions, graphics and other means that are readily accessed and referenced are critical.

Information sessions and demonstrations with typical waste items will improve the occupant's ability to understand and use the system.

For innovations like telephone-based lighting controls, acquire instruction cards or stickers that can be put directly on phones to ensure the occupants can use the system when they need it. Posters or floor plans in the elevator lobby with instructions are also useful.

Maintain the Steady-State

Once you have implemented your initiative, you have to continue communicating in order to maintain interest and participation. This communication should include information about how successful the programs are and, where necessary, clarifications. For instance, if you find that certain recyclables are still commonly not sorted properly, re-communicate about those items specifically.

Don't neglect the new tenants or employees. They should be given the appropriate communication when they arrive.

Communication about the success of the program should focus on the original messages that mattered to the occupant. Reinforce the issue and congratulate the occupants for making a difference. To maintain interest, you can even try some competitions within the building or between buildings, using waste diversion rates or consumption reductions as the measurements.

Quick Summary

Key Points	➡ Communicate several times to get best results.
	➡ The message has to be meaningful and have impact, not just deliver technical information.
	➡ A user group/focus group can help identify issues before they are raised by occupants.
Executive Tips	➡ Get buy-in and support from decision makers first, including colleagues and departments.
	➡ Use more than one method to communicate.
Traps to Avoid	➡ Using technical information to show benefits instead of relating it to the occupant.
	➡ Issuing a communication without having it checked to make sure it will hit the mark.

18

Developing Procedures

Procedures are a strategic tool to manage services.

"We should work on our processes, not the outcome of our processes."– W. Edwards Deming

Having procedures for your FM services improves results and consistency, enables training and cross-training, provides you with a means to audit your staff or service-provider performance, and ensures results.

Documented processes, policies and procedures are important, but simply writing detailed documents isn't the answer. The longer a document is, the less likely it will be used or followed. Unfortunately, organizations tend to lean in one direction. They either have little or nothing documented, or they have massive amounts of standard corporate documents that nobody actually uses.

Excessive documentation comes from the belief that more is better and that the heavier something is, the more value it has. A long procedure document is better. A long business case is better. A long strategic plan is better. Realistically, that approach says more about show than results. If your documents are long and difficult to follow, they won't achieve these results. Instead, they will absorb valuable time and take up space.

Michel Theriault

If you haven't developed your procedures, take a simpler, shorter approach to developing them. If you already have a bookshelf full of Standard Operating Procedures, Operations Manuals and other similar documents, leave them on the bookshelf and develop an overlay with the key parts of the processes in an easy-to-use, easy-to-reference format. Then use them for your training, performance and continuous improvement processes.

Your main goal is to provide staff or suppliers with guidance and to identify key things that are critical to the organization's success. Always provide some latitude for them to take the best possible approach to any given situation. Quality procedures and processes empower staff and suppliers to be successful based on their own knowledge and experience.

Focus on useable information. Refer back to this section frequently to keep your communications effective and influential.

Key Principles for Developing Procedures

Through my own experience in using and writing process and procedure documents in FM, including so-called "best practices" and personal research, I've developed the following set of key principles for developing procedures and practices. Here they are:

1. Develop them with input from staff and users

Real world experience beats theory every time. What you think is being done by your technicians, facility managers, planners, call center staff, etc. may not match what you think they should be doing for very good logistical reasons. If the issue is what's being done wrong in the field, understanding why the disconnect exists is the best way to change it in your practice and get buy-in from the field.

Your end users, whether they are tenants in a commercial building or occupants of corporate facilities, may also have very good ideas and observations about how services are being delivered, particularly where they interface with your users. Listen to them carefully as you may not have considered some of the options and you may need to introduce revised or new processes.

Involve your staff and users in the initial discussion when you develop your procedures. Ask them to review the documents afterwards to ensure they are easily understood and aligned with the reality of the process, not just the theory.

2. Keep them short and simple

This doesn't mean dumbing them down, it means making the documents easier to use by busy people with little time to read long documents. It's especially important for staff who aren't sitting at a desk all the time, such as technicians. They simply can't take the time to read large documents.

3. Use a format that is logical, visually easy-to-follow and quickly provides the needed information

This means using simple flowcharts, tables, illustrations, meaningful headings and clean, well-structured documents. Suggested checklist, flowchart and document formats are provided below. Try to get away from a simple text-based, narrative-focused, paragraph-dominated structure.

4. Include checklists

Checklists are a simple, visual tool to outline key steps required for any given procedure. They are already used frequently in preventive maintenance work orders, which often include a list of tasks.

Paragraphs, narrative and other formats aren't as effective, since they take time to read and understand. When you use a checklist as an overlay to the overall procedure, it makes the procedure much easier to follow.

Involve your FM staff and develop checklists that have the items that really matter, not everything you can think of. With their input, you are more likely to get buy-in and end up with a better final product.

5. Make them easy-to-access

If nobody sees them or if they aren't easy to reference when needed, new procedures and processes documents won't do any good. Make them easy to find on your company server, logically grouped and easy-to-access.

For paper copies, use a binder or booklet format with tabs that list the common activities, processes, etc. Check with your staff to figure out a structure that makes sense. Provide a quick reference with the most common issues and a summary with the overall process and references to each step that's broken out into more detail. For simple processes (which could include safety guidelines) provide simple pocket sized reference cards. Laminate them so they will stand up to field use.

If you follow these five principles, your procedures and practices documents are more likely to be helpful to your FM-services function. These will help your staff deliver the results you expect.

Checklists

The simplest implementation of a process or procedures is a checklist. They can be a stand-alone guide or be part of an overall process.

The best implementation of checklists is in the aviation industry where they are used for training and to provide quick, efficient guidance during an emergency.

With experience and knowledge, some people don't think they need to follow a checklist. Research shows that even experts make mistakes, so checklists have proven their value time and time again. In the book, *The Checklist Manifesto*, Atul Gawande provides compelling statistics with very clear examples of where a simple checklist gets results even for seasoned, well-trained specialists who supposedly know what to do in every situation.

Mr. Gawande discusses examples of how using a simple checklist in the operating room has reduced infections and medical errors by significant margins. It shows that even the most highly-trained and skilled professionals can benefit from a checklist.

The key is to use simple, short and easy-to-use checklists. In many cases, a checklist provides quick assurance that the key elements of the process are being followed or have been done.

You can create checklists on a word processer using bullets or tables or in a spreadsheet.

This can be used in many aspects of FM, including the following situations:

✓ To verify that all information has been collected for a process such as issuing a monthly parking pass.

✓ For a move to verify that all the steps required before the move have been done.

✓ As a quality-control inspection after a project has been completed.

✓ To verify all safety-related steps have been taken before performing work, confirming action, such as a lock-out/tag-out, has been done.

✓ To ensure the technician has all the supplies and tools necessary for a task.

Here is a simple checklist that can be used by the service provider or technician after a work order has been completed.

☐ Did you clean up the work area?

☐ Did you put the customer's furniture back in place?

☐ Did you leave a comment card on their desk?

☐ Did you advise the Call Centre that the work is complete?

☐ Did you check the room to identify any other issues to correct?

Graphics & Diagrams

In addition to checklists, include simple flowcharts and diagrams to illustrate the process, steps and decision-making process. Flowcharts are easy to make with standard word processing, spreadsheet or presentation software, so use whichever you are most comfortable with. You don't need specialized software, although it can make graphics and diagrams easier.

The following sample process diagram is called a Swim Lane diagram or Cross Functional Flow Chart and it clearly identifies the steps in the process for each individual. It was developed using a spreadsheet program, so while specialty software will make it easier, it isn't a requirement for good flow diagrams.

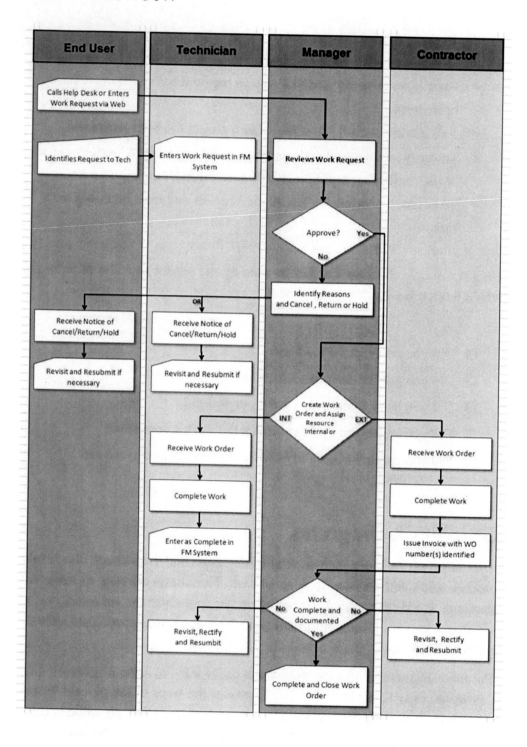

Format & Structure

The reality is, the easier you make it to read and the easier it is to see what they should do or not do, the more effective your procedures will be. Long, dense text won't be read.

A table structure similar to the samples shown below also makes it easier to read and understand work processes and directions. This approach forces you to think about the processes in a logical, structured way that will improve your documentation.

The sample below shows the overall structure. Instead of headings that are on top of the text, the headings are to the left, making it easier to find what you are looking for. Other information is presented in the same way, but nested within the original table.

While the structure could result in a longer document, it will also be easier to read. If you shorten your text to only what's necessary and structure it this way, you may find that the overall length of your document won't be very much longer.

1.1 PURPOSE

1.1.1	OBJECTIVES	Work Orders address maintenance or service requests which require the repair or replacement of building components, finishes or systems which have failed in order to bring it back to original standards, restore services or prevent service failure.
		Work orders include service requests which may not be related to building system or component failure however must be performed by suitable qualified staff and are required to enable ongoing activities at the schools.
1.1.2	OTHER REFERENCE DOCUMENTS	The following lists other documents you may need to reference related to this procedure:

Reference Document	Why you may need it
SR-23 - Purchasing Procedures	Provides direction on when a separate procurement initiative will be required to procure a contractor services for any given work order requirement.
Level of Approvals	Documents authority levels for approving contract work / invoice payments
FM System manual	Provides detailed information on the use of the work order management system.

Here is another example of using a table to present information. This clearly identifies the types of priorities and their related description. Note that the wording is stripped down to the key information. There is no need for long paragraphs.

PRIORITIES	Priorities are assigned to each work request based on the following criteria:	
	Priority	**Description / Guidelines**
	High	Will cause damage to persons, structure or equipment if not corrected. Will have a negative impact on core business activities if not corrected.
	Medium	May cause future damage to persons, structure or equipment if not corrected. May have a future impact on core business activities if not corrected.
	Low	Does not have an immediate impact however should be corrected to preserve asset life

This example lists specific actions that each work order can go through. Again, it is simple, clean and easy to reference.

WORK REQUEST ACTIONS	There are a number of actions that can be taken with any given work request. These are described below:	
	Action	**Description**
	Return	The work request is returned to the originator for more information or clarification. The originator can re-submit or cancel.
	Hold	The work request is on hold pending additional information before processing.
	Cancel	The work request is cancelled because it is a duplicate, the work is no longer required, the request does not fit the criteria of the work performed by Facilities Management.
	Assigned	The work request is approved and the work order is assigned to a resource who will complete the work.
	Complete	The work identified in the work order has been completed
	Closed	The work has been completed to satisfaction and no further activity is required.

The responsibilities of each individual in the overall process are described similar to the one for the facilities manager below. It uses simple, shortened descriptions. Details for each of the specific steps or responsibilities can be outlined separately in the process. If needed, the list could be split into two columns with additional information for each responsibility added. The table format lets you easily structure information.

FACILITIES MANAGER	
	1. Reviews new Work Requests
	2. Respond to all related requests and issues
	3. Determines whether to use internal or external resources.
	4. Distributes Work Orders to Internal; and External resources
	5. Reviews work orders that have not yet been completed
	6. Closes work orders following verification of work complete and correct invoicing as appropriate
	7. Review completed work orders and if additional work is required, authorizes the work

This is a text version of a work flow, along with a brief description. This could be accompanied by a Swim Lane flow diagram, similar to the one shown above.

OVERALL WORKFLOW STEPS		
The following chart outlines the main steps involved in the complete cycle of a work order, along with who is involved and a general description of the step.		
Each of these steps is further described in more detail in the next section, along with decision points, information requirements and handoff.		

Step	Who is Involved	General Description
Generate Request	Tech or User	This step generates a work request for work to be performed and is the initiation of the work order process.
Review Request	Manager	In this step, the work request is assessed against established criteria and a decision is made on how to handle the work request. This may include returning it for more information or clarification, denying the request or cancelling it.
Assign Work Order	Manager	If a work request is approved, the next step is to create a work order and assign it to a resource who will complete the work. Resources are either internal Facilities staff or external contractors as required. There may be more than one work order created from a single work request.
Complete work	Tech or Contractor	The resource who has been assigned the work order completes the work identified on the work order.
Verify completion	Tech	Where the work is done by an external resource, the work is to be inspected or otherwise verified that the work is complete satisfactorily before closing the work order and paying the external resource.
Close Work	Manager	Once the work is complete and verified, as appropriate,

Take Action

Developing procedures doesn't have to be a long, complex process. Start by asking the people currently involved in the process to write down the steps they take or to quickly draft a flow diagram to get you started. Ask them about the key steps and the decision making required during the process. Be sure to ask them what they would do differently if they could.

Compare the flowchart and steps from everyone involved in the process and then meet together to go over the steps to ensure you have common ground and have clearly identified hand-over points and information requirements.

Then, use the tools above to document the process as described. After it's done, walk through it with your team and make sure it reflects the correct procedures. Improve it where necessary.

Finally, make sure you make these documents easy to find and reference. Whether it's on your company's intranet site or in binders, key processes and steps should be easy to find and reference and not be buried in the complete document. Use separate files or use tabs in binders. Include an index and provide references to the relevant procedures.

Where one procedure interacts with another procedure, identify the reference and the location of the other procedure to make it easy to follow the full process.

Quick Summary

Key Points	➡ You need procedures for consistency, improved results, training and auditing.
	➡ Involve your staff and users when you develop procedures to ensure accuracy and buy-in
	➡ Procedures should be simple and easy to use.
Executive Tips	➡ Use modern techniques to develop effective procedures.
	➡ Focus on the key steps and decision points and give your staff more latitude to use their expertise.
Traps to Avoid	➡ Don't develop procedures in isolation.
	➡ Don't make them long and tedious to use.

Your Strategic Plan

Based on this section, what strategic initiatives do you plan to implement that will help you manage your assets better and when do you expect to accomplish them?

What are you going to do?	When?

Notes

_____

_____

_____

_____

_____

_____

_____

_____

_____

_____

Using FM Systems

Introduction

Having an FM system for your services, assets and resources is a key contributor to managing successfully and should be a basic tool for every FM professional.

Regardless of the acronym you use or the functionality you implement, a computerized system provides you with the control, consistency and the information and knowledge necessary to run a professional facilities department.

There are systems available for every size or organization, type of assets and range of services, from inexpensive web-based applications to large enterprise systems.

Just remember that your software is still just a tool. It isn't a solution that will solve issues with your resources, procedures, supplier management or service delivery. You have to start with a foundation that works in the first place, otherwise implementing an FM system will simply magnify existing issues. As always, strategy and planning will give you results.

19

Can an FM System Help Me?

FM Systems are critical to service delivery.

"I do not fear computers, I fear the lack of them." - Isaac Asimov

In the FM profession, good information is the important ingredient often missing in otherwise excellent organizations. Good information can help you make decisions and improvements with internally-delivered services and with your suppliers.

The kinds of systems you should consider for your operation are wide and varied. They are applicable to managing facilities for any type or size of organization across the entire spectrum of responsibilities that FM professionals are involved with.

The functionality of FM systems includes Asset Management, Lease Administration, Help Desk services, Preventive Maintenance, Corrective Maintenance and Work Order management, Capital Planning, Financial Management, Chargeback and Project Management. You can even get key control, conference room booking and more.

These services are all available as stand-alone systems or can be integrated to varying degrees, but there is no single solution that applies to all facilities; you have to do the legwork and consider your business needs, organization, culture and the level of support you need before taking the next step.

While the functionality is more important, various systems have different names and acronyms. Here are some common examples of system names and their acronyms. Keep in mind that these are just names - the specific functionality isn't always consistent. I expand on these further below.

- Computer Aided Facility Management (CAFM)
- Computerized Maintenance Management System (CMMS)
- Computer Aided Facility Management (CAFM)
- Facility Information Management System (FIMS)
- Integrated Facilities Management System (IFM S)
- Building Automation Systems / Building Management Systems (BAS / BMS)
- Energy Monitoring & Control Systems (EMCS)
- Integrated Workplace Management Systems (IWMS)

There is an impressive array of vendors and software consultants who provide these systems. They range from single-dedicated functions to fully integrated systems and from desktop- to server- and web-based access.

The bottom line is that CMMS and CAFM aren't just about the software. They are valuable tools, but you need to put everything in place and that's often beyond what the software vendor or consultant will do. This is necessary to make sure the tool is used effectively and puts wind in your sails instead of being a boat anchor.

How Can I Improve Results?

Implementing FM systems, including CAFM, CMMS, Work Order management and Help Desk systems, for example, is the most important thing you can do to improve service, reduce costs and preserve your assets, including reducing future costs.

The range and flexibility of available systems, including stand-alone, integrated or hosted web-based systems, put this capability in the hands of even small organizations.

Information from systems helps you manage your responsibilities better and make decisions based on evidence, not assumptions and anecdotes.

Information is the most important ingredient to managing facilities and buildings successfully and will help you get better results. Without it, you are working blind and relying on inaccurate or misleading anecdotal information, sometimes from staff that have been doing the same thing the same way for years or decades.

The business case for implementing a system includes at least four key benefits, however you need to consider the impact on your business process before you decide which system to buy and how to effectively implement your new FM system in your organization.

Simplify Delivery and Process

You can make your end-to-end processes for your service delivery more efficient, less prone to communication errors and more consistent by using computerized processes and planning, web-based work request entry, automated work flow and even direct dispatch and updating of work orders to contractors or your own staff through handheld devices.

Better management of space enables efficient planning, space use and move management. You can even give your customers direct access to the status of their requests.

Reduce Time and Costs

You get access to important data and information such as the number of work requests by a variety of useful characteristics, response times, equipment information, churn, workstation allocations and more. You can use this data to shorten and simplify your capital and space-planning processes. It can automatically calculate chargeback and eliminate the manual processing and manipulation that costs time and money.

As an example, your FM system can record new maintenance requirements and related costs that come from your technicians and contractors who identify issues after their preventive maintenance and inspection activities. This information helps you manage your assets and understand your activities better.

Add Visibility into Your Operations

You can see what's going on in your operations with the right system. They enable you to track work orders issued, who is doing what activity, see comments on work and know who or which department is absorbing most of your resources.

This data helps you understand the volume and type of moves and relocations. You can use it to monitor conference room uses, track spending on equipment repairs and immediately know whether your legislative compliance requirements are met.

Systems also provide tracking and evidence of completing legislative requirements, ensuring compliance, and demonstrating due-diligence.

Information for Decision Making

Since everything is tracked, you can generate reports and access raw data to analyze for patterns and issues that identify areas you need to take action on, providing the information you need to decide on key responsibilities such as resourcing, communication, process issues, bottlenecks and costs. It can also provide the evidence you need to justify initiatives and business cases, in addition to performance management and benchmarking.

For example, tracking corrective repair work and occupant requests, provides you with data you can analyze and turn into information you use to make decisions that reduce costs, improve services and manage your suppliers better.

By using this information and analyzing it with simple tools such as pivot tables using your spreadsheet software, you can pinpoint trends and develop strategies for your facilities and buildings. You can also track lamp replacement to identify when a re-lamping exercise will be cost effective, compare work order costs by vendor or service to see where synergies or new contracts are can save money, compare in-house work with subcontracted work to ensure limited overlap and that contractors are doing what is in their contract, identify call-backs on equipment to assess supplier quality, or indicate replacement of equipment to reduce maintenance costs.

Consider This

Information is the most powerful tool you have. You can use it to justify your business cases and your initiatives, and to demonstrate the value your FM or operations department provides to the organization.

What Kind of FM Systems are There?

The range of systems available to help FM organizations continues to grow. Vendors are expanding their software capabilities with additional integrated modules or with increased functionality within existing software.

The first thing to consider is the actual application or solution you need. This will depend on your set of responsibilites and the size of your organization and what makes sense to automate with a system.

Before we review the functionality, it is important to understand the different technology and approaches taken by software vendors.

In most cases, FM software is provided on a licensing basis, meaning ongoing annual or monthly fees. Some will sell the software for a single up-front fee and then provide a maintenance service for a monthly or annual fee.

More and more systems are moving to an Application Service Provider (ASP) model where the software (and usually the data) resides on the vendor's system. This gives you web access to the software from anywhere and means your own IT department does not need to manage the system.

This approach has reduced the initial costs and provides very attractive ongoing fee structures that even smaller organizations can afford.

Deciphering the Alphabet Soup

There are many acronyms and terms used to describe FM Systems. Some of these have been around for a very long time, while others are relatively new and are used to describe functionality that has evolved over time.

It's important not to focus on the acronyms and names. Instead, focus on the tasks and functions the software can do. The most common ones cover one or more of these six fundamental activities:

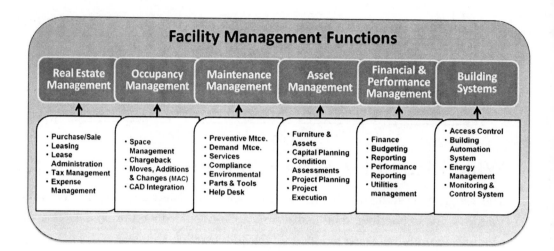

Terminology

The terminology and acronyms in common use include the following, all of which are used generically to describe types of FM systems. Note that this list only covers the most common terms:

IWMS   Integrated Workplace Management System

This typically describes an enterprise system that includes all the key areas of FM, including real estate management, occupancy management, asset and maintenance management and even project management. Actual functionality will depend on the software system itself.

CAFM   Computer Aided Facility Management

This has typically been an integrated system that primarily includes occupancy-related information such as work station layouts, assets, building information (like LAN, telecom and others), space usage, signage, etc. The term has evolved over time and may also cover integrated systems with building maintenance included.

CMMS Computerized Maintenance Management Systems

This is traditionally focused on preventive and corrective/demand maintenance planning and tracking. It may be as simple as a work order management system and scheduled work orders, or include call centre functionality to enable users to receive and record facility calls and turn them into work orders. Systems can often integrate with hand-held devices and provide work order entry or tracking for occupants on the web.

Modern systems include both preventive and corrective/demand-based maintenance and requests received from occupants on a variety of maintenance and service issues. They are flexible, adaptable, easy-to-use and usually employ web-based with systems available for small to large portfolios.

FIMS Facility Information Management Systems

This can have several meanings. It may refer to what is essentially a financial system that includes operations budgeting, capital renewal and possibly leasing and lease administration. It may also be used to describe an overall set of FM systems, whether integrated or not, including CAFM, CMMS, etc.

IFMS Integrated Facilities Management System

This is another term for IWMS (see above).

EDMS   Electronic Document Management System

This enables the electronic capture, storage and retrieval of documents such as building plans, layouts, leases, etc. The functionality may be included in CMMS, CAFM or an integrated system, but it can also be available separately.

Isn't it Expensive?

The cost of systems varies widely, as does the pricing model. Fortunately, pricing is often very flexible based on the size of your organization and even smaller organizations can now access more sophisticated systems. By minimizing the customization, you can also reduce your costs.

The more scope and services managed by the software and the more integrated a system is, the more expensive it will be in general. Keep in mind that the cost of the system may not be the largest cost when you are implementing new systems. The cost of resources to capture information, validate it and enter it into the new system can be high. In addition, customization of the system can add costs. You can trim your costs if you start small and gradually add functionality and data.

Pricing models include purchase and licensing. The licensing will sometimes be based on the area (total portfolio) which is managed by the system or by the number of unique users, often referred to as "seats."

If the system resides on your system, whether it is web-based or not, you also need to consider the IT costs associated with the implementation. Otherwise, the system will reside on your vendor's IT systems, reducing the issues involved with hosting the system yourself.

We Already Have a System

If you already have FM systems installed, you need to ask whether it is being fully used and providing you with the benefits it should. It is good management practice to do an audit to ensure that the implementation is working and giving you the benefits you need.

Often, older implementations aren't used properly, information has not been maintained or work-arounds have been put in place by users because it wasn't implemented well the first time. Because older implementations are more likely to have been driven by the vendor or IT department, they may fail to consider the real-world issues around processes and people, including change management and follow-up. These systems may not adequately address feedback from users or enable data to be audited to ensure the information is up-to-date, consistent and provides follow-up training as needed.

The first and most important test is whether you are getting the kind of valuable and reliable information from your system that enables you to make decisions that improve services and reduces costs. If the system is being used but you aren't getting anything from it, then you should question the value it provides in its current implementation.

If it isn't living up to expectations, it's time to re-implement. This includes assessing why it isn't doing what it should, adjusting processes, re-training and demonstrating value to your staff so they will buy-in to the system. If it is an old system, it may be time to upgrade it or replace it.

Quick Summary

Key Points

➡ Systems are a key part of effective management of physical resources, regardless of your size.

➡ A wide variety of systems are available that fit almost every need.

Executive Tips

➡ Understand why you are using the system and make sure it gives you the results you need.

➡ Use it to gain visibility into your operations.

Traps to Avoid

➡ Don't get hung up on system acronyms and names. Focus on the function.

➡ Don't select a system that significantly exceeds your requirements.

20

Information from your FM System

Get information and manage work processes with your FM systems.

"Everybody gets so much information all day long that they lose their common sense." – Gertrude Stein

Implementing with information in mind will ensure you have a system that provides you with information you can use to make decisions.

Information is the most important ingredient to managing facilities and buildings successfully and to getting better results. Without it, you are working blind and probably relying on inaccurate, missing or misleading information.

If you are like most FM professionals, you are inundated with data and information on a daily basis yet not much of it helps you make decisions.

The trend with facility managers, including those with systems already implemented, is a lack of visibility into crucial aspects of their costs and activities.

While they may have implemented systems and processes for managing their facilities, visibility in terms of management information is often lacking. That's unfortunate, since visibility would enable FM professionals to take the next step towards improving their operations.

Aberdeen Group, a leading provider of research into supply chain and other business processes, reports that real estate and FM costs represent over 30% of non-payroll costs, yet 40% say they have poor or no visibility into the costs of this important function.

Costs are one part of the visibility required, however few have visibility into key processes, work loading, work order activity, maintenance activity, moves, projects, etc. This strategic information can be used to build business cases with senior management and make strategic decisions related to process, resourcing and subcontracts.

The key is focusing on one area at a time and gathering only the data and information you need to make decisions. Too often, initiatives and systems are implemented which overwhelm FM with excessive process, time requirements, integration and excess data that doesn't provide meaningful information on which to make decisions.

The best approach is to decide why you need the information and what decisions you expect to make from that information and then implement processes and systems that get what you need. Instead of starting with processes and systems that give you more than you need, focus on increased visibility of information that yields results.

Consider This

Many FM systems aren't used to their potential after implementation. Some may not provide the information you need. Don't let yourself be confused. You want management information, not data.

Focus versus Quantity

The most fundamental problem we all face is that we have too much data and not enough of the quality information we need to facilitate effective decisions.

Make the "right kind" of data a priority so it can be compiled, compared and analyzed properly.

Implementing FM systems is among the most important thing you can do to improve service, reduce current and future costs and preserve your assets. The range and flexibility of available systems, including stand-alone, integrated or hosted web-based systems, put this capability in the hands of even small organizations.

Information for Decision Making

The next time you look at implementing a process, system, report or survey to gather and track data or information, take a step back and ask the fundamental question: Will this data or information help me make decisions that will improve services and reduce costs? When you understand the answer to that question, you will be in a better position to get the information you need to make decisions.

Successful executives understand this issue and focus only on information they need to make decisions. Eliminate the clutter and improve your decision making.

Since everything is tracked, you can generate reports and access raw data to analyze for patterns and issues that identify areas in which you need to take action. This builds the information you need to decide on key responsibilities such as resourcing, communication, process issues and costs. It can also provide the evidence you need to justify initiatives and build business cases, not to mention benchmark results.

Implementation Makes it Hard to get Information

Most organizations run into a common problem after they implement, as systems are typically not as easy to use as they first seem and chances are, organizational roadblocks make it even harder. These can include existing processes that make it difficult to integrate into your operations and interface it with current systems. There can also be organizational design and operational challenges related to the effort needed to populate it with accurate information up-front, the cost of maintenance and upgrades, resources to enter information and keep it up-to-date and even resistance from the staffs who needs to use it.

All these problems make it hard to get the necessary information into the system accurately and in a timely manner. This means that getting the information out will also be a problem.

These problems are magnified when systems are implemented without first understanding why you need the system, what you will use it for and how it will integrate with the rest of your operations, including effective processes and training to ensure your staff buy-in and support the initiative.

You need to recognize and plan for the resources required, provide refresher training, audit the system and the processes after implementation to make sure it's working as intended, and make the appropriate changes to adjust and improve the processes. You may even be collecting too much data or find you have installed a system that is too comprehensive and complicated for your needs.

Decide what Information you Need Up-Front

Problems are created when you don't clearly establish what information you really need and how you will use it to improve your operations. Built-in reports may not be enough. The information you get from your system, along with the ability to improve management of work and processes, are the most important features of a good system. Still, information overload can be paralyzing. If you already have an under-utilized system in place, there are things you can do to get better value from it. Simply return to square one and fix the things that aren't working. Aim to make deliberate changes so your system can start working for you instead of against you.

If you haven't purchased and installed a system yet, there are ways to ensure your new investment will deliver the benefits you expect and the results you need.

In addition to considering the business implications, needs and priorities, you must ensure your overall implementation plan addresses some of the fundamental problems organizations face when they implement new systems. This needs to be in addition to the software implementation process your software consultant or vendor specializes in.

The bottom line is that FM systems aren't just about the software. They are valuable tools, but you need to put everything in place to make sure the tool is used effectively and isn't a boat anchor that weighs you down. A well-implemented system should move you forward towards lower total cost improvements and enhanced efficiency and service.

Quick Summary

Key Points
- ➡ You need information to make good decisions.
- ➡ Your FM systems should support you, not hinder you when it comes to getting useful information.

Executive Tips
- ➡ Without good information, not just data, you can't make good decisions.
- ➡ Ensure your system can deliver the information you need.
- ➡ Instead of reports that are just lists of data, get analysis that helps you make decisions.

Traps to Avoid
- ➡ Don't collect more information than you actually need to manage your business
- ➡ Don't implement a system and hope for information - decide what you need before you select the system.

21

Implementing an FM System

It's not just about the system.

"Management manages by making decisions and by seeing that those decisions are implemented." – Harold S. Geneen

FM Systems are the most important tools a facility and property manager has to manage his or her responsibilities. They provide critical visibility into the operations, information for decision making and analysis and improved processes and efficient services. All of this results in lower costs and better services.

The value of FM systems aside, the reality is that many systems may not achieve expected goals because they are implemented without consideration for the true business needs the FM systems serve. By considering all the factors and developing a business implementation plan - and not just a software implementation - you will ensure success.

What Steps Do I take to Implement?

Many organizations encounter problems after they implement a new system, when difficulties with implementation are exacerbated by organizational roadblocks ranging from the operational processes to issues related to populating the system with current data.

These problems are magnified when systems are implemented without first understanding why you need the system, what you will use it for and how it will integrate with the rest of your operations. This includes effective processes and training to ensure your staff buy-in and support the initiative.

You need to recognize and plan for the resources required, provide refresher training, audit the system and the processes after implementation to make sure it's working as intended, and make the appropriate changes to adjust and improve the processes. You may even be collecting too much data or have installed a system that is too comprehensive and complicated for your needs.

Other problems are created when you don't clearly establish what information you really need and how you will use it to improve your operations. Built-in reports may not be enough. Again, if you already have an under-utilized system in place, there are things you can do to get better value from it. Go back and fix the things that aren't working. That means changing your system so it can work for you and your FM goals.

If you haven't purchased and installed a system yet, there are ways to ensure your new investment will deliver the benefits you expect and the results you need.

Consider This

Make sure your FM system implementation considers operational issues as well as business needs and priorities. Staff must be trained and willing to assist with implementation. Your software consultant and vendor may specialize in the technical side of implementation. Make sure you also support the people side of the equation.

Some of the things that may jeopardize an implementation are:

- ☒ No advance communication to establish why the system is needed; no effort to build implementation into the strategic plan and a lack of communication about what the information will be used for and how it can help staff do their jobs better.
- ☒ Not selling the idea directly to staff; showing them the benefits, giving them training, building it into their daily schedules and processes in a way that makes it easy and shows benefits.
- ☒ Not supporting change management; no effort to change pre-conceived notions, weed out roadblock issues and promote change.
- ☒ No recognition and planning for the effort needed to keep it up-to-date with processes, resources or support.
- ☒ Not monitoring usage, tweaking procedures, or doing quality control on the information.
- ☒ Not using or sharing the information to support and demonstrate that it's useful.
- ☒ Not getting any real value out of their investment.

Three Phases

Work on the business requirements first and then combine those with the software vendor to develop an effective implementation process that involves the following phases:

1. Before you implement

Don't use an FM consultant connected with software vendors to make the software decision. Use them (or the vendor directly) only for implementation after the selection is made.

Spend time understanding your business requirements first. If you understand what you are trying to accomplish and what you really need, you will be in a better position to decide on a system. Those who focus on the software features first risk buying technology they do not need - and missing out on technology that can revolutionize a work environment.

Decide what your objectives and requirements are before you search for a system, including what you will do with the information you get from it. Strategically plan for the business implementation and understand how that differs from a software implementation. This requires an assessment of your business needs versus software features. Don't rely solely on your software consultant or vendor for a successful system implementation.

Establish objectives and requirements, decide what information you need and what you will do with it, figure out how to integrate it with your business processes, personnel and resources and establish the real integration requirements.

Don't use a consultant connected with software vendors to make the software decision. Use them (or the vendor directly) only for implementation after the selection is made.

Consider This

Start looking for a system that fits your needs and avoid customization packages that "solve" specific problems. Before you customize, look at your processes for things that can be changed. This often yields process improvements that won't require software customization. Only customize software after you've exhausted other avenues.

2. During Implementation

Spend the time to implement it right. Use the principles of change management by involving your staff and getting their input before and during implementation. Change your processes to match the new tool, populate it with accurate data from the start, train everyone, etc. Also be prepared to change things after implementation. Once people know how to work with the new system, you may identify processes that would benefit from a new approach.

Communicate the changes and the reasons. Make sure it's meeting objectives by putting auditing and evaluation procedures in place. Give your staff training and re-training. Educate everyone on its value to promote support and ensure success. Listen carefully to your administration and field staff as their insight will be a valuable addition to your implementation plan. Tweak and adjust the processes to make it work better.

When possible, implement in stages. Start with one building or portfolio and with one element, such as corrective or demand maintenance work orders. Once that implementation is successful, add preventive maintenance, space management, asset inventory, performance measures or whatever other integrated FM elements you are implementing in your system. Involve your best staff. Show results and demonstrate the benefits. Then implement the rest, building on success.

3. After you implement

Do an audit after six months or so. Check with all the stakeholders and staff to find out what works and what doesn't. Do a quality assurance test on the data and process. Listen to your staff, they know best about what's working. Tweak processes, re-train your staff, conduct quality assurance on the inputs and continue to sell its value to your organization.

Schedule follow-up audits to ensure is the system is working as expected and take action to make changes as necessary.

Make sure you take the raw data the system generates and convert it to information you can use to make decisions, including those related to maintenance, occupancy, capital replacement, staffing and resourcing, etc. If you don't use what you put into the system, people will stop bothering with it and you and your organization will gain nothing from its implementation.

Avoiding the Traps

Beyond the technical issues related to new systems, many organizations will encounter significant roadblocks pre- and post-implementation of a new system. Many of these roadblocks are rooted in staff frustration. Existing processes can be difficult to integrate. The interface between different systems can be more complicated than expected. The need to populate and then maintain a new system with accurate data is time-consuming. Some staff may resent the new system's impact on their jobs.

Here are some of the main traps to avoid when implementing an FM system of any kind:

Not enough advance work

Advance work establishes why you need the system. Build the implementation schedule into your strategic plan. Make sure people know what you will use the information for. Clearly and honestly assess your current organization's ability and willingness to work with the new system and then develop a plan to make it work. Include integrating the plan with your current practices, staffing and resources and then seek the system that matches.

✓ Take action to help your staff understand how this system will help them work with you to improve FM practices.

Not selling the idea to staff

You may have sold the idea upwards with a business case and got the money you need to implement a system, but how much effort was spent selling the idea to your staff, showing them the benefits and giving them training? Engage your staff in decisions about how they will build system use into their daily schedules. Work with them on processes that make system use easy.

✓ Demonstrate the system's benefits to staff as well as the organization.

No change-management

Most organizations and staff resist change. Along with everything else, you need to consider the process, communication and personalities you need to deal with and build change management into a flexible implementation plan along with your complete business process. You may need to counteract pre-conceived notions about systems and weed out those who are roadblocks to success. After all, the software is just one part of implementing a system.

✓ Take a structured approach to managing the changes involved with implementation. Focus on a successful transition.

Not planning for upkeep and maintenance

Implementing and populating the system in the first place can take a lot of effort, but so the does the amount of time needed to keep it up-to-date and accurate after it's up and running. Make the processes, resources and support needed for upkeep and maintenance part of your strategic and implementation plans.

✓ Support the long-term success of a system implementation by looking for ways to optimize its value to your organization.

No follow-up

You can't introduce something new and then let it run on its own. You need to build follow-up into your plan to verify that the systems, processes and resources are working as designed, just like commissioning a new building. This includes revisiting the procedures, conducting a quality control assessment on the data, listening to the staff using the system and then making changes that ensure the system works like you expected it to.

✓ Engage. Communicate. Demonstrate commitment. Work with staff to assess and improve the system's value. Focus on solutions and continuous improvement.

Not using the information

Some managers are content to just "know" the data is being collected and is available for the analysis that will turn it into valuable information. That's short-sighted. Unless you actively use the information you won't benefit from it. Expect staff to question why they bother feeding the system with data and expect senior management to question your commitment to quality management and leadership. You need to analyzing the information your system provides, communicate what it tells you, and make changes as a result.

✓ Using a system to its full potential demonstrates the system's value and showcases your decision making and management prowess.

Customization

Everyone likes to think their organization's needs are unique. In reality, FM is very similar across all types of organizations and facility types and FM systems have been designed to meet the fundamental requirements.

Customization is expensive during implementation and can become even more expensive later when you want to upgrade the software.

Instead of customizing up-front, examine your processes and requirements and look for ways to accommodate your needs without costly customization. Where possible, only customize FM systems where they are designed to provide customization through built-in tools, such as modifying field names, creating different work order types, establishing your own work order tasks, adjusting work flow and other similar built-in customization

✓ Keep current and future costs down by using systems as they were designed when possible.

The bottom line is that FM systems are valuable tools, but you need to put everything in place to make sure the tool is used effectively. A well-implemented system should add value to your organization by tracking and feeding FM professionals quality information about processes and facilities. The end results should equal measurable improvements, lower total costs, improve efficiency and enhance service.

Quick Summary

Key Points

➡ Sell FM Systems with concrete service results.

➡ Implementation starts well before you buy the software.

Executive Tips

➡ Develop your business needs and business processes before you start looking for software.

➡ Involve your staff and audit it after implementation to make sure it works as designed.

Traps to Avoid

➡ Don't buy a system until you understand your business requirements.

➡ Implementation without effective change management will lead to failure.

➡ Customization is expensive and should be unnecessary.

22

How do I Sell it to Management?

It's more than just the right thing to do.

"In the modern world of business, it is useless to be a creative original thinker unless you can also sell what you create. Management cannot be expected to recognize a good idea unless it is presented to them by a good salesman." – David M. Ogilvy

Executive approval is often the biggest hurdle to implementing an FM system. You need approval for the investment and sometimes for organizational changes or increases, depending on your organization.

Getting senior management to approve system implementation is tough, whether it's Computer Aided Facility Management (CAFM) or a Computerized Maintenance Management System (CMMS).

To start, they may not understand the FM function and its importance, so they may not recognize the benefits of having a system. Rather than trying to focus on the facility-related details, focus on information as a key selling point.

Let them know how quality information about your business responsibilities and one of your organization's largest assets and expenses will be used to make decisions that improve efficiency and reduce costs. Information - and its connection to revenue and expenses - is the things most execs understand well.

Consider This

> Never assume an executive audience understands FM. Where possible, talk up the benefits of very specific information. Tell them how others are using improved maintenance and upkeep systems, or tracking efficiency data, and what the results are.

The Business Case for an FM System

The business case for implementing an FM system includes at least five key benefits. We will review those, but remember to always consider what your business needs are before you get caught up in what a particular software package offers. System purchases also require keen attention to system features and effective implementation.

Simplify delivery and process

A system's capacity to reduce costs is not always easy to quantify. Focus on the savings related to reduced time and effort, reduced mistakes and quicker service. For example, you can make your end-to-end processes for your service delivery more efficient, less prone to communication errors and more consistent using computerized processes and planning, web-based work request entry, automated work flow and even direct dispatch of work orders to contractors or your own staff through handheld devices.

How these translate into specific cost savings will depend on your organization.

Reduce time and costs

With improved information, you can manage your processes to reduce waste, ensure effective and cost-efficient capital planning and workstation planning, and automatically provide information and calculations that may have previously required a manual process. Depending on your implementation, you may also reduce manual input and processing. This may enable a net reduction, or allow you to implement the system with improved results and no additional staff requirements.

FM systems will give you access to important data and information such as the number of work orders by service, floor, department and other characteristics, response times, equipment information, workstation allocations, and more. You can use it to shorten and simplify your capital planning and space planning activity. It can automatically calculate your chargeback charges and eliminate manual processing and manipulation that costs time and money.

Visibility into your operations

FM systems provide knowledge and visibility into the details of your operations rather than relying on incomplete, anecdotal or inaccurate feedback. This allows you to respond to issues and make changes and adjustments based on facts. Those changes will reduce costs and improve services.

The right system also improves your ability to see what's going on throughout the FM operation. You can track work orders issued and who is doing what activity, see comments on work and know who or which department is absorbing most of your resources, track spending on equipment repairs and immediately know whether your legislative compliance requirements are met.

Systems also improve your understanding of the volume and type of moves and relocations.

Information for decision making

Information is the most important tool a facility manager can have and FM systems provide that information.

This information can be used to analyze your operations and costs and to drive improved services and reduced costs. In addition, the information is used to make decisions and justify business cases, giving you the evidence, via facts and data, to support your initiatives.

Since everything is tracked, you can generate reports and access raw data to analyze for patterns and issues that identify areas you need to take action on, building the information you need to decide on key responsibilities such as resourcing, communication, process issues and costs.

Reduce risks

An FM system can help you manage and reduce your risks. You can inventory your hazardous materials, particularly those that are controlled through environmental legislation. You can also include any legislative requirements for inspection and testing within your preventive maintenance or work order system, thus ensuring they are performed as scheduled and then tracked to provide proof for audit purposes or for the relevant authority. Demonstrating due-diligence is not only a wise corporate process, it is imperative for defending legal actions.

Focus on each function

Focus on each one of the functions your (future) system will do for you and identify specific and relevant information you will get and what you can do with it that results in dollars saved. Then highlight the woefully inadequate information you currently have and identify the risks of not having quality information. Again, risks are another thing executives understand. Keep your business case high level and results oriented. Many executives don't care much about FM details as long as the core business is operational.

Here are some simple examples of how you can approach the business case for an FM system. Always understand your organization and what the approval authorities think is important. Then adapt your approach as required.

CMMS system (preventive maintenance):

- ✓ Provides evidence that you have performed your legislative compliance responsibilities. You can produce a report at any time easily without doubting the information. It is auditable and defendable in the case of a lawsuit or audit by the authorities.
- ✓ Tracking repair activity and costs by asset provides data you can use to make better capital replacement decisions as well as decisions about maintenance practices, all of which can save money (i.e., lifecycle, energy, etc.)

Help desk (work orders and demand maintenance):

- ✓ Tracks the work orders (i.e., costs) by type and department. You can pinpoint departments who access costly services more than others and take action to reduce.
- ✓ You can spot trends such as departments who have high move/add/change (MAC) requirements and implement alternate accommodation / workstation / technology approaches that save move and reconfiguration costs as well as reducing the staff's downtime (inefficiency = cost) that result from MACs.

CAFM (space, furniture, assets)

- ✓ Tracks all vacant and underused space efficiently and up-to-date and helps you manage down the total requirements by giving you visibility into an expensive commodity – real-estate.
- ✓ Time you and your client department spends on reconfigs, shuffling, etc. will be reduced because you have the current information.
- ✓ Reports on department use of space will help put pressure on reduction or justify tighter standards. Information is used for benchmarking, which can prove your business cases.

If necessary, compare it with other parts of your company. Highlight the fact that they have systems (if they do) which provide them the information they need to run their responsibilities. You have the same needs. Ask how they justified them, if possible, to see what sells in your organization.

When you start going down the FM system path, be sure you understand what information you want, how it will fit in your work processes and staffing, what you will do with it and what you really need (your business requirements) before you even think about the process of selecting or procuring a system.

Quick Summary

Key Points	→ Focus on information and its value to your effectiveness and efficiency.
	→ Compare your operation with others in the organization if they have systems for their business processes.
	→ Develop a business case with quantifiable benefits and risk mitigation.
Executive Tips	→ Facts and figures are the best tool you have to sell your business case.
	→ Talk their language – time, money and risk.
Traps to Avoid	→ Don't push for an FM system unless you have a solid business case.

23

Surviving the Integration Trap

Don't let integration drive your system decisions.

"In a few minutes a computer can make a mistake so great that it would have taken men many months to equal it." - Unknown

Integration can save you time and effort, providing you with information that is coordinated between applications and linked to various operational processes, enabling cost savings and better strategic decisions. That's the sales pitch and generally, it's true. But rushing into integration can sometimes be costly and counterproductive. Invest in the process so you avoid the integration trap.

Keep in mind there are different types of integration. Built-in integration within the same system is common with large CAFM systems, however even these systems may interface with systems you already have, such as financial and HR. Integration between different systems can be a live, one-way transfer of data on a periodic schedule, or two-way synchronization where changes on either system are updated in the other.

The complexity and issues related to these different types of integration are very different. Integration within a single system is much easier and a Swiss army knife of a system that is fully integrated out of the box is tempting. Be careful to assess each tool, however. Some tools aren't needed and other multi-function tools are a poor substitute for the dedicated tool. If you have to compromise functionality or usability, reconsider the need for a single system and at the same time, carefully assess the need for integration between systems.

Does it have to Integrate?

Integration can save you time and effort, providing you with information that is coordinated between applications and linked to various operational processes, enabling cost savings and better strategic decisions.

But integration can also be costly and counterproductive if it's done without considering the reason for integration.

There are two different types of integration:

- ✓ Built-in integration within the same system is common with large integrated systems, providing live integration between modules performing different functions.
- ✓ Integration with existing systems you already have, such as financial and HR, or between different vendor systems.

There are three different ways to integrate:

- ✓ Live sharing of common data between systems where changes are instantaneously available to each integrated system.
- ✓ Two-way synchronization where changes on either system are updated in the other on a periodic or scheduled basis. This is similar to synchronizing your handheld device with your desktop email and contact program.
- ✓ One-way transfers of data on a periodic or scheduled basis, where the data is not modified and is sent back to the original system.

What do you Really Need to Integrate?

The best approach is to decide why you need integrated information and what decisions you expect to make. Then, implement processes and systems (with integration when it makes sense) that get what you need, rather than starting with systems that give you everything else.

The most important consideration is whether the systems you buy do what you need them to do for your processes and services, so consider that first.

If integration isn't possible, is costly or technically difficult, consider alternatives to real-time integration between systems. This can include third-party software for integration and reporting/analysis of data or for download/upload techniques where real-time synchronization isn't needed.

To help you with the decision-making process, consider all factors related to time, effort and cost versus real benefits to your organization. Ask these questions:

- ✓ What will you do with the integrated information – will you make better decisions?
- ✓ Is the size of your portfolio (and related information) large enough that integration will truly save you money with reduced resourcing?
- ✓ If you want integration within a system (i.e., a new CAFM), will the software do everything as well as two or more separate stand-alone systems?
- ✓ If you are integrating between systems, do you really need live and/or synchronized data to meet your needs, or will daily or weekly uploads work just as well?

What are the Benefits?

Integration, like the system itself, should provide you with clear benefits, both financial and non-financial. If you are assessing integration based on reducing double entry, carefully assess whether you will actually reduce costs in real-life, not just on paper.

If integration is driven by a need to have identical information for multiple uses, reconsider how important this is based on the decisions that need to be made, how easy it is to integrate and the requirements for timeliness and accuracy of information.

An example is utility management. An integrated system can enable single entry for processing payments of utility bills and entering utility consumption/rate information for analysis. But the information for each is very different. Another is maintenance costs related to work orders. Often the financial chart of accounts doesn't track the information you need to make decisions based on maintenance activity, labor and costs. Also, the skills and knowledge needed to enter payment information and maintenance information are different. Carefully look at what the information will be used for and what trade-off you will be making.

Challenge Vendors and IT Departments

Challenge your IT department and the system suppliers about integration. They sometimes prefer complex, expensive solutions. Bring them back to your core needs. This is about FM, not IT.

An issue with live integration between systems is that you may end up with a customized system and the risk of increased costs related to future software upgrades. If you feel a single system meets your needs with customization, take a step back and look at separate systems that meet your needs out of the box. If integration is no longer as important as you thought, this approach may save money and effort.

What are the Alternatives?

Consider alternatives to real-time integration between systems, such as third-party software for integration and reporting/analysis of data or for download/upload techniques where real-time synchronization isn't needed.

Industry Initiatives

Moving forward, there are two related initiatives in the industry that will make transferring information between systems easier.

One is the Open Standards Consortium for Real Estate (oscre.org) organization who is working with industry, including IFMA, to develop standards for electronic transfer of information. The other is a concept called Building Information Modeling (BIM) which also relies on information exchange standards, being developed by the National Institute of Building Sciences (nibs.org).

These initiatives will have a fundamental impact on how we use and manage information in the future through improved integration and sharing of facilities-related information both for current management and over the life of the building.

Quick Summary

Key Points	➡ Functionality and usability are the main objectives, not integration for integration's sake. ➡ Not everything needs to be integrated.
Executive Tips	➡ Challenge your IT department or software vendor about the need to integrate. ➡ Validate proposed cost and resource savings with integration.
Traps to Avoid	➡ Integrated systems can be at the expense of functional systems. ➡ Integration can be complex and expensive between different systems.

Your Strategic Plan

Based on this section, what strategic initiatives do you plan to implement that will help you manage your assets better and when do you expect to accomplish them?

What are you going to do?	When?

Notes

Procuring Services

Introduction

Your success depends on the success of your service providers and it's even more critical with customer-facing services where the service provider and its staff represent you and your department or for services that affect reliability and critical assets.

That's why procuring services shouldn't be a decision driven by the lowest cost. It should use a balanced decision-making approach that leverages leading industry techniques to qualify, assess, select and manage the service providers who essentially become partners in your success.

Make the right selection in the first place based on a balance of costs, risk sharing, experience, capabilities, culture and their solution, then build a working relationship that assures mutual success instead of fostering conflict and eventual failure.

24

Procuring Facilities Services

Adopt leading practices to get the results you need.

"There is scarcely anything in the world that some man cannot make a little worse, and sell a little more cheaply. The person who buys on price alone is this man's lawful prey." – John Ruskin

Procuring services for FM is not the same as buying widgets or tendering project work. You will live with the results, and the people who come along with the supplier, for the term of the contract.

FM service providers can impact your image with tenants and occupants, your tenant organization and your organization itself. Virtually every aspect of their performance will reflect on you. When they are successful, you will be successful.

This means it is just as important to get the right service and the right company as it is to get the right prices. The technical approach used to procure a construction project and the simple price-based process that applies to buying office supplies do not apply here.

Getting What You Need

Defining what you want is the first step and then you need to make sure the service provider can deliver what you want within the price they quote. You also need to make sure they are a good fit. This includes their level of sophistication, culture, how they deal with their staff, training, image and more. Again, their performance will have a far-reaching impact on your reputation with all of your FM stakeholders. Their success is your success - and vice versa.

Your procurement department, if you have one, will probably use a formula approach that's sometimes geared to squeezing the lowest possible price out of the suppliers. While this is may appear admirable, it may also be false economy. They will look good up-front, but issues with taking the lowest-price supplier may get worse over time, particularly with multi-year contracts.

Procuring FM services is a complex process that includes documentation, request for proposal (RFP) questions, site tours, supplier interviews, specifications, evaluation criteria and working knowledge of your overall FM process.

Focus and Flexibility

Focus first on getting the correct level of service you need for your facilities' services. Then introduce flexibility in the contract terms that will enable you to increase or decrease services with a defined pricing approach. This avoids having them under-price reductions and over-price increases in scope or service levels down the road.

Pricing

Get your pricing with details you can use to effectively assess bids. This is particularly important in labor-intensive services such as janitorial. Knowing their rates, loadings, proposed hours, etc. will let you compare properly between bidders and weed out any suspect pricing practices. It also provides you with more information to negotiate or modify scope if the prices you get are more than your budget will permit.

A key question to ask when evaluating a bid is whether the price they propose is sufficient for them to deliver the scope and service levels you require. While you don't necessarily have to eliminate the low bidder or bidders, always compare their bids with your current costs and the other pricing submissions.

If you've asked for enough detail in the RFP submission, you can do a quick comparison and establish whether the price is right. Accepting a bid with a price that's too low will cause service problems. Few companies are willing to lose money and they will end up struggling to deliver what you need, putting your own success in jeopardy. It's better to get the right price and work with a successful service provider.

Consider This

FM professionals show superior leadership and managerial skill when they make sure service contracts meet their FM needs for service and price. The benefits you receive after accepting a low bid for service delivery will quickly turn to risks if your FM service needs aren't being met because your service provider is cutting corners to meet their price.

Can they Deliver?

Assuming that you will only invite qualified companies to bid in the first place, they should know how to deliver the service. In your RFP, you need to let them know you want details in certain areas because their knowledge and skill in those areas will help you (and them) be more successful. How tech savvy are they? Do they have systems in place to analyze and improve services? What's their quality control? Do they provide you with information and knowledge, or useless lists and reports? Do they keep involved with industry trends and innovations? Do they properly train and re-train their employees? What is their reputation? Ask about these things and any other issues that are important to you.

Finally, learn to expect more from your facilities service providers and to make it your business to find out whether they can deliver. Instead of telling them exactly what to do in the bidding process, invite them to propose approaches and changes to your specifications that can save you money. They are the experts, so tap into their knowledge.

Value their Expertise

If your specifications are wasting money and a supplier can suggest solutions, cost savings ideas and other approaches to improve results and potentially save money, you want to know about it.

Forget about the old-style traditional supplier without any sophistication. You do not want a supplier who simply does what you tell them, whether it's wasteful or not. You want suppliers who think about how they can make you more successful.

When evaluating service providers, ask questions that give them a chance to differentiate themselves from others. The best FM/supplier relationships are built on mutual support.

Consider This

Your success depends on the suppliers you bring into an organization. You want someone who will do the job efficiently, give you the service you need and use their experience and knowledge to help make you more successful.

Who Should Make the Decisions?

If you are responsible for your budget, responsible for results and manage the supplier for the duration of the contract, you should be the one responsible for purchasing decisions, as long as they are conducted based on your organization's procurement policies.

More and more purchasing managers or purchasing departments are taking ownership of the decision process, which is driven by cost-reduction pressures. In the ideal situation, the purchasing department supports FM by providing a professional procurement service. They put together a great RFP with the right contractual terms, establish good evaluation criteria and processes (not just low price), integrate the scope/specifications effectively, vet the bidders and manage the actual procurement process.

In most cases, a low initial price (the bid price) is not necessarily the lowest total price over the term, since services have to be handled differently from commodities like office supplies or products. The "low price wins," approach may drive behaviours that you may not want – and no matter how iron clad you think your contract terms and specs are, the suppliers know more than you do about their business. This may result in additional costs or lower service levels and can even affect your organization's overall production and success.

Many procurement groups have a mandate to cut initial costs and may even be rewarded based on how much they save. As they don't have any stake in the future performance of the suppliers they've contracted, they may also not pay enough attention to a contract's total cost over the life of the contract or worry about the issues that can develop with a service provider engaged at a price too low to deliver the services you need.

That's why it's so important that the decision-making process ultimately be in the hands of the facility manager, with support from the procurement professionals. Your procurement support should make sure the process is fair, professional and effective. But final decisions should be based on a supplier's ability to meet FM needs, including future price increases, after the contract is signed.

Old way	New Way
☒ Procurement drives the process	✓ Operations drives the process
☒ Inflexible	✓ Flexible
☒ Price & nothing but	✓ Value above all else

Quick Summary

Key Points

➡ FM service procurement cannot follow the same processes as those used for construction or buying supplies.

➡ Your success depends on your FM services company - so make sure they can be successful.

Executive Tips

➡ Your procurement department should support your procurement, not drive it themselves.

➡ The lowest initial price isn't always the lowest overall cost.

➡ Make it your business to be able to show the procurement department the long-term costs associated with FM service contracts.

Traps to Avoid

➡ Don't accept a bid that's too low to believe.

➡ Don't use the same approach as you use for buying supplies or tendering projects.

25

Developing Effective RFPs

Get what you need with an effective RFP.

"Quality in a product or service is not what the supplier puts in.
It is what the customer gets out and is willing to pay for."
– Peter Drucker

For any new procurement or renewal, you should find the best service provider using a Request for Proposal (RFP).

The RFP document communicates your requirements and expectations to the service providers so they can respond with a solution and price that meets your needs. It is not the same as a tender. With an RFP, you get more than a price, you get a fully-proposed solution.

An RFP also provides the information you need to select the best provider. A poorly written RFP will make it harder to choose a provider, and you may not get the results you need.

There are a number of reasons a well-developed and managed RFP will provide you with benefits. These include:

✓ You get the best service provider and the best solution.

✓ You can manage cost and value.

✓ You control the process.

✓ You can balance price and service.

✓ You get innovation from the service provider.

✓ You make your selection based on criteria that matters.

✓ You end up with a better relationship and ongoing management.

There are four stages of an effective procurement exercise. Three are directly related to the procurement and the fourth is the management phase, during the life of the contract.

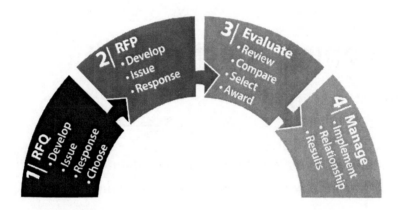

Qualifying Bidders

First, assume the service providers are capable of providing the service. Either conduct a Request for Qualification (RFQ) to establish their credentials, or select and invite only the best players in the marketplace. The RFQ is the first gate in the process and allows you to weed out bidders who are not really qualified before you issue the RFP.

If you are required to conduct your procurement publicly and anyone can submit a proposal, conducting an RFQ usually satisfies the public requirement. Then, you invite only the companies who passed the RFQ process. You can even pre-establish how many companies will be invited to bid on the RFP. This reduces your overall effort and doesn't waste the time of companies who simply won't have a chance to win your business.

The RFQ should not ask about the solution or price. Establish the minimum requirements you expect of a successful bidder and use those as your criteria. This could include their geographic presence, their resource base, experience, technology, financial strength, company size and other criteria.

Differentiate Bidders

Your RFP should focus less on getting details about how they deliver the core services and more on the aspects of the service that matter the most to you in a new contract relationship. This could be data and information exchange, reporting, performance measurement, working interfaces, their proposed organization and staffing, their ideas and approaches to improving service and reducing costs, how they will transition the service and more.

Some of these are standard while others depend on your business and the reasons you are outsourcing.

Understand What Is Important to You

Your ability to assess and select a provider is directly related to how well you develop your RFP and the information you provide. Before you begin, you must know what is important to you, what the key comparisons should be between suppliers, how you will assess the bids and what information you need to provide bidders. You also need to have an effective approach to managing the process.

The RFP

There are two key aspects of the RFP you need to develop. This includes the information you provide to the service provider and the information you want to get back from them.

Your RFP should solicit solutions and approaches from a proponent rather than set a rigid, prescriptive structure where little more than price matters. You need to focus on the outcomes you want, not just how the provider will achieve them.

Give a relatively tight page limit, along with minimum font size and margins. Shorter RFP responses are easier to evaluate and will force the bidders to eliminate most of the marketing fluff while giving you solid information you can use to evaluate. It's harder for the bidders, but easier for you.

Your RFP should clearly state that their RFP response forms part of the contract if they are the successful bidder. Usually, the contract supersedes anything in the RFP. However, if they propose a value-added service or techniques that aren't specifically asked for in your RFP specifications, including the RFP response as part of the contract makes their promises a contractually-binding document. This is where a careful assessment is required when you evaluate their proposal. Look carefully at the wording to ensure they are committing to what they say, not just explaining what they could or may do yet. You want a contractual commitment.

For an effective RFP, you need to provide clear, concise and complete information to the bidders so they can deliver a well-written and well-priced proposal response. Here are some examples of information you should provide for the bidders and information you want them to give you in their proposal.

RFP Information You Provide	RFP Information You Request
✓ Company background	✓ Company background
✓ Your goals/objectives	✓ Proposed delivery model
✓ Selection process/criteria/schedule	✓ Proposed organization structure
✓ Portfolio / facility details	✓ Proposed staff and qualifications
✓ Scope and specifications	✓ Innovative solutions
✓ Service levels /performance indicators and management	✓ Benefits you will receive
✓ Report and integration requirements	✓ Implementation approach
✓ Questions	✓ System/information integration
✓ Pricing model	✓ Examples of past success
	✓ References
	✓ Price

Make it Fair & Transparent

The principles of fair and transparent procurement are important for all organizations, but your ability to select the right service provider shouldn't be jeopardized by your organization's procurement rules.

By establishing and following fair yet flexible rules for your procurement process, the bidders understand the rules before they bid and you can apply them in a way that works for you. Make sure you fully document your process and the RFP rules so you have a fully-informed bidder. Then, follow your process and document what you do so you can demonstrate that you've followed it.

Part of this is the issue of mandatory requirements mentioned earlier. By including a clause that gives you the right to waive or rectify minor, non-competitive mandatory requirements, you won't have to eliminate a bidder just because of an administrative error, for instance.

Include language in the rules that gives you flexibility, yet adheres to a fair process. For instance, include language so that you don't have to accept the highest-total scoring bid if the price is higher than your budget and lets you negotiate scope or service levels to bring down the price to a level that meets your needs.

Include Scope & Specifications

Your RFP includes the scope and specifications for the bidders. This enables them to answer your RFP questions in the right context, develop a solution that meets your needs and establish pricing that matches the level of effort required. Here are a few of the characteristics that your RFP should include:

Tell them what you expect

Provide enough details so they understand what will be expected of their service. This can be results based or prescriptive. In some cases, telling them the outcome you expect and enabling them to use their own experience and capabilities to decide how to do it most effectively is the best approach, particularly if you can define the outcome in a service level or some other measurement.

There will be other areas where you need to be very specific about the requirement, either because it's unique, hard to define in an outcome or is driven by an organizational requirement.

Regardless, the more accurate and detailed you make your scope and specifications, the more successful your RFP process will be and the easier it will be to manage the services.

Make them easy to understand/organize

Just providing the information isn't enough. You need to make sure that it's clearly read and understood by the bidders so that their solution in their pricing matches your requirements. If your documentation is complex, fragmented and difficult to follow, it's likely that the bidders will misinterpret, misunderstand or simply miss key aspects of your requirement. This will cause problems during the life of the contract.

The way specifications are organized in the information provided needs to be as clear as possible and directly related to the services that are being requested. Instead of using the traditional approaches to developing specifications, including specifications used for construction projects, use a more modern approach.

Organizing them in a logical, clear, and easy to read format is critical. Use the techniques discussed in the section, *Communicating to Influence*.

Split requirements by management/technical

Many specifications combine technical and process requirements together with management requirements. Instead, deal with them independently in two separate sections. Focus the technical and process requirements on the specific outcomes and prescriptive requirements of service delivery. Separately outline your management requirements for delivering, managing and controlling the services provided by the bidder. This includes reporting, quality control, requirements such as security and confidentiality, management, escalation, inspections, performance reporting and more.

Consider your management requirements and make sure your service providers are able to feed you the information, data and analysis you need to effectively manage the overall facilities function.

Refer to standards, legislation, etc.

Wherever your requirements are covered by industry standards or legislation, refer to the standards or legislation instead of repeating the requirements unless there is a specific nuance or different requirement in addition to the standard ones. For legislation, you can cover it off in the general specifications by indicating that the requirements of any legislative authority must be adhered to, or you can list them. If your organization is in a unique position where some regulations don't apply to you, then specifically address these. Let the bidder know whether you voluntarily comply and need the bidder to adhere to these regulations or not. This is particularly important where the requirements have a cost impact.

Reference the most current version of the standard or legislation and add "or most current" in the requirement. Your contract should include provisions for addressing the impact of changes that increase costs. This allows bidders to avoid building-in costs to deal with uncertainties over the term of the contract.

Require analysis, not just reports

If you want valuable information from your service provider, don't simply ask for reports that don't tell you anything. Include a requirement to provide analysis and summary about their services on a periodic basis. Link this with your own internal reporting and information systems so you can use the information to make decisions.

Where you have other reporting requirements, such as greenhouse gasses or carbon emissions, for example, be sure to include these requirements as well if they are applicable to the service.

Don't leave gaps for misunderstanding

Carefully review your specifications and ensure you covered all the requirements and identified what is not part of the service if there may be doubt. Have someone else review the specifications to make sure they are complete and don't have misleading or conflicting requirements. The tighter your document is, the fewer the misunderstandings.

Include performance management

This is your opportunity to include performance management requirements for the service. Performance management goes beyond service levels and KPIs, however. The most important part of managing performance is the management process, tools and communications. Refer to the section, *Getting Performance.*

Ask the Right Questions

Evaluating RFP proposal responses is a critical yet often painful process. You want enough information to evaluate the bidders, yet you get widely varying responses that don't always answer your questions and sometimes don't reflect their true capabilities. This makes RFP responses hard to evaluate.

Understand that bidders aren't usually very good at writing about what they do. You will get proposals filled with generalities and marketing pitches, text that is difficult to read, narrative that is hard to follow and responses that don't really answer your questions.

As you need to evaluate bidders on their ability to deliver the service, not their ability to write a proposal, make it easy for the bidders to give you what you need to evaluate their capability, not their proposal writing skills.

The quality of the questions you ask is critically important to your evaluation process. Quality questions make it easy for them to respond to your RFP and that eases your evaluation. It's one of the key ways you establish whether the supplier is capable of delivering what you need.

Develop RFP questions that will meet your objectives, fit into your strategy and enable you to make a decision. Don't leave questions open to interpretation – make their purpose clear and you will get clear and concise responses that are easy to evaluate.

Carefully structure the questions so they are not repetitive and are logically grouped. This makes it easier to respond and easier to evaluate. You can ask some specific and pointed questions that have short answers as well as open questions that require much longer responses. But the actual questions you ask should be short, clear and concise. Don't ask a question with several sub-questions buried in it. Separate them out into separate questions or use a list to indicate the items you want them to cover.

If you have pre-selected the bidders, either in a formal request for qualifications (RFQ) or by reputation, don't ask basic questions about whether they can deliver the services - you should already know this, or you wouldn't invite them to bid.

Here are five things you can do in your RFP to get better proposals from your bidders:

1. Ask clear questions

Don't make the bidders guess about what you want from them with ambiguous or broad questions. Each bidder will interpret a broad question differently and provide you with diverse answers that don't match your expectations. This makes it difficult to differentiate and evaluate bids. Use language that doesn't leave any doubt about what you want. Don't ask for a "detailed summary," if you want to know the steps they take to deliver service or maintain quality. Ask for exactly what you want.

Don't repeat the same question in different sections. Look at the flow of information and the questions you are asking and make it easy for them to respond and easy for you to follow the same logic when evaluating. If you ask questions and the bidders refer you to their answer in another question, you haven't organized the questions effectively.

2. Use few but focused questions

When you invite companies to bid who have been by pre-selected by reputation or by an RFQ process, you should know they have the qualifications to provide the services you need.

Your goal is to assess their approach and capabilities in important areas that differentiate the bidders in key areas. For instance, asking a question like "describe your approach to...." is very general and will get a wide variety of responses.

Instead, ask specific questions that are key to your own success, such as "when delivering the service, what technology do you use to communicate the status to us on a timely basis?"

3. Separate multi-part questions

Long questions with multiple parts are difficult to fully answer. Answers to these questions are also hard to evaluate. Don't make it hard for you to find the information you need. Instead, break the complicated question into separate questions.

For instance, don't ask a bidder to "describe your approach to reporting, including formats, distribution, and revisions." Decide what key points about reporting are important to you and ask specifically about those points as separate questions or sub-questions. This ensures concise answers that give you the information you need in a consistent structure that is also easier to evaluate.

4. Ask for evidence

Ask questions that enable the provider to demonstrate what they will do for you and what they have accomplished with other clients. Think of this as a job interview and don't rely on what they say they will do – make sure they have a solid track record of delivering. Let the proponents tell their story.

Anyone can tell a good story about what they will do for you in general terms. To evaluate bidders, you need details and specific approaches they will use to meet your needs. You need to know the tools and techniques they use and how well they understand and can adapt to your specific issues and requirements. In your instructions, tell them you are looking for detailed responses that demonstrate how they will provide the services for you. Ask them to avoid motherhood statements, theory and marketing material.

Where possible, ask them to describe a specific example of where they have done a particular job, for whom, how long, how they deliver, etc. If relevant, ask for samples of existing documents, such as the table of contents of an existing quality assurance program, training manual, process document, etc. If they do not have those kinds of documents and you require them, ask them to explain how they will develop them.

It's easy for a bidder to describe what they will do for you without demonstrating that they have a track record of doing it for others or exactly how they will do it for you.

Since you already know they have the capability to do the work, focus on differentiating the bidders by assessing the specific approach, tools, techniques and resources they will use to meet your needs.

5. Tell them why you are asking

Try to identify the intent of your question where possible and word it so it is easy to understand and interpret.

Answers to your questions give you information to evaluate and differentiate the best bidder from the others.

Don't make them guess what you want. Since even the most carefully-worded question could be interpreted slightly differently by bidders or their focus in responding may vary widely, tell them why you are asking the questions and what you are looking for, either within the question, or as a preface to the question or the section in the RFP. This makes it more likely that you will get the response you need to evaluate their bid. As indicated earlier, ask for evidence to avoid answers that are given simply to tell you what you want to hear.

By implementing these five techniques, it's easier for bidders to respond to your RFPs and it will be easier for you to evaluate the responses. In the end, that will make it easier to select the bidder who is best suited to your requirements.

Pricing Information

The pricing you request should be detailed enough to analyze and compare between providers, yet not so detailed that it's irrelevant or excessive. Do allow providers to submit options as long as there is enough structure to enable a reasonable comparison and a basis for negotiations. Depending on the service, this information will allow you to assess pricing and understand whether it is reasonable. It will also let you compare separate parts of the competitors' bids, letting you determine whether they fully understood the requirements. The old approach of accepting bids that are too low, either by design or by mistake, contributes to service failures.

Evaluation Criteria

To effectively assess the RFP responses, clearly establish your evaluation criteria and provide a structure with guidelines. You should also consider setting a page limit for the response. Include a schedule in the RFP that identifies site visits, access to information rooms (or data sites on the web), a process and deadline for questions and a clear time and date for submitting the response.

When procuring a service provider, the more effort you put into the RFP document up-front, the easier it will be to select a proponent, negotiate, transition and then enjoy a smooth operational phase that gets you the results you want. Refer to the next section for more information.

Sample RFP Table of Contents

The following is a sample of an RFP's table of contents. Use it to provide some guidance on the type of information you should include and how to organize it. Of course, the details will depend on the service and you will have some material that your corporation expects to be included in all RFPs. Make sure that it enables you to select the best provider.

Section A - General Information
A.1 Purpose of this RFP
A.2 About the Facilities
A.3 Definitions

Section B - Rules and Special Provisions for this RFP

Section C - Instructions to RFP Proponents
C.1 General Information
C.2 RFP Schedule
C.3 Proponents' Conference & Site Visit
C.4 Communications during Proposal Period
C.5 Detailed Site Information
C.6 Contract and Pricing
C.7 Submission of Proposals
C.8 Proposal Format

Section D - Evaluation
D.1 Step 1 - Evaluation of Mandatory Requirements
D.2 Step 2 - Evaluation of the Technical Proposal

Alphabet Soup – RFPs and More

The RFP is one of many different tools. While they are the most effective for FM services, there are other potential options and other tools you can use before you issue your RFP to ensure you have interest from bidders, consult with bidders and prequalify bidders. Understanding these options puts you in a better position to develop your own approach.

Request for Information (RFI)

The RFI is typically used when a client wants to gather information from the market to help develop an RFP approach, make decisions about the procurement process, and help develop the RFP document and even the scope.

The RFI presents an opportunity to try to shape the client's final RFP to your benefit. Take the opportunity to identify approaches, bundling of scope, pricing structure, technology the client should request, and any other elements you would like to see in the final RFP that will give you an edge over your competition. Take the process seriously, and use the same techniques you would in a proposal to convince the client that the information and suggestions you're providing should be incorporated in the final RFP.

Request for Expressions of Interest (RFEI)

This process is used to identify potential bidders and establish their level of interest. It is issued in advance of an RFP and should include enough information for you to decide whether you're likely to pursue the final RFP. If this will be followed by an RFQ process, keep it light and focused on client requirements. However, if the client will be going straight to an RFP, you need to demonstrate that you should be included in the RFP process, otherwise there's a risk you may not be on the client's final list for the RFP.

Request for Qualification (RFQ)

This step is used by the client to pre-qualify bidders and narrow the field to a small number of companies who will receive the RFP itself. It's usually a shorter, simpler process that's open to all interested service providers. It uses a straightforward series of questions and qualification requirements that require lower effort to evaluate than a full RFP. It does not include pricing or require identification of a final solution.

Organizations required to conduct a public bidding process use the RFQ to narrow the list of bidders invited to respond to the RFP. It also minimizes the number of RFPs they'll need to evaluate. Even with organizations not required to use public procurement processes, RFQs are used when the number of capable bidders is too large to manage in an RFP process.

An RFQ process minimizes the level of effort you need to make as a bidder, and prevents you from expending efforts on an RFP you aren't likely to win. But while it's a shorter, simpler process, you need to employ a process similar to the one you use for an RFP since it's just as important. If you don't pass the RFQ process, you will be eliminated from further consideration.

It's important to note that some organizations use the acronym RFQ for a different purpose, known as a Request for Quote. This is similar to a tender where your response is evaluated based on price and some mandatory requirements such as bonding and insurance. A formal written submission is seldom required.

Request for Proposal (RFP)

The RFP is a flexible process usually used for services where the delivery of services can be accomplished with various approaches. The RFP structure and approach can vary widely, so reading the documentation is important to understand the process being used by the client, including procurement rules, evaluation processes, and negotiations.

Rather than predefining the methods of delivering the service, the client provides required guidelines and outcomes and allows the bidder to design a solution that meets their needs. The requirements will vary widely. Some have a very detailed scope of work or detailed specifications for certain areas, while others are very general and broad, requiring a great deal of interpretation and a wider range of possible solutions.

The approach will depend on the client's specific situation and how much they want – or are able to – define their requirements. The requirements are often outcome-based and may include some form of service level agreements and performance measurements, with a financial risk/reward structure.

The RFP process may include negotiation of the technical solution and pricing. A proposal that suits the client's needs but has some details the client may prefer to do differently can be negotiated with changes. A preferred bidder may have a higher price that exceeds the client's budget, but that may be negotiated, either with smaller margins or by changing the elements of the solution or scope to bring the price down.

Sole Source

This method is typically used for lower-value procurement initiatives that require unique or specialized services. These may be available from only one company, or where a specific supplier's knowledge, experience or approach has a great deal of value to the service being required. Even organizations required to use an open, competitive process are sometimes able to procure using this method if it meets their procurement policies and fits within certain criteria.

This method is quick and easy for the client, but requires the bidder to fully understand the requirements and still provide a compelling proposal, not only to convince the client they have chosen the right company, but also to provide the evidence they need to justify their decision.

Request for Quotation (RFQ)

The RFQ is sometimes used for low-to-medium-valued procurement requirements where the requirements are clearly defined and well understood, and where a competitive pricing process is required. Often a select number of known companies are asked to quote, but sometimes the client will add in some new ones. The only requirement from the bidders is a price, which typically provides the basis for the decision. The RFQ itself is usually a very short description of the work and other related requirements, sufficient for the bidders to provide a quotation. The quote may be for a fixed price or for time and materials.

Request for Tender (RFT)

A tender is typically used for defined requirements, which enable the bidder to provide a firm price based on clear, detailed specifications. While some written response may be required in addition to the pricing, it's more for compliance and to validate qualifications than to evaluate a proposed solution. The lowest price is typically the winning bid as long as compliance and qualifications meet requirements. There are either built-in criteria for compliance and qualifications, or only known bidders are invited to participate in the tender. An RFQ process may precede the RFT to provide for the compliance and qualification stage, with the RFT evaluated solely on price.

This approach is commonly used for construction projects and commodity products rather than for services, however some services may also lend themselves to this type of procurement approach.

Quick Summary

Key Points

➡ Selecting a service provider isn't like selecting a contractor or product. It's a long-term relationship.

➡ Use more than just price to evaluate your suppliers.

Executive Tips

➡ Focus on their fit, technology, management, staff, training approach and other key organization alignment items.

➡ Use an RFP, not a tender, keeping your options open. Communicate your process and criteria to keep it fair.

Traps to Avoid

➡ Evaluation criteria that doesn't help you to get the best bidder.

➡ Asking questions that don't enable you to differentiate between bidders.

➡ Asking questions that let the bidders give you a sales pitch, not solid information.

26

Evaluating Your RFPs

Get the service provider you need with an evaluation process.

"True genius resides in the capacity for evaluation of uncertain, hazardous, and conflicting information." – Sir Winston Churchill

Issuing the RFP is just the first step. Once you receive the proposals, you need to evaluate the service providers.

Your organization may dictate how your evaluation process is conducted to ensure fairness and transparency, however you need to make sure it meets your needs to select the best service provider, not merely the lowest-price service provider.

Clearly outline the process in the RFP, including the option to negotiate, and take steps to ensure the evaluation is fair and objective.

There are several approaches to the evaluation. Where possible, postpone the pricing evaluation until after the proposal is evaluated to prevent the evaluators from being influenced by the pricing. In the final steps, you should give yourself the ability to negotiate with the top scoring bidder, so how they approach the work is more important initially.

The steps you should take to evaluate an RFP include:

1. Mandatory technical evaluation

2. Proposal evaluation

3. Pricing evaluation

4. References

5. Presentation/interview

Proposal Evaluation

The fundamental process includes using pre-established evaluation criteria to evaluate the proposals and assign a score to each of the service providers.

This enables you to compare proposals. The highest score is likely your leading provider, but before you make your decision you must also consider the relative scoring for the parts of the proposal that are most critical to you. You could manage your evaluation process so that minimum scores are required in certain areas. This ensures that the things most important to you will count and won't be minimized because a particular bidder was very strong on other areas that are less critical.

Depending on the scope and size of the RFP, you should have subject matter experts contribute to the evaluation as applicable. Include IT, finance and HR, for instance, to evaluate sections dealing with their specialty if necessary.

When possible, have several different people with knowledge and understanding of the service and the requirements score the RFP and then come to a final overall score. A consensus score between the evaluators is a more relevant process than an average score. This process should include a discussion when scoring between individuals is significantly different, since the different perspectives and the discussion they generate enables you to better evaluate the service providers.

Step 1 - Evaluation of mandatory requirements

An RFP is a formal document so it's important that the service providers have submitted all the elements required for evaluation.

In this first step, the mandatory requirements are reviewed and evaluated. If the mandatory requirements are not substantially met, the bidder could be disqualified. Be sure to reserve the right to request clarification or seek additional information as necessary so you don't disqualify on minor issues. Since you've selected the bidders through an RFQ or by invitation because you know they can do the work, you want to ensure their bid is included in the evaluation process.

This step should not be used to eliminate a provider on a minor technicality. While you identify it as mandatory, be sure to give yourself some latitude in the RFP rules to correct typos, administrative errors and other simple issues. You don't want to eliminate an otherwise good bidder over an administrative error or other minor technicality.

Once bidders have met the requirements, their bids will be evaluated based on the technical and pricing proposal.

Where possible, include a list of mandatory items within the RFP itself to make it clear what you need them to submit or to follow, such as page counts. You can include a list similar to the following:

Mandatory Criteria	Requirement
Proposal form	Submitted fully completed with signature
Certificate of independent proposal	Submitted fully completed with signature.
References form	Submitted fully completed with signature.
Declaration of subcontractors form	Submitted fully completed with signature.
Conflict of interest declaration	Submitted fully completed with signature

Step 2 - Evaluation of the Technical Proposal

The next step is to evaluate the technical submissions based on the submitted response to the RFP requirements questions against the evaluation criteria.

Have each evaluator review and score the submissions independently. They can then get together to discuss and develop a consensus score for each bidder.

Scoring scale

You would use an evaluation scale similar to the one shown below. Each of the responses to the RFP questions would be scored using this scale. The description of the scale helps each reviewer fully understand how to use the scale.

Here is a sample scoring scale ranging from zero to five:

Score	Description
0	Not addressed - There is no response to the RFP requirement or it has not been answered in accordance with the question.
1	Minimally addressed - The response is not complete and/or does not meet the evaluation criteria.
2	Partially addressed - The response is partially complete and/or only partially meets the evaluation criteria.
3	Satisfactorily addressed - The response is complete and meets the evaluation criteria to an acceptable level.
4	Well addressed - The response is complete and meets the evaluation criteria to a very good level.
5	Excellently addressed - The response is complete and meets the evaluation criteria to an excellent level.

Evaluation criteria & guidance

Since it's important for each evaluator to evaluate based on similar criteria, the expectations for each question that are scored should be further outlined. Again, this ensures clarity and consistency between bidders and you can include the criteria in the RFP document to guide the bidders so you get better responses.

The description of the criteria below illustrates some factors you can use to evaluate the proposal response.

In order to demonstrate the required criteria, the bidders should provide sufficient details to clearly identify the resources, processes and approach to providing services. General statements and marketing material are not sufficient to demonstrate that they meet the criteria.

Benefits of this approach include:

- ✓ Helps evaluators
- ✓ Ensures consistency
- ✓ Focuses on what is important for evaluators
- ✓ Provides backup for audit.

Here is a sample list of criteria the evaluators should look for when evaluating the bidder's answers and the expectations for each one:

Criteria	Expectation.
Understanding requirements	The question has been answered completely and demonstrates an understanding of the requirements.
Approach	The answer identifies a reasonable, well managed and effective approach, backed up with experience, process and resourcing to providing services for The College in accordance with the requirements.
Details and information	There are sufficient details and experience provided to support the successful provision of services and eliminate doubts or potential issues that might result in services that don't meet the scope or detailed requirements.

In addition to the general criteria above, you can develop more detailed evaluation guidance for each of the questions to use internally. This is more detailed information for the evaluators on how to evaluate each question as it relates to your specific needs. This detail is generally not shared with the bidders.

Here is an example from one section of an RFP. It shows the original RFP Question as well as the more detailed guidance for each question:

2.6	Service Request Response	
	RFP Question	**Evaluation Guidance**
2.6.1	How will you provide 24-hour response?	Clearly outline the methods for emergency and routine, business hours and after hours. Process appears workable and should result in proper response.
2.6.2	How will you dispatch and track building operations and maintenance work orders?	Provide details for effective dispatch to their own staff and subcontracted services.
2.6.3	How will you dispatch accommodation and move work orders?	Provides details that should meet requirements. Demonstrates an understanding of this requirement by referencing the spec requirements.
2.6.4	How will you receive, dispatch and complete occupant requests and provide billing information?	Provides details that should meet requirements. Demonstrates an understanding of this requirement by referencing the spec requirements.
2.6.5	Provide examples of existing reports.	Examples include the required information. Examples are existing reports, not made-up for the response.

Weighting

To develop the overall score for each bidder, you need to match the score you assign to each question the bidders answer (i.e., a score from 0-5) with the relative importance of each question. Some things are more important to your service and its success than others so should have a higher weight in the total.

The best way is to start by assigning a weight to each section, then further sub-divide each question in the section. While it may seem that this approach is too detailed, it will provide an effective, easy-to-manage evaluation process that is more accurate and more defendable.

The sample table shown below identifies the weight for each of the main sections in an RFP.

Proposal Requirement	Weight	Max Points
Service delivery organization	20%	100
Resource management	10%	50
Management of service delivery	15%	75
Service delivery approach	30%	150
Previous experience on similar work	20%	100
Contract start-up	5%	25
Innovation & value add (Bonus)	5%	25
Total available points	105%	525

This information indicates the relative weight of the requirement based on its proportion of the total available points for the technical proposal, which in this RFP was set as 525 points and is simply a multiplication of the highest score of five by the weight (i.e., the highest possible score of 5 x a weight of 20 = 100 points)

The absolute number of total points isn't critical, but make sure you have the right balance between the total points for the technical scoring versus the financial scoring.

The benefits of using a weighted approach include:

- ✓ Based on individual questions
- ✓ Assigns relative importance to the responses
- ✓ Balances important / not important
- ✓ Provides consistency
- ✓ Documented and auditable
- ✓ Provide to bidders.

Scoring method

Using the examples above, you establish the score for each question by multiplying the score for that question by the weight for that question. This allows you to arrive at the assigned points for the question.

The assigned points will be totaled together to arrive at the total points for each bidder's technical proposal. The weighting helps to focus the points on things that matter the most. However, as discussed earlier, you may want to set a minimum for specific sections or even questions if they are critical to a successful service provider.

You can also set a minimum total score to be considered. For instance, you may require that bidders achieve a minimum total score of 350 out of the maximum available 525 points to have their financial proposal evaluated in the next step.

Step 3 - Evaluation of Financial Proposal

A well-structured pricing model provides enough detail to effectively evaluate their pricing and compare it to the proposal evaluations. If bidders achieve your minimum score in the technical evaluation (if you've set one), you then evaluate their financial proposals.

You should have asked for their total price and some details that enable you to understand where the differences are between the service providers and whether they line up with your evaluation of their proposals.

If there is a large discrepancy, use the details and the proposal to understand why. There may be provisions of the RFP that increases cost unnecessarily, the level of service may be higher than needed, or their start-up or staffing costs may be over- or under-estimated. Knowing this enables you to enter negotiations well prepared.

There are a number of methods for evaluating pricing. Depending on the service and the size, you should decide which one works best for your situation. In any case, you don't want to set up an evaluation model that weights price so much that it makes your technical evaluation irrelevant. Your intent shouldn't be to get the lowest price, it should be to select the best overall bidder.

Consider This

The right RFP rules and processes allow you to fairly evaluate and select service providers while ensuring that you aren't obligated to select a bidder with a price higher than your budget or lower than what is reasonable to provide the service.

To evaluate the financial submission, the proposal with the lowest price is assigned the maximum available points. Each of the other bidders is awarded points based on the ratio of the lowest price to their price. Divide the lowest price by the bidder's price and multiply by the available points to arrive at the bidder's score for their financial submission.

This process works well where the scores are all within a similar range. If you have an exceptionally low bid, it may significantly skew the score. If the low bid is too low, validate that that price is sufficient to deliver the services first. If it's not, consider rejecting the bid and eliminating it from the evaluation.

You could also establish the average of the scores and award points to the bidders based on how far they are from the average, regardless of whether they are higher or lower. An average score would receive 100% of the available points and you deduct points from each of bidder based on their percentage away from the average. This method helps to prevent a low bid from significantly affecting the evaluation. It also rewards the bids that are closer to the average.

Which method you use depends on your overall evaluation, goals, values and other factors. Where possible, test various scenarios before finalizing an evaluation method to make sure you understand how it affects different price variations.

References

Using references to help you make a decision is just as important with an RFP as it is when hiring staff.

Ask for references in the RFP and speak to specific clients (such as their last new client with similar size scope) to ensure you aren't hearing only from their most satisfied clients.

Also ask for a reference from a contract they recently lost. This may tell you more about the service provider than existing clients. In any case, use this information cautiously.

Establish a list of questions to ask every reference, enabling you to evaluate the feedback. The questions should be directly related to the evaluation criteria and scope to ensure you get comments on the areas that matter the most to you.

Presentation/Interview

A presentation by the service provider, preferably in their offices, is the final step in the evaluation process. At this point, you should have narrowed the field down to the top two or three at the most. A presentation enables the service provider to summarize their proposal, introduce you to their delivery team and make their sales pitch.

If you have questions or want clarifications, submit them ahead of time so the service provider can prepare. If you ask key clarification questions, be sure to record the presentation or request the service provider re-iterate their answers in writing for you.

You may also want to conduct interviews with key individuals within their organization to ensure the right fit and validate some of the RFP details.

In the end, a well-developed RFP document followed-up with an effective evaluation process will help you to meet or exceed your objectives.

Selection

A well-structured pricing model will provide enough detail to effectively evaluate their pricing and their technical submission to select the best overall service provider. Build in flexibility, as long as it's fair and transparent, to enable you to make your choice based on the score and your overall requirements. Avoid being trapped by your own process.

To decide the preferred bidders, summarize and rank the scores on a simple spreadsheet. The table shown below is a summary and is populated from more detailed spreadsheets for each bidder, with scores for each question and the calculations to establish the financial scores. The ranking is done with a simple spreadsheet formula.

Evaluation Summary	Bidder1	Bidder2	Bidder3	Bidder4
Service Delivery Organization	68	60	72	64
Resource Management	40	35	30	35
Management of Service Delivery	55	51	31	48
Service Delivery Approach	75	67	75	105
Previous Experience on Similar Work	80	70	100	80
Contract Start-up	22	22	25	25
Innovation & Value Add (Bonus)	15	0	0	15
Total Technical Points	355	305	333	372
Technical Rank	2	4	3	1
Financial Evaluation Points	241	256	175	210
Financial Rank	2	1	4	3
Combined Evaluation Points	596	561	508	582
Total Rank	1	3	4	2

Once you've made your selection, you would begin negotiations with the highest ranking bidder. Only after you've made a formal agreement should you notify each of the other bidders and advise them they were not selected. This gives you some leeway to go to the next highest ranking bidder, if for some reason things don't work out with the highest ranking bidder.

If the pricing you get is higher than your budget, consider revising the specifications by negotiating with the selected supplier. Discuss how the pricing can be reduced through reductions in scope. If you asked for enough detail in the pricing, this will be a simple and fair process. Keep in mind that reducing cost while maintaining the original scope will often lead to problems.

When you notify the unsuccessful bidders, offer to give them a short debrief about their technical submission. Give them insight into the areas they could improve so they are a better bidder the next time.

Consider This

Bidding is a complicated process with winners and losers. As an FM professional, see the process of evaluating bids as a way to understand the market for service providers. You want to be seen as professional, fair and committed to excellence in your organization and to the industry suppliers.

Quick Summary

Key Points

➡ Start with a qualification process to get bidders that can do the job.

➡ The RFP should enable you to document requirements and enable bidders to differentiate themselves.

Executive Tips

➡ Once you've qualified bidders, your focus should be on differentiating them.

Traps to Avoid

➡ Minor mandatory requirements that eliminate an otherwise ideal service provider.

➡ Looking at price before you evaluate their capabilities and fit.

27

Selecting a Janitorial Service Provider

Get the right service at the right price.

"What separates two people most profoundly is a different sense and degree of cleanliness." – Friedrich Nietzsche

Janitorial is a commonly procured service that is highly competitive and often causes the highest level of issues since it's a front-line service that your occupants or tenants encounter daily. While the issues are somewhat unique, they can be applied to other services as well.

Establish your Needs

When selecting a service provider, the first step is to decide what you need. It sounds straight forward, but cleaning is a very labor-intensive service that's largely based on the frequency cleaning tasks are performed.

Your needs are usually identified through a specification, which outlines the tasks and frequencies you want performed daily, weekly, monthly, quarterly and annually. The specification should also identify special requirements, finishes and levels of service you need. Providing floor plans showing the flooring surfaces, office density, room uses and areas will ensure the prices you receive are based on correct information.

Get More than Cost Information

Since the cost is driven by labor, with wages representing 70% to 72% of the total price on average, don't ask for a bottom-line price. A good service provider will disclose how their pricing is established through a simple yet detailed cost sheet. The cost sheet shows the distribution of costs for wages, benefits, equipment, supervision, materials and supplies, profit and overhead. It should also show the shifts for each classification of janitorial employee along with total projected hours. This allows you to compare productivity via a review of the square-foot area cleaned per labor hour.

Unrealistically low wages or high productivity is a sign the contractor will not be able to maintain staff or provide the appropriate service. Combined productivity from 4,100 to 4,300 square feet per hour is a good standard for a general level of service. In addition, light-duty cleaning should not exceed 5,700 square feet per hour unless there is an investment in special equipment and techniques. Compare prices with the productivity and wages disclosed by the service providers and make sure they add up.

Match Scope and Specifications to your Budget

In some areas, existing staff are protected when the management company changes. This means service providers should factor in wages that are at least the same as the current staff are paid. Check with your local authorities.

Leave Room for Price Increases

Be sure to structure the pricing and the term of your service to allow for natural increases in wages and supply prices. A fixed price for three years may sound good, but the service provider has to guess about increases and blend their cost increases over three years, meaning they get a much higher margin in the first year (adjusted for start-up and equipment costs) and very tight margins in the last year. That may influence their staffing behavior and when you re-tender, you may have a sudden jump in your costs.

Handling Supplies

Washroom paper supplies are often excluded from the price, due to the high cost and uncertainty of usage. If the service provider includes this in their base price, they may underestimate the cost and run into problems; or overestimate, leading you to pay more than you need. As well, if you increase density on the floors, add additional shifts, or otherwise impact the usage of washroom supplies, the service provider may request an adjustment to the pricing. These supplies can be provided to you through a resale arrangement with your provider on an actual usage basis, or you can provide supplies directly. Usually, your provider has better buying power than you do, so ask for unit pricing.

Other Factors

So far, the focus has been on pricing, however there are other factors to consider.

The use of illegal labor or violations of the labour code are cost-saving techniques that put you and your company at risk. Check the reputation and professionalism of the service provider before selecting them. In addition, check for good standing with local authorities like workplace safety and insurance boards or government labour departments

The ability of the company itself to support the services they deliver with responsiveness and professionalism is also important, as is the technology they use. Well-maintained equipment, qualified supervisory staff and good communications are all critical.

Technological capabilities may need to be considered, depending on your needs. Can the supplier work with your facility's work order system, can they provide appropriate reporting and quality assurance results through the web or other electronic means, and how will they monitor their own services to ensure you receive the service quality you are paying for?

Depending on your organization's goals, you may also want a supplier who can use "green" cleaning processes, which includes cleaning products that are certified by environmental organizations in your area.

Since cleaning has such an impact on your facility's occupants, spend the time to select a provider who can deliver the best service at the right price with the professionalism you need.

ault

Quick Summary

Key Points

- ➡ Selecting a provider includes more than just total price.
- ➡ Enable the provider to propose staffing and innovations.
- ➡ Consider management, track record, image, training and supervision as part of your evaluation.

Executive Tips

- ➡ Getting information on individual pricing components will enable you to compare and negotiate.

Traps to Avoid

- ➡ Not allowing price increases to keep in line with inflation, particularly labor costs, will cause service problems and sticker shock when you retender.

320

Your Strategic Plan

Based on this section, what strategic initiatives do you plan to implement that will help you manage your assets better and when do you expect to accomplish them?

What are you going to do?	When

Notes

Outsourcing FM Functions

Introduction

Outsourcing usually refers to subcontracting out a full range of services as a bundle, including the full FM function, but for many facility and property managers, it's also associated with specific functions such as janitorial or maintenance.

Regardless of the scope, outsourcing is a well-accepted and commonly-used business model that you shouldn't discount until you've investigated and analyzed the options.

Outsourcing can be a good business decision, provide more personal growth, professional challenges and opportunities for you and your staff to be successful in their roles as a "stay-back team" or within an organization whose core business is FM.

Even if you don't outsource, it can be professionally-rewarding to study how outsourcing companies get results.

28

Make your Organization Flexible through Managed Services

Using an outsourcer or sub-contractor has its benefits.

"Do what you do best and outsource the rest." – Tom Peters

While cost savings are one of the initial reasons organizations hire an outsourcing company to provide managed services for non-core elements of their operation, flexibility quickly becomes one of the biggest benefits.

The flexibility comes from the secondary reasons organizations use managed services. Beyond saving money, outsourcing enables organization to focus on their core business and access resources, world-class business processes, additional scope and improved scalability of the services.

The FM profession is becoming more complex, and responding to those complexities with managed services is easier and exposes you to fewer risks.

The complexities include more stringent regulatory oversight, emerging environmental issues, increasing risk and liability, technological changes, complex energy management coupled with increasing costs and difficult HR-management issues resulting from accelerated business changes.

Because FM is typically a small part of the organization, it lacks the concentration of resources, technology, experience and buying power that a large outsourcing company has. That makes it more difficult for FM professionals working inside an organization to provide flexible, cost-effective service to the core business.

Strategically, improved flexibility is just as important as reducing costs when implementing managed services. The business environment organizations face in today's economy requires quick action, frequent changes in direction and easy scalability of services and facilities. Organizations know they need that flexibility to change priorities and increasing competitiveness - but they may not be in a position to meet all of the FM-related needs in-house.

Switch from Tactical to Strategic

With managed services, organizations gain flexibility through the size of the outsourcing company and the ability to focus on strategic core business issues instead of managing tactical business processes and issues.

As an example, let's say the outsourcing company becomes responsible for HR related to facilities staff. Daily issues, including providing continued services when a vacancy arises and staffing up or down in response to business changes, are no longer an FM responsibility. This frees up internal HR and management resources to focus on the needs of your primary employee base; the one that directly supports your core business. Scalability becomes effortless when you purchase, sell or lease new properties, or acquire or divest a business unit.

Get a Technology Boost

Another area where you gain flexibility is technology. A large outsourcing company has the resources and size to use flexible enterprise systems. It is also able to provide them at unit costs a smaller FM department can't match. By eliminating the direct management, expense and investment inherent in the technology necessary to manage facilities and by focusing your IT department on your key business, you free resources to become more flexible in response to core business needs.

The increased concentration of resources that result from managed services also provides the flexible analysis, reporting, technical solutions and advice needed to support key decision for your core business. This includes effective preventive maintenance, capital planning, asset management, financial analysis, environmental stewardship and the increasing legislative initiatives that impact your facilities.

Transition and Management are Key

While managed services will provide benefits, a successful transition and a strong ongoing relationship with the service provider is essential. As an important business strategy, it is worth spending time planning the initiative and ensuring key elements are in place to ensure success. To ease transition and ongoing management you need:

✓ An effective contract management team or individual to manage the outsourcing relationship and provide oversight to the managed services.

✓ Well-defined scope and contract provisions that give you contractual flexibility as your company changes.

✓ A procurement process that ensures the company you select can deliver the results you expect, and is a good match for your organization.

✓ Effective performance measurements focusing on results that are important to your organization as well as providing key management tools.

✓ A transition plan to smoothly shift people, processes and other resources over to the outsourcing company in addition to ensuring the business and information interfaces are in place.

✓ A contract management structure and culture that leverages the benefits of managed services and ensures a partnership approach to the relationship.

Financial Models

The financial model you use for your outsourcing initiative will drive price, behavior and risk. While pushing risk to the service provider may seem ideal, it results in some potential issues that may not be worth it.

There are three basic financial models you can use for outsourcing. The characteristics and risk profile are shown below:

Fixed Price

- ✓ Need a high level of baseline information
- ✓ Risk moved to service provider
- ✓ Less flexibility

Management Contract

- ✓ Moderate/low level of information needed
- ✓ Some risk retained by client
- ✓ Moderate flexibility

Flow Through/Transaction Based

- ✓ Low level of baseline information needed
- ✓ All risk retained by client
- ✓ Very flexible

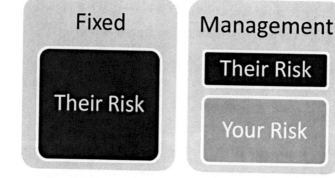

With the cost and complexity of providing facilities management services, managed services can be an effective business strategy to reduce costs and increase your organization's flexibility. By focusing on your core business, you can leverage the benefits to enhance your competitive advantage.

Quick Summary

Key Points	➡ Managed services offer a tried and true way to get results. ➡ Your decision point will be the size and complexity of your FM portfolio and team. ➡ You can outsource or subcontract a portion of your overall scope and still get benefits.
Executive Tips	➡ Good management practices require looking at managed services to see if it fits your needs. ➡ Even if you don't outsource, reviewing options will provide information you can use internally.
Traps to Avoid	➡ Don't underestimate the costs of a transition or managed services. ➡ Ensure you have a strong stay-back team to manage the service provider and strategic requirements

29

One Step Re-Engineering through Outsourcing

A new organization provides immediate change.

"Re-engineering is the radical redesign of business processes for dramatic improvement." – Mike Hammer

Re-engineering is one of the main strategic tools for staying competitive. Staying competitive so that you support your organization's core business means you must constantly look inward and examine the opportunities to improve processes, systems and ultimately, results.

The concept of re-engineering began in the 1980s as large corporations began to re-think the way they did business in order to adopt the powerful new computer systems that were emerging.

Re-engineering, as a label for what was happening, was introduced by Mike Hammer in his groundbreaking article, "Re-engineering work: don't automate, obliterate," in the *Harvard Business Review*.

The definition put forward by Mike Hammer defined the nature of re-engineering as a radical change. Since he coined the phrase, re-engineering has played a large part in improving the competitiveness of corporations.

At the same time, the mere mention of re-engineering often invokes fear. Not just because it means changing the status quo and a potential risk to individuals within the organization, but also because since the 1980s, organizations have come to realize that it is difficult o get the results they need from reengineering. Moreover, the task itself consumes a great deal of resources.

These concerns are well-founded. Since reengineering took root, organizational studies have come to show that it requires more than a shift in technology. Indeed, effective re-engineering requires change management to work. In other words, re-engineering is about technology and processes, but it's also about people. Ignore the human element in the re-engineering equation and you risk certain failure.

Re-engineering Principles Still Apply

This does not mean the basic principles of reengineering have changed. That is, you still need to recognize that your organization's core business is what makes it successful. In fact, it is often the most important part of an organization's competitive advantage.

For non-core parts of your company, including many of the functions of FM, re-engineering that occurs via outsourcing can yield almost immediate results. With outsourcing, you can effectively change all technology and processes with one fell swoop.

In this case, outsourcing a business process provides a quicker, more effective way of achieving the same, or even better, results as an internal reengineering project might accomplish. This is why *The Outsourcing Institute* considers outsourcing to be a central management tool for the fundamental re-engineering and re-energizing of businesses. They cite accelerated re-engineering benefits as one of the top ten reasons companies outsource non-core business processes.

Consider This

Don't be confused by what outsourcing offers. Outsourcing means turning over a specific or suite of business processes to an outside service provider as part of a contractual relationship. With outsourcing, you turn over the work and the management of the work, in such a way that it still integrates with your core business. You do not lose control, you gain functionality. Many FM functions are commonly outsourced and the FM professional guides or makes outsourcing decisions based on what works for the organization. Here, saving money and improving workplace efficiencies are key leadership and management skills.

Pre-Engineered Services

By bringing in a service provider who has already engineered their processes and management to world-class standards, you benefit immediately.

Since your service provider's core business is the service they provide to you, they have already designed it to be as efficient and effective as possible. In addition, the scope and scale of most service providers ensures improved efficiency and seamless access to enterprise systems, technical knowledge and resources, including personnel, you may not otherwise have access to.

What stays? What goes?

How do you know what to outsource and what to re-engineer? Those decisions are based on your core business. A core business is your primary purpose; it's what gives you the advantage over your competitors; it moves you from raw commodity status to essential service.

And your core business may not be immediately obvious. For instance, you might think Motorola's core business is making devices such as radios, cell phones and pagers. In fact, much of their manufacturing is outsourced. Their real core business is designing products that consumers will want - and then convincing consumers to buy them.

Non-core elements of your business include all the internal services that support your core business. What those services are will depend on your business. For property managers, this may include IT and payroll, for instance. For facility managers, it often includes the full range of property or facility management services, depending on whether they occupy their own space.

The core parts of the facilities or property management role that are traditionally retained by the organization involve strategic aspects such as asset management, planning and the all-important interface between the organization's needs and service delivery. After an outsourcing initiative, this is usually the function of the stay-back team, but it can be as simple as someone to manage specific subcontracted services.

Of course, successful outsourcing takes some time and effort, but it's typically not as complicated as a re-engineering initiative.

Changing Culture

One of the difficult parts of change is always culture. While re-engineering usually retains much of the built-in culture, an outsourcing initiative quickly results in a culture change.

Along with this comes a true sense of customer service, since the people now providing your non-core internal service are part of a different organization, your service provider. These people are governed by a contract that establishes a formal business relationship. That relationship requires all the elements of a service culture to be in place and that's something that's not always as easy to achieve with internal services.

Implementation

Implementing an outsourcing initiative as a re-engineering tool means you only need to focus on the inputs and outputs of the business process, and the related results you need for your core business to be successful. Internal processes, technology, training, personnel and a myriad of other management issues no longer need to consume your time and effort, giving you more resources to direct to the core business that makes your company successful. Of course, you will need to deal with employee issues related to outsourcing your staff, but the extensive change management required for a re-engineering initiative is significantly reduced.

To successfully implement an outsourcing initiative, you need to consider a number of elements, including the following:

- ✓ An effective stay-back team to manage the outsourcing relationship.
- ✓ Well-defined scope and contract provisions that also give you flexibility as your company changes.
- ✓ A procurement process that ensures the service provider selected can deliver the results you expect.
- ✓ Effective performance measurements that focus on the results and provide management tools to both the service provider and your company.
- ✓ A transition plan to smoothly shift people, processes and other resources over to the new way of operating.

Clarify your objectives

The FM professional takes responsibility for the successful implementation of an outsourcing initiative. Like re-engineering, successful outsourcing has to be looked at as a project with clear objectives and requires a plan to get there. By using the above elements as an anchor point, your outsourcing initiative will get you where you want to go sooner, and get you the results you need.

Staying ahead of your competitors is the only way to be successful. Rather than focus your time and energy re-engineering non-core areas of your business, consider an outsourcing option and then spend your own resources improving your organization's core business and competitive advantage.

Consider This

The FM professional should zero-in on his core objectives, too. That is, what competitive advantage do you offer your organization? When you use your leadership and management skills to identify ways to improve efficiencies, reduce costs and improve performance, you prove your competitive advantage. While re-engineered solutions may be helpful in some areas, consider your outsourcing options as well.

Quick Summary

Key Points

➡ Internal re-engineering an FM department has a higher risk of failure than outsourcing.

➡ Outsourcing can be easier to implement and yield quicker results by providing ready-made solutions to business issues.

Executive Tips

➡ If you have to make major changes to the organization, outsourcing may be the easiest path.

➡ The business case for outsourcing is still an important part of a re-engineering decision.

Traps to Avoid

➡ Moving your major problems to an outsourcing company without planning for the transition and culture change.

30

Outsourcing Integrated FM Services

Choosing the right company is critical.

"The other part of outsourcing is this: it simply says where the work can be done outside better than it can be done inside, we should do it." – Alphonso Jackson

Selecting the right company to manage your property is critical to maintaining your asset value while continuing to deliver the service that's expected. These principles, combined with an effective procurement process described earlier, will position you for success.

For residential and commercial properties, you need to satisfy your tenants and maintain your brand value. For corporate buildings, you need to establish and provide a productive, efficient work environment.

Managing buildings is an important and complex service. Getting the right company requires well-defined objectives, scope and specifications, performance and contract management provisions, procurement process and selection criteria. Once you select the company, you still need an effective transition/start-up and management process going forward to maintain a strong and productive relationship.

Finding the Best Company

To procure a facility or property management company, first pre-qualify a select number of companies and then issue a request for proposal (RFP), followed by an evaluation process that uses several of factors to make a final decision.

Establish your requirements for scope, size, experience and coverage up-front and invite a wide variety of companies to qualify. Prepare questions for them to complete, asking for information that will enable you to select three to five bidders for the next stage.

Basic qualifying requirements should include their size (facilities, total space managed and staff), the scope of services they provide, their experience with your type of facilities and their presence in your area.

The size of your facility or portfolio will also make a difference in who you select. A large global firm may not be as effective as a smaller, local firm for a single facility. If you are looking for consistency and improved systems and management information for a large portfolio, however, particularly one that includes facilities in other regions, you may need a global firm.

The next step is to develop your RFP. Unlike a traditional tender, the RFP enables you to ask questions about aspects of the service or the company that matter to you and to ask how they will deliver the services. These answers will be the differentiators you use to make a final decision.

Develop the questions carefully. If you have pre-qualified the firms, you should be confident they can provide the services. You should find out what innovative or value-added services and experience they will provide for you, make sure they can deliver on your specific expectations and validate that they can do what they say.

The RFP process enables them to propose additional services, methods or techniques you may not have considered. Your ability to assess and select a company is directly related to how well you develop your RFP, the background information you provide and the questions you ask.

A formal evaluation

Evaluate the responses using pre-defined criteria with values associated with different questions based on their relative importance. (This approach is addressed in *Procuring Services*). As part of the evaluation, check references and request one or more meetings and presentations from the top bidders to get a feel for whether there will be a good fit between their company and your organization over the term of the contract. Don't limit this to the executives or sales staff. Meet with the individuals at the front line who actually deliver the service.

These factors should be combined with the proposed price to arrive at a score for each bidder, thus enabling you to make a decision. Their capabilities, value-added services and the overall fit with your organization going forward will have a higher impact on your real costs than a marginal difference in price.

Document Requirements and Expectations

While the contract structure is critical for ongoing service performance and management, the RFP process must also inform the bidders of your requirements and provide background on which they can base their responses.

This will make it easier to formalize the deal once you have selected a provider, since they will have already seen the contract and specifications.

The document should be created using a straight forward modular approach that is easy to understand and reference, and easy to use going forward. The documentation should include the following elements, which work together to describe the services you expect.

Legal contract language

This part of the document contains all legal and contractual requirements of the relationship, including all of the typical language around liability, insurance, payments and financial issues, dispute resolution and, most importantly, clauses that provide a mechanism for change. This ensures you have the ability to add, remove or change services, with suitable mechanism for price adjustment as well as the ability to change the performance management framework to match your organization's changing needs over the term of the agreement.

General management & administration

This section describes the responsibilities, processes and expectations from a management and administrative perspective for the services being delivered. These work in conjunction with the detailed service specifications identified below. Rather than repeating expectations around each service, this section provides the information in one place. A good example is reporting, which is included in this section and would define all reports required for each service in one place.

While this list is not inclusive, the structure should include the following elements:

- ✓ Start-up / transition-in
- ✓ Standards, policies, standards and compliance
- ✓ Staffing, training, key personnel, etc.
- ✓ Management processes and expectations (generally and as needed for specific services)
- ✓ Reporting
- ✓ Management meetings
- ✓ Auditing and quality assurance
- ✓ Systems, information, security and access.
- ✓ Communication and relationships
- ✓ Subcontracting expectations, limits, etc.
- ✓ Ad-hoc requirements, additional projects, etc.
- ✓ Hand-back / transition out.

Specific service definitions

These describe the levels of service and specifications of service delivery for all services. This supplements the management and administrative items above. Included in this section would be a list of services covering the entire scope of the services. There could be only one or two listed services (for a simple subcontracted service), or there could be a long list for an all-inclusive, full-scope service.

The descriptions may include detailed technical specifications, such as maintenance or janitorial tasks and frequencies, as well as results-based descriptions of the service outcome that is expected, ranging from a visual description of cleaning, to your tolerance for fingerprints on glass entrance doors. Sample items in this section would include:

- ✓ Maintenance of HVAC systems
- ✓ Grounds maintenance
- ✓ Parking management
- ✓ Janitorial sServices
- ✓ Backup systems maintenance
- ✓ Call centre services
- ✓ Security, patrol and access control services.

Performance management framework

Based on the specifications, management and administrative requirements, the performance management framework defines the key measurements and outlines the management approach to enable proactive management of performance. The key is to manage performance, not just measure it. That doesn't mean that you do all the work. Much of the performance management tracking, reporting and activities should be performed by the service provider, with suitable information and reporting provided to you along with the ability to review details and audit the results.

Since your needs and expectations will be specific to your own goals and the type of facility you are responsible for, the details need to be carefully developed to match your needs. The performance management framework, however, should include the following elements:

- ✓ Key business objectives
- ✓ Measures & ondicators
- ✓ Processes and reporting
- ✓ Penalties and incentives
- ✓ Proactive management processes.

Given the importance of the property or facility manager in the current market place, selecting and managing the right company must include a well-developed strategic approach. This company will be managing your asset and will represent your organization to tenants, residents and employees, thus establishing and maintaining your building's reputation. You will also interact with them for the length of the contract.

Using the approach identified above will improve your ability to select and manage a company that meets your needs in the short and long term. The investment in time and effort needed for this process and the related documentation will be worth it in the long term.

Quick Summary

Key Points	➡ Your success depends on your supplier's success, so selecting the right one is the first step to success.
	➡ Document what you need and expect from your supplier. Get information from the marketplace if necessary about capabilities and scope.
	➡ Build service level definitions and performance management into the contract.
Executive Tips	➡ Ensure the FM service provider fits your needs related to coverage, size, sophistication and even culture.
	➡ Use a structured approach to selecting the supplier.
Traps to Avoid	➡ Don't base your decision on the lowest price.
	➡ Don't believe the sales pitch. Get beyond their marketing and make them demonstrate what they can do.

31

The Outsourcing Stay-Back Team

Your role - making outsourcing work.

"There is no security on this earth. Only opportunity." –
Douglas MacArthur"

Successful outsourcing is about more than selecting the right service provider;
successful outsourcing requires an effective stay-back team to guide the initiative.

An effective stay-back team can be the cornerstone of any outsourcing initiative.
The stay-back team includes the senior FM representative and staff that remain
with the core organization after an outsourcing initiative. They form an
important link between an organization's business and the service provider. That
link starts with the onset of the RFP process, continues through the ensuing re-
organization when the contract is awarded, and covers the ongoing management
of the services provided. In summary, the stay-back team manages the contract
with the new service provider and performs any facility functions that have been
retained in-house.

They also coordinate the activities of the service provider within the activities
and needs of the organization. This ensures that the service provider's activities
support the goals and objectives of the organization's core business.

Stay-Back Team Role

The role of the stay back team varies depending on the overall goals of the organization and the exact nature of the outsourcing initiative.

However, the core role related to the outsourcing initiative will remain the same – managing and administering the contractual relationship between the organization and the service provider.

Generally speaking, in any large outsourcing initiative the SBT performs the following important functions:

✓ Asset management / strategic planning.
✓ Contract management / administration (including performance management).
✓ Coordinating the linkages between the service provider and the corporation.
✓ Other FM functions retained in-house.

The stay-back team should be established early in the process so the team can be involved from the beginning, giving it the knowledge it needs to manage the service provider after start-up. This is an important consideration, since an outsourcing initiative includes many steps from the initial decision to outsource to the selection and transition of the successful service provider. As these steps are sequential, the stay-back team needs to be involved in each step along the way. This ensures the continuity and knowledge necessary to effectively manage the contract and maintain a good relationship between the organization and its FM functions.

Flexibility is required

Managing the outsourcing relationship requires flexibility, since not everything can or will be reflected in the contract. Indeed, the relationship between the service provider and stay-back team must be flexible enough to enable changes as the contract progresses.

When a professional organization is hired to manage facility functions, it's important to let the service provider do the job. The stay-back team should then concentrate on long-term activities like asset management and strategic planning, in addition to managing the relationship and monitoring the service provider's performance. Even if asset management/strategic planning activities are outsourced to the service provider, a member of the stay-back team should oversee the activity and interface with the corporation due to the strong interrelationships between the facilities functions and the core business.

Fundamental Shift

Those who stay back to become members of the stay-back team often encounter a fundamental shift in their work and work culture. This shift includes learning to "let go" of the details of service delivery to focus more on the strategic facilities issues and outcomes. As members of the stay-back team, their core business shifts to functions that add the highest value to the organization and its core goals.

To fulfill that role, interaction with the service provider is critical, since the service provider generally delivers a broader scope of services than with subcontracting or outsourcing, and includes a larger management component to the service. The stay-back team also interfaces with the service provider to align the contractual relationship and objectives so that they meet the organization's objectives.

Skill Sets

Since the role of the stay-back team members is a significant shift from their previous roles within the organization, it requires a careful matching of skill sets and even culture. For success, stay-back team members must move beyond the day-to-day operations and assume the role of owner representative and strategic planner. It's important to assess individual skills and abilities in this new context.

This ensures individuals will be successful and considers whether new resources from outside the organization should be included.

With a focus on contract management and administration and a significant focus on asset management, a number of skills should be present in the stay-back team, particularly within its leadership. To help members of the stay-back team be successful, additional training should be considered in relationship management, contract management, performance management, strategic planning and asset management.

Effective linkages

The stay-back team needs to be able to link the activities of the service provider and other in-house services with those of the organization and its core business. This requires a broad knowledge of the services being provided and sufficient knowledge of the organization and its core business. The stay-back team leadership must also have the ability and the status necessary to interface with other groups within the organization's core business. That interface with others ensures FM can influence and be effective at managing the linkages between service providers and the organization.

Cultural change

The outsourcing initiative itself is a cultural change that needs to be effectively supported by people who can adapt themselves to the new culture. They should also be able to lead others through the cultural change. It is important when selecting the stay-back team members that they fully support the initiative and can work in the new environment. The stay-back team leaders in particular must be capable of influencing a significant change in the culture.

A critical mass of internal knowledge and expertise

The stay-back team needs to have a critical mass of knowledge related to the services being outsourced and the services that continue to be provided in-house. If possible, this knowledge should include knowledge of the core business as well. Detailed historical knowledge is also very useful, however many of the staff with this type of knowledge will be retained by the service provider and personnel and other records will be accessible.

Structure

The size and structure of the stay-back team depends on the size and scope of the outsourcing contract, as well as the services, if any, which remain in-house. Through the stages of an outsourcing initiative, the composition of the stay-back team will change, since staffing levels and skill sets will be different throughout the various stages.

When establishing your stay-back team, consider where they report within the corporation to ensure they have sufficient influence and can effectively participate in FM business strategies and decision making. The outsourcing initiative provides an ideal opportunity to reassess the existing reporting structure and influence necessary changes.

Interaction with the service provider is another important element of the stay-back team. There will usually be important interactions at many different points between the service provider, the stay-back team and even other departments within the organization. Still, it is important to formalize and maintain a single point of contact for issue resolution, contract interpretation and central coordination.

Quick Summary

Key Points	➡ The stay-back team is an important interface between the service provider and your organization.
Executive Tips	➡ Provide your team with the training and skills they need to be successful. ➡ Shift their focus from delivery to strategy.
Traps to Avoid	➡ Staff continuing to work as if they are hands-on with the services.

32

Developing an Outsourcing Partnership

It won't come naturally – you need to build it in.

"If we are together nothing is impossible. If we are divided all will fail." – Winston Churchill

Outsourcing FM services works best when there is a partnership developed that ensures your goals are met and your needs are realized while also respecting the service provider's business goals.

Many outsourcing deals are called "outsourcing partnerships" and since the word "partnership" is used by clients and service providers, it's easy to believe outsourcing is about partnership. But are these partnerships real or imagined?

The reality is not so clear, since the notion of "partnership" includes some elusive qualities. In some cases, the arrangement isn't a partnership, nor will it ever be one. This is more the case in out-tasked or subcontracted services, but even with outsourcing, partnerships don't develop unless the conditions are right.

Before we worry about whether there's a partnership or not, we should understand what it means. In a legal context, a partnership is a formal, contractual arrangement where the partners share in the profits or losses of a business activity. Usually, it's a joint business venture where the parties contribute to an outcome, whether it's a product or service they both profit from.

Since outsourcing involves a buyer/seller relationship, this formal definition doesn't apply. We have to look at a more general definition of the word, which is the mutual cooperation towards achieving a goal. The two key words are "cooperation" and "goal."

In FM, the service is complex and constantly shifting based on the client's organizational needs. Partnership means there is some give-and-take in the service and the relationship that allows both the service provider and the client to easily adapt without being constrained by rigid key performance indicators (KPIs), strict contract terms and inflexible financial models through mutual, cooperative agreement and trust. It's this flexibility that makes the difference between a partnership and a traditional buyer/seller relationship.

If you look closely at outsourcing, you see that it typically includes the overall management of more than one facility services function with a specific responsibility for the outcomes. These are often enshrined in service levels or KPIs. Progressive outsourcing doesn't constrain the service providers with detailed specifications or procedures; they focus on the end result and let the service provider achieve the goals using the experience and abilities you chose them for.

That should cover the "goal" part of the general definition of partnership, but the only way for a partnership to succeed is for the goals to be met. If that doesn't happen, it becomes a traditional buyer/service provider relationship very quickly. That occurs because trust and flexibility are abandoned in favour of a formal, inflexible contract management approach that brings performance in-line and initiates due diligence to support penalties, withholding payments or termination. The key to maintaining a partnership is to ensure the goals are realistic, achievable and aligned.

Are Your Goals Aligned?

There are three distinct goals and misalignment of any of them gets in the way of a real partnership, jeopardizing the results you need for your organization.

Often, only two goals are considered critical to the outsourcing partnership relationship; the basic goals of the client and the basic goals of the service provider. For the client, this includes service performance and budget objectives. For the service provider, it's their profitability.

These goals are more readily aligned when the procurement approach enables alignment and the goals are achievable. One of the problems in meeting both financial and performance goals for the client occurs when the service provider over-promises savings and finds itself unable to deliver the savings and maintain service levels. Here, there's a direct relationship between service levels and resources - and resources cost money. Just consider the differences between various organizations you see in other markets, from the low-cost budget services and products to high-cost premium services and products. The service you're outsourcing is no different.

Increasing competition and the large scale of many outsourcing companies reduces costs. But that doesn't attract from the fact that outsourcing companies are in business to make a profit. The reality is simple, when your service provider is losing money, they can't give you the service you need.

Your expected goals must be realistic and achievable and the service provider must also promise results that are realistic and achievable. The procurement process must recognize this and make sure these goals are aligned when a deal is done. If not, once the procurement professionals are gone, you will be left with a very challenging service management issue that impacts your success.

The third goal is usually overlooked, yet has a significant impact on the success of the outsourcing initiative and the partnership. This third goal is that of the client's staff. Also known as the stay-back team, they remain with the organization to manage the outsourced services. They are also accountable for the results.

Like any business situation, outsourcing involves people and partnerships are always between people. In an outsourcing partnership, that includes the service lead from the outsourcing company and the client's stay-back team. Outsourcing isn't a "set it and forget it" proposition. It requires effort to make it work the way it should.

Managing the outsourcing relationship is usually left to the stay-back team. This is where a real partnership can be built regardless of the other factors involved in the outsourcing relationship. If outsourcing is new, the stay-back team should be trained on how to manage and know what is expected from them.

The stay-back team members must also support the outsourcing initiative and the goals without letting their own internal or personal goals conflict with the organization's goals. When that doesn't happen, the stay-back team (or individuals on that team) may try to demonstrate their own value by over-managing the service provider or competing with the service provider's team to maintain credit for initiatives or service delivery. The KPIs, service levels and the penalty/reward systems may be inadvertently designed to create this misalignment. Be wary of cost pressures or how the individual performance of the stay-back team is evaluated as these factor may encourage stay-back team members to find reasons to penalize the supplier rather than rewarding work well done.

Consider This

While it may seem counter-intuitive, you need to support your outsourcing service providers to ensure they are successful. After all, when they screw up, you screw up. It's simply not possible to blame the service provider since you selected them and are managing them. In this way, they become an extension of you. Work with your stay-back team and service provider to build a relationship based on trust and support.

Is Your Procurement Process Designed For Partnership?

While the goal of many procurement exercises is to reduce costs, the reduction must be reasonable and a flexible contractual arrangement provides more opportunity for a partnership while also meeting overall goals and reducing costs. This includes recognizing that cost, service levels and scope are part of a triangle. If you change one, you usually impact the others.

First, the goal needs to be clear and understood by both parties. For instance, if your procurement process is designed to save money and that's it, then be honest and expect your "partner" to manage appropriately.

For a partnership approach, start by selecting the company with the best fit by asking the right questions in your RFP and evaluating them on what matters to you and what ensures successful and efficient delivery of services. Include meetings with each service provider during the process if your organization or governance allows it, and build an interview stage into the process. The detail and depth depends on the scope and size of your initiative. Selecting the right company in the first place creates the foundation for your partnership and outsourcing success.

The second stage is to establish a realistic cost based on your organization's financial goals and performance priorities. Ask specifically how cost reductions will be achieved and what impact they will have on service levels, including what modifications the service provider would make to specifications, service levels and KPI targets to balance your financial and performance goals. In most outsourcing contracts, the delivery methods, staffing and other factors are left up to the service provider as part of their bid. As most service providers are bidding based solely on what you tell them in an RFP document, it's impossible to be perfectly accurate - and that's a problem since the details impact cost and, by default, the cost estimates in a bid. Include a flexible process that enables you to discuss and negotiate these factors with the selected service provider to balance goals and costs. A cooperative approach right from the start will be advantageous to you, your organization and your service provider.

Does your Contract Model Support it?

It's nice to believe that a good partnership doesn't depend on the contract, but the contractual and financial arrangement will definitely have an impact on the relationship. Without a fair, balanced and flexible contract, you may not get the cooperative relationship on which to build a partnership

The contract includes clauses designed to manage risk between the parties as well as clauses designed to make decisions and disputes easier. In other words, contracts manage the grey areas that always surface. Include clauses that identify what will happen when scope, portfolio, specifications or legislative requirements change or other unknown pressures arise. A partnership is built with clarity and fairness about how these issues are dealt with. By eliminating uncertainty, you also enable the bidders to provide a more accurate price.

While there are many contract types, a complex outsourcing arrangement with many subcontracted services is better managed with a management fee and a flow-through arrangement for most of the costs. This enables flexibility, visibility and control over the resources, costs and the specifications of the subcontracted service. It also eliminates some of the issues involved with a fully-included fixed price. You can build in a sharing arrangement for savings, but as continuous savings simply won't be sustainable if you want to maintain the same service levels, this shouldn't be the way the service provider expects to make their profits.

The contract model can also stifle innovation, continuous improvement, introduction of new techniques and technologies. These are areas where your service provider can provide some of the best value as a partner. The financial model around costs and savings should foster innovation and new ideas, not limit them. Build a flexible approach to implementing your service provider's ideas so there is incentive for both parties. For instance, if the service provider can implement innovations that improve your results or save you money, yet the financial model means related costs must be absorbed by the service provider, they are not likely to implement these innovations. To facilitate flexibility, include a cost/benefit sharing mechanism or a way to fund these types of incremental costs in your contract.

Contract length

The length of the contract also impacts the partnership. A contract that's re-bid every two years isn't designed to build and sustain a partnership. A longer contract with extended renewal options is more likely to foster a partnership, all else being equal, simply because of the longer time horizon.

By building in some renewal periods, you can extend the contract easily if things are going well. You can still renegotiate pricing, but won't have to re-bid the service.

Are You Investing in the Partnership?

Managing the outsourcing partnership requires flexibility since not everything can or will be reflected in the contract. The relationship between the service provider and stay-back-team must be flexible enough to enable changes as the relationship progresses and your needs change. A narrow adherence to the contract will be detrimental to the relationship. With flexibility, be sure to document agreements and changes so when you move on, your replacement understands why things are the way they are.

When problems arise

There will always be problems and sometimes the service provider will make mistakes. In a partnership, the service provider is given a chance to fix the mistake and make sure it doesn't happen again. How they recover is almost more important than being perfect in the first place. Blaming and punishing the service provider won't foster a strong working relationship and may cause them to hide things or stop communicating about important issues.

Enabling a service provider to improve on past performance or fix mistakes can only happen if there is a level of trust between the service provider and stay-back team. Establish this early through regular and open communication. Both sides must be open and honest to build a relationship since even a hint of mistrust will destroy it with little chance to rebuild. If possible, co-locate their key staff with yours to foster a better and more integrated working relationship. This will also help you communicate your issues, goals, and problems. Include key service providers in meetings so they hear information directly and can contribute their experience to help you with issues.

Don't rely only on SLAs and KPIs

Tools developed to manage outsourcing relationships, including service level agreements (SLAs) and key performance indicators (KPIs), were meant to ensure the service provider outcomes are aligned with the goals of the client organization.

Don't think, however, that you can depend on SLAs and KPIs, with their dashboards and red, green and yellow stoplights, if you are serious about developing and managing quality relationships with service providers. A rigid measurement and reward/penalty system that tracks intermediate results, reports on them after the fact and delivers a financial penalty or reward focuses both parties on those specific issues with less regard for the bigger picture. A dependency on measures and a reward/penalty system can also drive bad behavior, even in people with the best intentions.

A true partnership goes beyond KPIs and uses a progressive, ongoing performance communication process, including less formal performance and service assessment tools, regular meetings and cooperative discussions about problems and solutions. Be flexible, adjust targets, add new measures, and drop the ones that don't provide any value. A better partnership moves towards managing and improving results while delivering the required services. Partners understand they must sometimes focus on what matters *now* versus what matters overall.

To get the full value of outsourcing, which is more than simply shifting the risk and responsibility to someone else at the lowest possible cost, you have to actively manage the relationship to get the best out of your partner. While outsourcing is often a way to reduce headcount, you should continue to use progressive performance management approaches similar to the ones you use with valuable employees.

What would you have done?

A partnership, just like a marriage, includes compromise and the realization that neither you nor your partner is perfect. When you deal with issues, consider what you would have done when you were managing the service yourself, probably with fewer constraints, and manage them accordingly. Flexibility is probably what enabled you to manage successfully. It's the same flexibility your service provider needs to deliver service to you and help you and your organization be successful with a working partnership.

Quick Summary

Key Points

➡ Success relies on a good working relationship with your supplier.

➡ Don't just rely on KPI measures and SLAs to get the service you expect.

Executive Tips

➡ Your success is tied to the success of your service provider.

➡ Managing performance is a pro-active process.

Traps to Avoid

➡ Don't create an adversarial environment with your supplier by emphasizing price over everything else.

Your Strategic Plan

Based on this section, what strategic initiatives do you plan to implement that will help you manage your assets better and when do you expect to accomplish them?

What are you going to do?	When

Notes

_____

_____

_____

_____

_____

_____

_____

_____

_____

_____

_____

_____

Getting Performance

Introduction

When most people think of performance, they think about balanced scorecards and Key Performance Indicators (KPIs).

Unfortunately, those tools are really just one part of managing performance – and they only measure results. In fact, measurements themselves don't result in improved performance.

You can't rely on a passive performance measurement system. Instead, you need a proactive system that works with your staff, contractors and service providers to assess and modify performance before they fail. When you link performance to bonuses and penalties, you can even drive the wrong behaviour.

Managing performance, and therefore results, takes more effort than simply measuring results against a target, but in the long run, you will get better results.

33

Managing Performance

Their success is your success.

"By measuring and managing a work process, you alter all the future results produced by that process." - Bob Frost

Managing the performance of the FM related services is key to minimizing your organization's risk and supporting its core business.

Your tools include proactive performance management and reporting, quality management, effective interfaces with the managers of the critical operations, and strict processes and procedures for maintenance activity.

Think of your facility as a jumbo jet, essentially a flying facility with zero tolerance for failure. On your next flight, how safe would you feel if the pilots didn't have instrumentation? What if all they had was the small, forward-looking window? What if instead of a flight manual and checklist, all they had was their memory? That's what it's like to manage a facility without effective performance management tools.

These tools are typically applied to an outsourced arrangement, but the principles should also be applied to individual subcontracted services and your own in-house services.

Beyond Performance Measurements

Managing performance isn't about introducing KPIs, tracking results periodically and penalizing failure. While some people like the carrot and stick approach, you need a more effective management approach that uses measurements and other techniques to get performance. Those who rely on a passive performance measurement system typically miss important management opportunities. In fact, measurements like KPIs can even drive the wrong behavior if you aren't careful. Rather than looking in the rear view mirror, you need to be looking forward.

Having KPIs and including service-level definitions with teeth in your contracts may seem like the right approach, and you can certainly point to these measurements as examples of the due diligence you apply to supplier performance. Just don't ignore the fact that the penalty/reward system isn't the most effective management tool.

Just looking at a KPI that isn't meeting expectations doesn't tell you what you need to do to improve results. For that you must understand what is happening in the complete process that leads up to the KPI result (which is typically an outcome from a process). You also need to work with your suppliers or staff to identify and fix the issues so that failure doesn't happen.

For that, you should track the parts of the process that impact results to give you more information. Where is the bottleneck? Is there a year-over-year explanation (i.e., seasonal)? Is it an anomaly or a trend? What needs to be fixed? How does one building, region, supplier or staff compare to another? What is the high performer doing that the others aren't?

Then bundle that information with good management techniques and communications to manage results. A simplistic "gotcha" system of KPIs and service-level definitions won't enable you to work together with your supplier and staff to identify issues and correct them before they become a problem. Communicate with them about what works and what doesn't, where the weakness is and where the strength is. Do it formally and regularly in a constructive way, being adaptable and understanding; after all, nobody is perfect. If you dwell on the small issues, the big issues won't get any attention.

Integrated Contract Management Approach

Start with an integrated contract management approach that works with your service providers to achieve joint success. This includes performance measurements that address current performance while providing forward-looking trends and measurements that are analyzed and acted upon proactively.

It also includes some form of service-level definitions which clarify the responsibilities and documents the extent to which the service is performed as expected. This is important whether you are hiring contractors or staffing-up internally.

A quality assurance approach should govern the processes and service delivery. Whether ISO-certified or not, a quality program provides consistency and monitors adherence to effective procedures and practices.

Finally, effective procedures and policies that seek to limit the possibility of failure must be put in place. These include traditional ticketing and change notification processes used in the IT industry, but extended and adapted to the maintenance and operations function in-house or outsourced.

The track record of the service company, combined with effective performance measurements, ensures you get better performance from your service provider. The key result of performance management is to:

- ✓ Foster a partnership, not an adversarial relationship. The service provider's success is your success.
- ✓ Support your organization's overall strategic goals.
- ✓ Focusing service delivery on what matters to you.
- ✓ Enable you to provide leadership and management on strategic issues and outcomes, not processes, practices, procedures or methods.

With carefully-designed and well-implemented performance measurements, you will get performance like you never did before. The measurements provide you with control over the results, establish common priorities and clear goals, provide feedback and management information, drive the behaviors you expect and most importantly, give you the results you need to be successful.

Performance Management, Not just Measures

Performance measurements are often associated with penalties. That's unfortunate, since the real objective of performance measurements is to ensure the desired results are achieved. If you have to penalize your service provider, it means the services that are important to your organization's core business failed to meet your needs.

It's better to implement a process that manages performance and helps your service provider meet their performance objectives.

This may mean a combination of incentives or penalties as well as performance measures that provide management information the service provider can use to proactively adjust performance and avoid missing performance targets. The real goal is to not have to apply penalties of any kind.

If you are already measured internally, mirroring those measurements with your service provider will help them optimize their performance and deliver the service you need to be successful.

Effective performance measurements include many measures, but should never dilute the ones that are key to your core business.

With KPIs, look at sub-measures that support the KPIs. These become the performance indicators or trends you use as management tools.

As a management tool, you can tie KPIs and trends to action plans. If a performance indicator fails to meet the target or a trend is tracking negatively, the service provider provides a plan describing how they will correct the issue.

Once you decide on the measures, establish the mechanism to measure and report performance results. Where possible, build them into the processes and automation used to deliver the service. To put this into action:

- ✓ Set the format and frequency of the reporting so that the information is timely and useful.
- ✓ Use clear and concise reports for performance management that provide forward-looking management information.

While dashboards are useful to represent performance management information, they are often used to provide static information that isn't much use for managing the services.

To optimize its value, your dashboard reporting format should include useful management information that is represented using easy-to-read formats with both trend and snapshot information that enables effective decision making.

Managing results is as important as measuring them. Establish regular meetings to review the performance results and discuss action plans where necessary to improve results that are not being met or where trends are pointing in the wrong direction.

Effectively implemented, performance measurements drive the behaviors you want, result in the performance you need and make the overall management of the contract easier. Providing the outsourcing company with clear goals and objectives will drive specific outcomes that support your organization's success.

The real key to effective measurement is to focus on results. Measuring process may be useful to track the direction things are going and provide an early warning system. But ultimately, the only thing that matters is results.

Building a flexible performance measurement framework into the contract is important, and ensures the outsourcing company knows and understands your expectations and performance targets in advance. There are a number of considerations that will ensure a healthy, stable, flexible relationship that gets you results:

- ✓ Define the measurement framework in the contract. The clearer expectations are, the better.
- ✓ The contract language and structure should support and encourage achieving performance.
- ✓ Maintain flexibility so your measures can change as your business evolves through the life of the outsourcing contract.
- ✓ Outline the fundamental areas of performance that are critical to your core business success.
- ✓ Define the measures, targets, measurement tools, incentives, penalties and management processes up-front.
- ✓ Set reasonable benchmarks or develop the benchmarks in the first year of the contract.

Most performance measurement frameworks involve penalties or incentives of some nature. Design these carefully to drive the behaviors you want while ensuring a fair relationship with your outsourcing company. Some key considerations include:

- ✓ Incentives are more likely to inspire performance.
- ✓ Incentives or penalties must be relative to the performance (outcomes or results).
- ✓ Not all measures should be linked to incentives/penalties.

When developing the measurements themselves, ensure the measurements relate to your organization's core business and meet your organization's goals and objectives. Start by identifying the key success factors that are important to your core business, then identify the related key success factors for the FM services provided by the outsourcing company and align your measurements with these.

The term KPI is commonly used for all measurements. In reality, it should be reserved for a small handful of critical measurements that relate directly to the organization's core business. The rest of the measurements should be used as a tracking and management tool, since they are typically related to process or simply roll-up into the KPIs.

There are some fundamental characteristics of good measurements. These characteristics include statistical relevance, objectivity and the ability to be quantified and be within the outsourcing company's control. For each measurement you develop, test it against these characteristics. If they don't match, you should re-evaluate the measure.

Proactive Performance Management

Effective management uses a proactive approach, not just the typical static measurements. Rather than simply reporting measurements such as call response time, maintenance backlog, temperatures and similar key measures against targets and penalizing the supplier, the information must be used to manage future performance, with trending and analysis by the service provider.

This provides advance warning when services, systems or processes are trending towards a failure and enables the service provider to correct them before that happens. Managing performance this way is more effective than the carrot-and-stick approach. Remember, you will be accountable for shutting down your organization's core business no matter who was responsible.

Measurements extend to key aspects of the system where trends and other management information are used to prevent failure. Frequently, equipment performance, such as current draw, is recorded during preventive maintenance tasks. However, this information is seldom compared to historical readings to see trends and initiate action. In a critical facility, this should be part of the overall management approach.

Other examples include temperature in equipment cabinets for a data centre facility, humidity in a printing facility or biomedical refrigerators in a hospital. These may be alarmed and even measured for supplier performance if they go outside a specified range. However, their functions should also be trended and more importantly, analyzed. If temperatures frequently rise to just below a critical threshold but don't exceed them, this indicates a performance problem that is likely to create a failure in the future. It is better to assess the root cause and fix it before a problem occurs.

For management purposes, include measures that predict reliability or potential performance issues. By requiring analysis and a corrective action plan as described above, you improve the likelihood of success instead of simply penalizing failure.

Consider This

In addition to using measures to manage your supplier, require them to investigate and report on causes and initiate corrective action for measures that are within a certain tolerance, but don't exceed the targets. Instead of penalizing for non-performance, give them a chance to assess and rectify the performance first. This creates a better relationship and gets you better results. If their action plan is not successfully implemented or the issues are recurring, corrective measures could then be applied.

Process and Procedures

The best intentions with managing performance, contract management techniques or quality management initiatives will fail if appropriate procedures and processes are not in place to mitigate issues and reduce potential failure.

Build these into the contract by focusing on potential failure points and addressing them up-front. If you don't have them in place already, develop them in conjunction with your service provider or with your own staff.

Integrate the FM maintenance and operations processes with the core business operations at the facility, particular with critical core business services. The best examples are the processes used by IT professionals to deal with change and issues management within their own systems and infrastructure. As an example, if an activity introduces risk, such as taking a backup system off-line, alternative backup or processes to quickly rectify failure during the work activity should be identified and planned as part of the process.

This planning and approval process is critical for major work to ensure ongoing performance. For instance, within a hospital, maintenance activities can have a serious impact if not planned accordingly, so hospital representatives are given advance schedules of activities, along with an assessment of potential risks and plans to mitigate the risk. The hospital representative can request changes to the schedule or modify work activities to suit hospital needs and schedules. This reduces the chance that a seemingly minor activity will compromise the hospital's critical clinical and patient-related activities.

You may notice that effective communications and a good contract management relationship are the main themes of the performance management approach described above. Since human error is responsible for the majority of failures, implementing this performance management approach in your critical facility can improve your chance to succeed.

Quality Management

A key responsibility of the FM service is to prevent failure and ensure the organization's core business isn't negatively impacted.

Implementing quality management principles provides an additional measure of protection against failure when implemented and used effectively. Even if you don't require ISO certification, implement a quality management system that is rigorous and follows the same principles.

Consider This

Quality management systems themselves don't ensure quality, they simply ensure that processes are put in place and used consistently.

As a result, effective processes and procedures that are designed to provide a quality service are the key to achieving quality.

Your quality management system uses checks and balances, including auditing and testing, to ensure that the processes and procedures you or your service provider have in place are consistently used as intended.

A good quality management system includes a process to identify changes that should be made to processes and procedures and enables flexibility.

Quick Summary

| Key Points | ➡ Managing performance is as important as measuring performance |
| | ➡ Use performance management to foster a partnership in delivering results, not an adversarial relationship |

| Executive Tips | ➡ Have an effective management process to support commitments to your organization's core business. |
| | ➡ Build performance management into your contracts. |

| Traps to Avoid | ➡ Don't use penalties to drive behavior. They may result in undesirable behavior |
| | ➡ Lack of process will waste your efforts. |

34

Supplier Relationship Management

Get success from your suppliers.

"Performance measurement systems should be positive, not punitive. The most successful performance measurement systems are not "gotcha" systems, but learning systems that help the organization identify what works and what does not so as to continue with and improve on what is working and repair or replace what is not working." - From: Serving the American Public: Best Practices in Performance Measurement

Being successful means getting what you need from your suppliers after they start working for you - not just during the procurement phase.

Supplier Relationship Management moves the procurement process from legal terms and specifications to an important tool between you and your service provider to ensure mutual success.

There are a lot of old contracts still being used that are difficult to follow, unclear on deliverables beyond technical specifications and don't provide the purchaser (and more importantly, the facility manager) with the tools they need to effectively manage and administer the contract and more importantly, get the performance they need.

Even worse, many managers still use the old-school approach to managing contracts and are failing to benefit from the opportunity to develop a stronger working relationship that enables the service provider to understand and help achieve the most important goals.

Outsourcing arrangements have introduced tools and approaches that can be applied to all types of facility contracts and subcontracted services. These are the leading practices you should be adopting for all your services.

Supplier Management

For subcontracted facility management services, your contract document is an important tool throughout the term of the contract; however your approach to managing the contract is just as important.

Your service provider has a vested interest in success, as does your organization. A constructive approach to managing the contract is key to establishing a relationship where the service provider understands and addresses your needs without always checking the contract. If you are inflexible, they will be inflexible. If you want flexibility, you need to manage the contract relationship accordingly.

The contract language itself must be flexible and enable you to adjust priorities, address issues and make changes that you need to be successful through the full term in a constructive, planned manner. While your procurement department will likely be responsible for the contract documentation, make sure it has flexibility built in that suits your ongoing management needs in addition to having the standard contractual, legal and risk clauses. This enables you to effectively manage the contract beyond start-up.

The contract must also include provisions for performance management, including the ability to adjust or change the measures and targets to adapt to your changing priorities.

Effective interface, communication, reporting and processes must be spelled out in the contract, with structured meetings that support your contract management approach and forward looking management.

The contract and related specifications, as well as the procurement process, must define the responsibilities and processes for the transition-in at the start of the contract and the transition-out to a different supplier at the end of the term. Just like takeoff and landing for a jumbo jet, these are among the most risky periods in a contract cycle, particularly for management of critical facilities. The key issue of personnel and training/knowledge transfer during a transition is one issue that needs to be addressed.

Identifying key expectations such as risk assessment and mitigation are also important. By identifying these responsibilities, you clearly indicate their importance and add their skills, knowledge and on-site experience to your overall risk-management initiatives.

Establishing Effective Contract Management

When developing an outsourcing solution, effective contract management is the cornerstone to success. Outsourcing is a major change for existing staff. They are often used to managing or even doing the work themselves and have a difficult time turning the responsibility for day-to-day activity over to a service provider.

The change requires your staff to manage a complex outsourcing contract and a new high-level relationship with a service provider. It's important to manage the change and equip your new stay-back management team with the tools and the skills they need to be successful.

These tools include a solid contract management process with an effective and flexible contract that has service levels, a performance management framework, defines reporting and interfaces, and features a built-in change management and conflict resolution process.

The change management process is needed since it is impossible to consider every situation that could arise. The simple reality over the course of a long-term outsourcing contract means your business needs will change. This addresses the most important aspect of the service triangle described above: cost. A change management process enables you to manage changes scope or service levels using a pre-defined mechanism to set a fair and reasonable price.

Putting a contract management team in place is more challenging. Since the contract management role is often a significant shift of your staff's current roles within the organization, it requires a careful matching of skill sets and even culture. Your contract manager must change from managing resources to managing results and focus on the strategic issues that add value to your company.

Develop new job descriptions that outline the change in roles and responsibilities. Provide them with guidance on the intent of the outsourcing relationship and the workings of the contract, service levels and performance management framework, and give them training or coaching on contract management principles.

The role is to manage and administer the contractual relationship between your organization and your service provider to get the results you require.

Penalties aren't the Only Driver of Performance

Unfortunately, the idea of punishing suppliers to get better behavior is an old-fashioned approach that still lingers. If services are not performed as expected, you need tools to deal with the failure, but that occurs as part of a performance management process, not as a "penalty." If they truly aren't performing and their bad behavior continues after proactive and constructive measures, including good communications, you need to exercise your termination clause and move forward.

However, before you procure someone else, carefully consider why they didn't perform. Is it the spec, a price lower than market, unrealistic expectations, conditions they didn't foresee, issues caused by your own operations, etc.

Unless you assess these issues and correct them, you will only repeat the cycle.

According to a 2002 study by Aberdeen Group, a 26.6% increase in supplier performance was realized by organizations that have formal measurement processes in place for suppliers. The type of improvements cited that can have an impact on your company's bottom line included aspects such as quality, on-time delivery, total cost, contract compliance, lead times and overall responsiveness.

A well-managed procurement process ensures you have the right supplier at the right price, but all too often, the process ends at that point and ongoing performance is left to somebody else. By building an effective performance measurement framework into the contract at the procurement phase, you get the service your company needs to be successful. With performance measurements spelled-out, your supplier will be in a better position to understand your priorities and deliver the results you need.

Performance measurements aren't new, but applying them effectively with a consistent, formal process and building them into supplier contracts of all sizes isn't common practice. As more and more products and services are contracted out, either using traditional contracts, out-tasking or even outsourcing, the need to rationalize performance and ensure you are getting what you need is becoming more critical to your success.

Quick Summary

Key Points	➡ Contract management techniques are evolving to a more partnership approach.
	➡ The supplier's success is key to your success. It's in your interest for them to succeed.
	➡ A positive relationship with your supplier starts with an effective contract and procurement process.

| Executive Tips | ➡ Penalizing suppliers without managing results will lead to increased problems. |
| | ➡ Ensure supplier relationship management is built-in to the procurement process. |

| Traps to Avoid | ➡ Don't use a forceful approach. Treat suppliers as valued partners in your success. |
| | ➡ Don't assume service providers are not performing because they don't want to. Find out why and fix it. |

35

Service Performance Assessment

Implement a process to manage performance.

"You cannot measure a man by his failures. You must know what use he makes of them. What did they mean to him. What did he get out of them."- Orison Swett Marden

All facilities and property managers use service providers to get results. Whether you subcontract some services or have outsourced the FM function, performance management and audit tools are necessary to enable efficient, effective assessment of performance.

Managing performance, not just measuring it, is important to getting success. It's easy to set up some KPIs or service level expectations and then measure the supplier against it. Unfortunately, by the time you measure something that's failing, it's too late to correct it. Implement a performance management process into your approach to the FM/supplier relationship and you will get better results from your suppliers.

We've included various checklists and forms in this section you can use as a model for your own process. The details are less important than the approach you use. You can keep the checklists simple or expand them and add issues that are important to you, and remove the ones that either aren't important, or aren't relevant to your facilities.

Checklists

In addition to providing an immediate feedback tool for the service provider, the checklists serve as a discussion and reference point during the supplier review meetings and results can be rolled-up.

The checklists are broken into two separate checklists, one for general management-related performance and the other for the performance of services within the buildings.

For specific facility or regional requirements, checklist items can be added as a separate page. Regardless, the existing checklist items should remain as-is for comparison and consistency.

Checklist process

Checklists evaluate and provide performance feedback to suppliers. While they can be completed independently, it is preferred that the service provider representative is present while the building-based inspection is undertaken and the checklist is being completed.

If any item is listed as doesn't meet" or "marginal" it must include comments to explain the deficiency.

Quarterly Management Checklist Process

This simple process ensures regular, formal discussions and interaction with the service provider at a more senior level. It should not exclude regular and ongoing discussions with the service provider.

Step	Action	Explanation
1	Complete checklist	Checklist is to be completed one month prior to the supplier review meeting for each supplier by each manager for whom that supplier provides services.
2	Review and consolidate regionally	For regional, national or global services, the checklists are to be reviewed by a central manager for consistency and consolidation.
3	Provide to supplier	A single checklist is to be provided to the supplier representative for their comments and response, which should be received one week before the supplier review meeting.
4	Review at supplier review meeting	The checklist is to be discussed at the supplier review meeting and any action items noted.
5	Roll-up results	The checklists will be included in the results that are rolled-up.

This Quarterly Management Checklist provides the basics you should consider about how they manage their service and interact with you.

The management checklist shouldn't be too long, however your requirements or issues may require different checklist items.

Provide suitable training to the staff using the checklist to ensure fairness and consistency. This is also very valuable where there are many interfaces, such as with a national portfolio. It allows you to compare relationships and performance in different areas to see whether it's a local issue or a companywide issue.

Quarterly Management Checklist	Meets	Marginal	Doesn't Meet	Comments (Required for Doesn't Meet or Marginal)
Reporting				
Reporting on-time				
Reporting meets requirements				
Fully compliant				
Communications				
Availability/responsive				
Availability after hours				
Issues reported in a timely manner				
Pro-Active Approach				
Issues resolution				
Bring forward ideas / innovations				
Energy management /efficiency				
Personnel				
Qualified and knowledgeable				
Personnel uniformed & professional				
Responsive				
Project Work				
Responsive				
Communication				
Quality and timeliness of completion				
TOTALS				

Monthly Building Checklist Process

This provides a regular process that promotes quality communication and provides information that can be used to manage performance.

Depending on your portfolio and the services, you could do this more or less frequently. If you have a large portfolio, you may also only do a certain number of buildings per month.

Step	Action	Explanation
1	Complete checklists	Checklists are to be completed monthly for [XX%] of the buildings.
2	Create CAR's	Any corrective action requests (see below) that are required as a result of a deficiency should be created.
3	Provide to supplier	The checklists are to be forwarded to the supplier, along with any appropriate corrective action requests (see below) for response. Where possible, a discussion with the supplier should be held.
4	Review at supplier review meeting	Building checklist results for the quarter will be summarized and presented at the supplier review meeting. The related corrective action requests will be reviewed for completion.
5	Roll-up results	The summarized building checklist results will be included in the results that are rolled-up.

This checklist provides the basics for a simple, easy-to-complete checklist. You can expand the checklist to include key aspects of your facility or issues and areas that are of specific importance to you or our core business. Don't expand it too much, however. It is meant to be a snapshot of performance, not a full audit of service delivery. The longer it is, the harder it is to use.

You should develop a checklist for each regularly provided service that focuses on the specifics of that service. Provide suitable training to the staff using the checklist to ensure fairness and consistency.

Monthly Building Checklist	Doesn't Meet	Marginal	Meets	Comments (Required for Doesn't Meet or Marginal)
Maintenance / Life Safety				
PM activities completed				
Work Orders completed				
Work orders used and filled-in				
Compliance routines complete				
Fire extinguishers up-to-date				
Cleanliness (visual observation)				
Exterior				
Entrance/lobby				
Public areas				
Washrooms				
Office areas				
Mech. Rooms / Jani closets				
Periodic routines				
Windows (interior)				
Windows (exterior)				
Grounds				
Summer - landscaping				
Summer parking/road/sidewalks				
Winter - entrance/sidewalk				
Winter roads/parking				
Tenant Comments				
Cleanliness				
Interior temp/humidity				
Exterior appearances				
Response and professionalism				
TOTALS				

Corrective Action Request

Corrective Action Requests (CAR) are a useful quality tool. They document issues and require the service provider to document their corrections and to ensure effective communication about relevant issues.

Instead of being used as a negative measurement tool, it should be used as an ongoing management and communication tool.

The form will be used to document issues and problems that persist. All CAR forms will be reviewed at the service review meetings (described later in this section) to enable the supplier to provide input and explanation as necessary regarding the solutions and changes made to prevent recurrence.

The use of these forms should be tracked and reviewed to ensure that the tool is being used to deal with issues. Roll-up of a summary should be done quarterly.

Use of this system will be part of the training activity to outline the purpose, use and importance of using a formal system for managing supplier issues.

Corrective Action Request Process

Step	Action	Explanation
1	Identify corrective action	Provide email/verbal instructions to correct deficiency and give time for completion.
2	Issue Corrective Action Request (CAR)	If not resolved, issue CAR.
3	Receive completed CAR	If completed: File for future reference. If not completed: Initiate action (if service provider has provided an alternative completion date, revisit and wait to take action).
4	Initiate action	Follow appropriate procedures for action taken.

Corrective Action Request

Date	Supplier Company	Supplier Representative/contact info

Building Name / Address or Number	Facility Manager

Section 1 – Request (Completed by FM)

Description of Issue / Problem	Description of action / communication to-date

Requested Action	Due Date : _____
	Possible Next Steps ☐ Escalation ☐ Hold Payment ☐ Make Good ☐ Termination

Section 2 – Response (Completed by Service Provider)

Action Taken OR Corrective Plan	Status
	☐ Completed Date: _____ ___ ☐ Pending - Planned Date:_____ ☐ Disputed

Section 3 – Follow-Up (Completed by FM)

FM Representative Comments	Status
	☐ Closed Date: _____ ☐ Take Action ☐ Escalation ☐ Hold Payment ☐ Make Good ☐ Termination

Next Steps (If Any)	

Quick Summary

Key Points

➡ A formal process improves your ability to manage suppliers effectively.

➡ Checklists provide important feedback to suppliers.

➡ Corrective Action Requests are a useful tool to document issues that need to be addressed.

Executive Tips

➡ Assessing supplier performance helps you and the supplier improve and get results.

Traps to Avoid

➡ Don't expand the checklists too much or they will become unwieldy and too detailed to be used effectively.

➡ Ensure consistency if more than one individual fills in the checklists.

36

Service Review Meetings

Structured meetings get performance results.

I have found no greater satisfaction than achieving success through honest dealing and strict adherence to the view that, for you to gain, those you deal with should gain as well." – Alan Greenspan

This provides a formal forum to review performance, discuss and resolve issues and communicate and work together.

Service review meetings are a forum to provide the service provider with important information about priorities and initiatives. They are also a good place to receive value from the service provider in terms of learning about and addressing management- and industry-related initiatives.

These review meetings should be held regularly with a structured format that includes a set agenda, outcomes and follow-up process to foster communication and exchange of information. A standardized approach will ensure effective communication and the ability to roll-up the results to the regional, national or global management as appropriate.

Why have Service Review Meetings?

The service review meetings are meant to provide:

- ✓ A snapshot of service delivery.
- ✓ A formal means to discuss and resolve issues.
- ✓ A forum to identify initiatives and for you to communicate priorities.
- ✓ A structure for identifying and documenting significant changes and decisions.
- ✓ An opportunity for the service provider to demonstrate their expertise and value to you.

There should be specific and meaningful outcomes from the meeting based on the intended purpose and the structure of the meetings. These outcomes benefit the local management of the contract and allow you to share key management information between regions. They are essential to rolling-up a summary to senior management.

The meetings are part of a continuous contract management process, not simply a one-time event. Follow-up from previous meetings and planning for future meetings is required.

Service Review Meetings Process

Step	Action	Explanation
1	Plan	Meetings are planned and scheduled annually for the year. Standard agenda is identified.
2	Prepare	You provide agenda items to supplier. Documentation is collected and provided in advance or available for the meeting. Supplier prepares and distributes agenda for the meetings, with required attachments. Supplier prepares a brief presentation of the past results, future plans and issues that need to be addressed.

3	Conduct	Meeting is chaired by the local or regional manager. Agenda is followed, no new business accepted – should have been identified in advance. Minutes are taken and action items identified, assigned and due-dates set.
4	Follow-up	Action Items are followed-up and updates provided to all participants.
5	Report	Result of the meeting is reported upwards using standard format provided, which identifies issues, decisions and notable items. Recommended or approved changes to contracts, services, etc. must be documented and reported. This report is compiled with other reports and used during senior FM executive management meetings.

Schedule

Meetings should be held at least quarterly with each major supplier separately. The schedule should be coordinated other operational meetings to enable roll-up of supplier meeting results.

Participants

Participants should include decision makers from the service provider who can deal with issues and make commitments as well as front-line staff who can provide first-hand information and insight into operational issues, solutions and recommendations.

Documentation & Preparation

Documentation is meant to provide historical context, support recommendations and changes and support any discussions and decisions that are required.

In Advance	At Meeting
✓ Previous minutes (with action items) ✓ New issues and initiatives summary	✓ Supplier presentation ✓ Backup reports (as needed)

Agenda Topics

The agenda should be structured and have these fundamental topics each time.

Review of the previous period

This review must provide an overall insight into the activities, issues and other general issues that impact the services or your goals and objectives. Items could include:

- ✓ Review the previous meeting's minutes and actions (overview only – issues discussion should be postponed until after review completed.)
- ✓ Service Provider Presentation
- ✓ Operational summary and recommendations
- ✓ Performance Results (with corrective action / plans identified)
- ✓ Financial Results / issues
- ✓ Overview and feedback.

Issues

Agenda items must have potential impact or ramifications across the region.

That means minor issues must be dealt with outside this meeting. They are brought forward to this meeting only to document decisions and identify the solutions. Issues discussed in this meeting should be provided to the other party in advance and be included in the agenda documentation.

Initiatives and News

These include technology, process or other changes the supplier wants to bring to your attention, either because they have a potential impact or benefit. This is an opportunity for the service provider to share market and industry information with you.

The service provider is encouraged to bring forward recommendations for service changes or improvements in this section.

Sample items include:

- ✓ Supplier news
- ✓ Industry news
- ✓ New technologies / new processes
- ✓ Changes to staffing, organization, delivery, subcontractors, etc.

Preview next period

A review and preview of upcoming activities, initiatives or work by the service provider such as staffing, major maintenance, project work, etc.

A review of upcoming initiatives, events or activities that the service provider should be aware of.

Formal changes and decisions

Any changes or decisions that impact the services, relationship or contract must be discussed and documented in the meeting. This documentation must be formally approved by both you and the service provider and should be incorporated into the supplier file and, when appropriate, be shared with senior management or colleagues. These items will be documented in a formal change management form.

In the agenda, this item is a review item to verify and confirm understanding of the change proposed.

- ✓ Service provider initiated
- ✓ Your initiatives

Decisions are recorded on a formal Change and Decision Log that is retained on file.

Action items

Action items either outstanding or newly assigned will be reviewed and confirmed at the end of the meeting to ensure they are recorded as intended.

Meeting outcomes

Outcomes are important to provide continuity, share information and document decisions. The following specific outcomes are required:

- ✓ Minutes of meetings (with issues tracking, due-dates and responsibilities identified)
- ✓ Formal presentation from service provider
- ✓ Change management forms
- ✓ Summary of meeting (for roll-up to senior management as necessary) using standard forms.

Schedule

This overall schedule will identify the suppliers and the schedules for meetings with the suppliers and your staff. The logistics (i.e., cross region, cross supplier) will be established in order to develop the schedule.

Service Review Meeting Notices

This form is used to clearly outline the participants, agenda items and material necessary for the meeting.

Service Review Meeting Notice				
Supplier				
Logistics	**Date**		**Time**	**Location**
	JFM ☐	A MJ ☐	JA S ☐	O ND ☐
Invitees: (Name, Title)	**Facility Manager**		**Service Provider**	**Others**
Documentation required	Previous minutes (with action items) New issues summary Other items summary			
Agenda items	Review of the previous period Previous minutes Service provider presentation Client overview & feedback Issues Unresolved issues from previous agenda Service provider new issues (from issue notice form) New client issues (from issue notice form) Preview next period Initiatives and news Other items Formal changes and decisions (review) Action items (review & confirm) Closure (verify next meeting)			

Issues Notice Form

This form is used to advise the other party of an issue for discussion at the next service review meeting. The intent is to avoid new issues raised at the meeting without preparation.

Using this process, a summary of which will roll up to higher levels, will enable an overview of all issues and promote escalation and resolution at higher levels where necessary.

Issues Notice

Date	Supplier Company	Supplier Representative/contact info

Building (specify building or General)

Issue Name	Issue Log #

Issue Description

Background

Problem or Risk

Recommended Course of Action

Action/Decision

Changes & Decisions Log

This form is used to document decisions taken as a result of the service review meetings or any other decisions which should be documented on file and also rolled-up or shared with other regions.

Attach any supplemental documentation as required.

Contract Change Notice

Date	Supplier Company	Supplier Representative/contact info

Building (specify building or General)

Change Name	Change Log #

Change Description

_____

Background

_____

Problem or Requirement

_____

Recommended Change

_____

Financial or Contractual Impact

Action / Decision

Title	Signature	Date

Report Roll-up Form

This form is used to summarize the results of the service review meeting to roll-up to senior management for issues or decisions that need to be communicated. It is particularly useful for a large regional, national or global portfolio or where multiple suppliers provide services.

Supplier Meeting Roll-Up		
Date of Mtg.	Supplier Company	Region or Portfolio
Attendees		

Summaries
Supplier Review Meeting
Performance Issues
Supplier Initiatives

Issues	
Resolved Issues	New Issues

Changes	
Agreed Changes	New Changes Requested

Other Comments

Quick Summary

Key Points	➡ Meet with your supplier to share performance results and discuss solutions for improvement.
	➡ Establish a formal process for service review meetings and follow-through on them.
	➡ Use the meetings to share your own issues, plans and upcoming events they should know about.
Executive Tips	➡ Communication is your most effective performance management tool.
Traps to Avoid	➡ Don't hold meetings and then not have any follow-up
	➡ Don't let the meetings become a complaints meeting.

37

Measuring In-House Performance

Performance management is not just for service providers.

"People and their managers are working so hard to be sure things are done right that they hardly have time to decide if they are doing the right things." – Steven Covey

You measure service providers, but how much effort have you put into measuring internal results and using the measurements to improve what you do?

Putting measures in place internally can be even more challenging, but it may be well worth the effort.

If you are already measured internally or have measurements in place for your service providers, mirroring those measurements will help you optimize your team's performance to meet your requirements. In some cases, it will also give you comparative information you can use to make improvements. Relying on anecdotal information and informal reviews of results simply isn't enough.

Develop measurements the same way you would for a supplier, using the same principles and approaches to deciding what should be measured and how it will be measured. Either set targets initially or allow the measurements to develop a trend that becomes the benchmark targets. You can eventually adjust them by focusing on percentage improvements later.

Drive Behaviors

Effective implementation of internal performance measurements will drive the behaviors you want and result in the performance you need while at the same time making the overall management of your responsibilities easier. Poorly implemented, performance measurement can inadvertently drive the wrong behaviors, focus attention on aspects of the service that aren't critical to your success, and make managing your resources more difficult.

While actual measurements may vary, the underlying philosophy for performance measurement remains the same, which is to influence the behaviors and subsequent results that are important to your success. You can do this by measuring the output of the service rather than the details and processes by which the output is obtained. At the same time, having information about the processes will help you to figure out what is going wrong when the results aren't being achieved.

Management Process

Establishing an effective management process around the measurements for your in-house team is important to influence results and maintain a partnership approach with your team. It gives them the feedback they need to identify issues and make improvements on their own, or to bring them to your attention. As much of the measurement framework as possible should be developed with them. The key is to separate much of the measurement process from direct consequences. The information on performance should be primarily used to guide decision making and improvements.

The management process includes a mechanism to review and discuss the results of the measurements in a way that provides for a collaborative approach. To be effective, performance measurements shouldn't be used as a "gotcha" mechanism to antagonize and penalize staff. The purpose is to implement a mechanism that will reduce the likelihood that your team will fail to deliver the results you need. After all, if they fail to deliver, it's already too late.

Measure Satisfaction

Satisfaction surveys are always a good idea as part of the performance management process. A simple transaction survey provided to the client representative (such as the move coordinator or senior department manager) is best, but for a large move, surveying all the occupants involved may be worthwhile. Develop the questions based on the type and nature of project, as well as the level of responsibility of the project manager. Keep the number of questions to a minimum and focus on things you can actually control or change.

The reason for asking questions is to identify things you can change to make it better. If there are some issues which you drive, for instance, like limiting their finishes choices, space standards, etc., don't hold the project manager accountable if the client wasn't happy about those things.

Incentives can Drive Bad Behaviour

Whether performance management is effective or not depends on the specific conditions, since measures can sometimes drive the wrong behaviour and cause unintended issues.

When it comes to performance pay, be very careful. It's powerful incentive that causes normal people to do things that are on the margins and may be contrary to your goals.

It's better to manage performance by measuring it and using it as a discussion tool for performance (i.e., manage performance, don't just measure it) and possibly as a decision maker about re-engaging them instead of as a reward/punishment mechanism. For contracted project managers, you should always have contract language that gives you tools to manage significant non-performance.

By implementing a strong management process that includes measures, communications, supplier meetings and action plans from suppliers to correct trending problems instead of waiting for failure, you will manage results and be more successful in your own goals and objectives.

Involve Your Staff

A small committee of your staff should be set up to review the performance results regularly. Include everyone involved in the processes and develop action plans to deal with areas that are problems. These meetings will allow for discussion and agreement of the plan.

The committee should look at the results, the reasons they are not meeting expectations, solutions that the team needs to implement, and possibly solutions you need to implement within areas you control to help improve results.

Allow for changes and adjustments to the measurements or the targets over time, since it's likely your needs or goals will change.

Quick Summary

Key Points	➡ You should also be measuring your in-house staff performance
	➡ Develop measures and implement a management process to foster improvements
Executive Tips	➡ Implement measures carefully and with a continuous improvement approach rather than for penalties.
	➡ Always consider what's outside their control and adjust your measures as necessary
Traps to Avoid	➡ Don't set unreasonable targets.
	➡ Some measures will be circumvented if they are threatening to your staff.
	➡ Don't let your measures drive the wrong behavior

38

Defining Service Levels

Service levels document your service expectations.

"Don't tell people how to do things. Tell them what to do and let them surprise you with their results." – George Patton

Service level definitions help document and quantify your service delivery requirements. Whether you develop them for internal use or for a subcontractor or outsourced services, their purpose is the same – to communicate expectations.

Service levels are commonly used to measure the performance of suppliers, usually in conjunction with KPIs. The real value is using them to document and communicate the level of service. With this approach, they give you a way to determine whether the service performance is meets your needs or not. It's important to build them into an overall management process, instead of simply using them as a "gotcha" tool.

You should also implement them for your own internally-delivered services as a way to help you manage your resources and services. You can use it as a communication tool between you and your tenants or occupants, so they understand what to expect.

Most facilities departments and property management companies don't define the level of service they provide unless they subcontract or outsource. They simply deliver the service, whether good or bad. When you manage the services and are accountable for the costs, you can balance and adapt the service levels on-the-fly.

A big problem with developing service levels and applying them is that they don't appear to take into account the flexibility you may currently enjoy. They are looked at as a ridged set of hurdles that must be jumped. This is understandable, since they are often developed at a very detailed level that dictates the overall outcome and many of the steps that must be taken to achieve the outcome.

If you implement service levels this way, you will set up your staff or suppliers for failure and you may also limit your staff and suppliers from fully achieving the best-possible results.

Setting Expectations

When subcontracting or outsourcing, defining service levels helps the service provider understand what is expected of them and how to develop both their service solution and their related pricing. Without accurately defining service levels, you leave the service provider guessing and you may not get what you need to be successful. You may get less than expected or more than necessary along with a higher cost. It's also harder to determine whether you are getting what you paid for and the service provider doesn't have clear service targets and objectives to achieve.

It's important to recognize the link between service levels and price. The service level, cost and scope are balanced. Changes to the service levels will often impact the costs if scope doesn't change.

Identify all key services and develop specifications that indicate the actual level of service you need using well-developed description and measurements where possible. Some services lend themselves well to objective measurable levels, while others require a more subjective approach.

Your goal should be objective, measurable service levels. Some services will be prescriptive in nature, where you will list specific work activities, for instance.

The majority should be performance based, allowing the service provider or your staff to use their experience and resources to meet the performance requirements.

Defining Service Levels

To define the services, use information from existing services, assess current delivery levels or use industry standards. Make them easy-to-read, consistent, short and descriptive. Combine them with your business objectives and measurements to focus performance. By going through this process, you may even find some service levels that are actually higher than needed, so adjusting them could save money.

Service levels define expectations, technical service specifications and performance requirements. They are similar to contract specifications but instead of providing highly prescriptive task-based requirements, they shift the focus to a results-based specification where possible. This gives the service provider the latitude to use their own skills, technology and knowledge to adjust the service and achieve the results rather than having to adhere to prescriptive specifications. As mentioned, don't use a rigid pass/fail approach to measuring achievement; use the more productive performance management approach described later in this book.

There will be areas where detailed technical specifications are necessary. For staff, they provide clear guidance. For service providers, they are an important tool for them to properly staff and price the service (for instance, specifying predictive maintenance activities above and beyond traditional preventive maintenance tasks). In the end, however, s shift to results-based specifications will get better results when combined with effective contract management and performance management techniques.

Service Level Template

The easiest way to develop your service levels is by using a simple table. For each separate service, you list different specific functions within the service that are important and then describe the service itself, any measurements that relate to the service and the expectations, which will either be outcome based or prescriptive. For some services, you will also have more detailed specifications as well.

Here is a sample matrix you can use for your own service levels. Use a table like this for each of the separate services.

Service			
This is the title of your service such as Project Management, Cleaning, Help Desk, etc.			
Function	**Service Description**	**Measurements**	**Expectation**
List the sub-part of the service, such as public areas, washrooms, offices in the case of cleaning.	Provide a description of what the function or service is in general terms.	Include things like response time, inspection or audit scores, incidents, number completed, etc.	Describe the outcome, such as no visible dust, washrooms always stocked, spills responded to within 20 minutes, etc.
Document the next function.			
Continue for all relevant functions within the service.			

Where you have different levels of service levels between types of facilities, their location or use, you can add columns to indicate the differences between the facility types and the associated difference in the expectations. The service description would usually be the same, but the measurements and expectations would be different. For instance, you may have a location where only basic preventive maintenance is performed and another where the full range of manufacturer's recommended preventive maintenance is performed. The difference may be due to your plans for the facility, your financial priorities or the different risks related to the facility or systems.

When establishing different levels of services, only identify service differences that are tangible and have a real impact on the cost of service delivery.

Other information you can add to each service or even function includes the following, which can be included on a separate form, one for each service:

- ✓ Objectives (what is the intent of the service, it's importance and impact)
- ✓ References (i.e., standards, policies, legislation)
- ✓ Responsibilities (especially where there are joint responsibilities or approvals necessary)
- ✓ Dependencies (where successful delivery of the service is dependent on something outside your staff or service providers control).

While the tendency is to only document the delivery of service, you should also include, where relevant, services like reporting, inspections, quality control, communications, etc. Having documented service levels for a large portfolio will help ensure a higher level of consistency, whether the service is internally or externally delivered.

Combine this with KPIs where relevant, good service management processes and well-documented procedures, will give you more control over the overall service delivery quality and consistency. At the same time, it's a good exercise to document and communicate service levels internally and to your occupants or tenants and help you ensure you are getting the correct level of service you need to successfully support your organization's core business.

Quick Summary

Key Points

➡ Defining services levels is important to get the results you want.

➡ They are a combination of results-based and specification-based expectations.

Executive Tips

➡ Service levels are tied to scope and cost. They can't usually be changed independently.

➡ Match your supplier's service levels to the levels of service you need to deliver to your organization.

Traps to Avoid

➡ Don't be arbitrary. Levels of service should be based on real or current service delivery.

➡ Don't set service levels that can't be measured and use them to determine whether standards are being met.

39

Developing Key Performance Indicators

Getting results means measuring and managing performance.

"How do you know you are doing well, if you don't define up front what doing well means?" – Phil Bernard

You can influence performance with well-developed performance indicators and measures that are linked to service levels and are used in a service management process.

Performance measurement applies both in-house to your own services and to service providers. Often, it's only really developed and implemented when a company outsources its FM functions. Ideally, it should be developed and implemented even with in-house service delivery because it is a critical tool to manage results.

Like service levels, performance measures should only be part of your overall performance management framework. They mostly provide information you and your service provider or staff can use to make decisions and changes that improve services.

Your staff and service providers both need to know that the performance goals you set are being met, and the service provider or employee needs to know what your most important goals are and what the criteria for success is. This way, they are aligned to your needs and support your objectives. Otherwise, you won't ever know if you are getting what you expected - and they won't know if they are doing what's necessary.

Performance measures should be treated more like a science than an art because they have a significant impact on your success. Key components of all your measures should be:

✓ Statistical relevance
✓ Objective measurements
✓ Quantifiable measurements.

Establish Goals and Business Objectives

Before you can develop performance measurements, you must clearly establish and quantify your business objectives. These must be directly related to the success of the organization, guiding your staff and leaving your service provider some freedom to implement the appropriate processes and sub-processes to achieve the goals themselves.

Ultimately, you want to measure the performance of facilities services that support the core business.

Once your goals and business objectives are established, determine how to measure their performance, how to find metrics that indicate what you need to know and how to track and report the results. This includes:

✓ Source
✓ Frequency
✓ Identify what you count (i.e., definitions)
✓ Allowable variance from target
✓ Tracking and reporting mechanism.

Developing Measurements

To develop your measurements, start with KPIs by identifying the key deliverables that impact your organization's success. Once you narrow them down, look closely at the deliverables and determine how you can measure them. This may be quality, timeliness, customer satisfaction, uptime or a number of other attributes. If these measures impact the service provider financially, make sure they are as objective as possible.

This is where you start to translate the goals and business objectives into performance measurements or KPIs. These are high-level results that if met, will support the goals and business objectives.

Once you decide which measures to use, establish the mechanism to measure and report the performance results. Where possible, these should be built into the processes and automation used to deliver the service. If your supplier will be measuring these directly, specify the requirement as part of the procurement exercise. At the same time, identify the format and the frequency of the measurements.

With KPIs developed, start looking at sub-measures that support the KPIs. These become the PIs or trends you use as management tools. Where possible, identify this in your procurement initiative to give the supplier an idea of the requirements you have for tracking and reporting.

There are three levels of performance measurement the KPIs should be focused on for performance purposes while the other indicators are more effective for management purposes and to ensure the support structure is functioning.

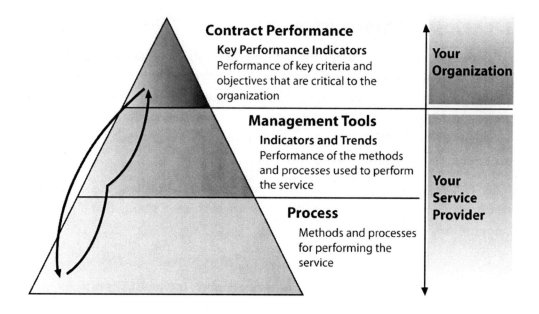

Key Performance Indicators (KPIs)

As outcome-based measurements, these are the most important measurements. Linked to the needs of your core business, they mirror objectives that directly impact your company's success. Relatively few in number, there should be from one single KPI to a handful of KPIs, depending on the service and your specific requirements. They must be outcome- or results-based, not intermediate process measurements.

With such high-level measurements in place, your supplier and staff will clearly recognize what your priorities are, and by setting targets to reach, the results you need will be clear.

Performance Indicators (PIs)

The next level of measurement becomes a management tool, however some PIs may roll-up and be aggregated into KPIs. Aggregation can provide cumulative results or measure regional results as PIs, then aggregating them nationally into KPIs. Your specific needs and the nature of the service will influence this.

Measuring at this level provides an early warning to identify performance issues that impact the KPIs and enable corrective action. These should be trended and analyzed to understand whether the service is being successful or changes are required in the delivery.

As a management tool, you can tie PIs into action plans for your suppliers or even for your staff. If a PI fails to meet the target, an action plan is provided by the supplier to correct the performance issue, ensuring effective management control is being applied and KPIs are not at risk.

Indicators/Trends (T)

Trends are managed like PIs, but are usually more detailed and process oriented. They also compare results over time, providing trend information and enabling continuous improvement and corrective action and to provide an early warning system for the KPIs.

While managed like PIs, they are not used as cumulative or point-in-time measurements. They are generally comparisons of the change in results over time, either from a specific PI or other measurement.

Performance Management Framework

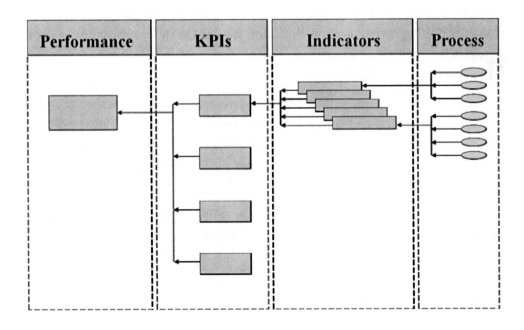

Baselines

Finally, in order to make your KPIs meaningful, they have to be measured against a target or baseline. If the target is obvious, for instance linked to an existing company or customer-related measurement, all you need to do is identify the targets to the supplier. If they are not clear, or you have no way of knowing what level of performance is acceptable, or even more importantly, achievable for the price you are willing to pay, you may need to develop these over the first year of the contract. This entails working closely with the supplier to develop reasonable baselines and then setting them for the balance of the contract.

Some measurements have readily-identifiable targets based on your organization's core business needs or market-related information. For everything else, you need to develop baselines to measure performance against. If possible, baseline measurements should be made before outsourcing. If not possible, baselines should be established early in the process.

Testing Performance Measurements

Performance measurements are one of the most useful management tools available. Getting it right is another matter. It's easy to develop ways to measure performance, but it's harder to assess how those measures will drive performance.

One way is to test the measures. First, use some trial data to see what the results will be and how different measurement techniques may affect the results. For instance, compare using calendar months versus rolling 30-day periods for averaging, or using weighted averages rather than simple averages when rolling up a portfolio of measurement data.

In addition, never put consequences in effect immediately. Give your measurements some time, perhaps six to 12 months, to establish a track record and develop a baseline before making the measures count. Remember, performance management is more about effective management than it is about penalties.

Once you determine the KPIs, test the measurement to validate that the result is meaningful, and rework if necessary. Be prepared to revise the KPIs as your needs change and the working relationship with your service provider evolves.

Before implementing measurements, you should ask two questions:

- ✓ What behaviour will this measurement encourage?
- ✓ Will this behaviour support my organization's goals?

Business Goals

If you focus on KPIs that ensure your business goals are being met, then the job of implementing, tracking and recording will require fewer resources. In fact, many of the KPIs you develop are likely to be part of existing processes. The results will then be easy to compile into the final KPIs, and easy to report for management purposes.

The key is simplicity and a focus on an outcome that supports your organization's core business.

An important aspect of measuring performance is how you manage performance. A measurement system isn't enough; it needs to be part of an overall strategic approach to managing and improving performance.

Best Type	Worst Type
Easy to understand	Difficult to understand
Few in numbers	Too many measurements
Quantifiable based on measurable values	Subjective or focused primarily on process rather than value creation
Drive action and motivate performance	Punitive rather than a motivator to enhance performance
Able to be benchmarked	Internally focused, not often benchmarked to external measures
Focused on client's objectives	Focused on service providers processes

Quick Summary

Key Points

➡ Measures must meet your corporate goals and objectives

➡ Use KPIs as part of an overall supplier relationship approach.

Executive Tips

➡ Keep the number of measures small and focused on results.

Traps to Avoid

➡ Measures that drive the wrong behavior.

➡ Measures that don't directly relate to performance results and corporate objectives

➡ Implementing KPIs without improving the measures themselves.

40

Applying Six Sigma in Facility Management

The principles of Six Sigma are valuable management tools.

> *"We're supposed to be perfect our first day on the job and then show constant improvement." – Ed Vargo*

The Six Sigma concept was designed for manufacturing with high-volume production. Six Sigma refers to mathematical equations that don't work for low-volume FM services. Still, the principles do apply.

First, it's important to understand where Six Sigma came from. The term itself refers to having less than 3.4 defects per million. It's pretty well impossible for any FM organization to have that kind of volume for anything they do. Luckily, Six Sigma is more than just math.

Born out of Motorola's desire to improve their product, Six Sigma uses disciplined management processes to achieve improvements. You can use those management processes and apply them to your operations. It's useful to note that this is really just a different take on existing quality assurance principles.

The Six Sigma process that applies is called DMAIC, which stands for Define, Measure, Analyze, Improve and Control. Once you get beyond the mathematical origins of Six Sigma and use these principles, you can easily identify areas for improvement, make change and improve results.

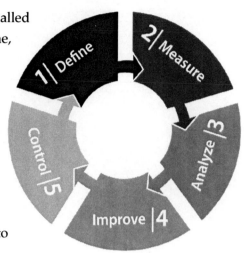

Let's look of these five steps in the process to see how they apply to facilities management

Define

This means defining what your customer needs for your product to be successful. In some cases you may link it to customer needs and expectations or you can link this to internal requirements and processes. The idea is to define exactly what the parameters are for the service.

For FM, you would define the service based on things like response time for work orders, turnaround time for moves/adds/changes (MAC), accuracy of completing a reprographics job, nameplates, service quality, KPIs, communications and more. All of these are important to a customer because if they aren't right, the customer won't have what they need to do their core business.

Example: Moves adds & changes (MACs)

MACs are important to your customers because it impacts their efficiency and down-time. So, you may define the service in terms of:

- ✓ Scope of FM involvement (i.e., compared to your occupant's involvement)
- ✓ Minimum lead time
- ✓ Maximum time to complete.

These may vary depending on the number of positions involved and the degree of physical construction or changes required.

Measure

Once you've defined what the outcome should be, you need to measure it. This way, you can see trends and identify when the measured result didn't meet the defined target outcome. You certainly won't be able to get the less than 3.4 defects per million, but you will be able to identify the problems where the service didn't meet expectations.

If you haven't already developed your KPIs and PIs, as described in a previous section, this is an ideal time to do them both for in-house services and subcontracted services. Use that information to measure your results.

With effective measurements that are relevant to the individual services and the results you need, you have something you can use for the next step.

Example: MAC

Since you have defined the scope, lead time and time to complete, you would then measure these for each MAC you complete. The scope can be measured with a checklist or survey to ensure you have actually done what you said you would do. For the lead time, you can measure whether you are able to meet your minimum lead time and whether you are able to do the MAC based on the customer's requirements. The time to complete could be whether the move is fully completed either overnight or over a weekend, depending on the size. You would define what "complete" means before you measure it.

Analyze

Once you have defined and measured, you now have information to analyze. This is very similar to other quality management approaches and you can use all the same tools, such as root cause analysis, fishbone diagrams, problem-solving teams and more. The key is to identify the cause of the poor performance, not just know that there is a problem. By knowing what caused the problem, such as communication, backordered parts, lack of resource planning, cumbersome process, unclear instructions on work orders, etc., you will be able to find out what you need to change so the problem won't happen again. This is essential to continuous improvement.

Example: MAC

Once you have measured the results described above, you would analyze the performance. If your survey comes back negative, you would analyze the response and pinpoint the issues. You may even interview the occupant's coordinator to see what went wrong. If you aren't meeting the required lead time, you would then investigate to understand why you are taking too long to initiate the moves and what can be done to correct the situation. The same applies for the maximum time to complete. If certain things are not completed by the next morning or the Monday, for instance, then you would identify what those are and the reasons they were not completed when required.

Improve

After the analysis is done, you should know what needs to be improved. This is the key step, since just knowing the problem won't change anything; you have to actually develop and implement a fix. Whether it's retraining, changing processes, verifying information, managing resources better, keeping stock of key parts or any number of other solutions, you must find out how to fix it and make the changes. Of course there are times when the improved results don't justify the cost of the solution. That's also part of the analysis.

Example: MAC

Based on the analysis, you would now be armed with the things that are preventing you from meeting your objectives. Since you have identified the problems, you would develop solutions that will correct them. It may involve having more resources on-site, adding longer lead-time, adding furniture components to inventory, better documenting the process and responsibilities, etc. These have to be implemented as part of a revised process so that the improvements actually happen.

Control

Making the change to improve results is the first step. Ensuring that the change sticks requires control. Especially in the early stages of implementation, there may be resistance or implementation hiccups that need adjusting. You may encounter a situation where those involved aren't bothering to follow the changes. With control, which includes monitoring and testing in addition to measurements, you ensure that the improvements you worked hard to make are implemented and sustained.

Example: MAC

Now that you've made these changes, you continue to measure and analyze. In particular, you assess your improvements to ensure they are giving you the improved results you expect and that there aren't other factors that were the real issue in not meeting your results. Sometimes you fix one obvious issue only to learn there are other issues that weren't revealed via the first analysis. You would also implement controls to ensure the improvements (and the entire process) is being followed. This may involve using new checklists or implementing spot audits, for instance.

As you can see based on the example above, the principles of Six Sigma can be applied to FM. If you want to take the time and formally learn the fine points and useful techniques for applying Six Sigma, follow up with formal training. In any case, apply the steps provided above and focus on making improvements using the principles.

Quick Summary

Key Points

➡ Pure Six Sigma can't apply to facility services - but the principles do.

➡ It is another version of a quality management system.

Executive Tips

➡ Six Sigma principles are an effective way to improve results.

➡ Don't expect that Six Sigma processes will solve all your problems.

Traps to Avoid

➡ Don't get hung up with the pure Six Sigma application. Use the basic principles.

41

Performance Dashboards

Dashboards provide management information at a glance.

"Some of the best lessons we ever learn are learned from past mistakes. The error of the past is the wisdom and success of the future." – Dale E. Turner

Measuring performance is only part of the job. Tracking, reporting and managing the results is an important part of any performance management framework. The best way to do this is with easy to read dashboard reporting.

A good dashboard will be a combination of simple snapshot information such as the overall KPI performance results like the one shown here, plus other dashboard elements that provide more useful information for making decisions and changes to service delivery.

You Need More than a Historical View

Don't simply use your dashboard as a historical view of results at a high level, or simply because it's expected.

This very simple dashboard registers the current status of overall performance. The bar shows current results, while the tick mark shows the target.

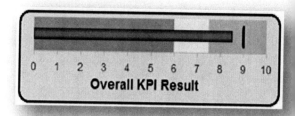

To be truly useful, your dashboard must give you information you can use to make decisions, even if those decisions require you to dig deeper into the results to understand them and make corrections that improve results or avoid failure.

Of course, this shouldn't be the only thing you do to monitor and manage performance. It's only one small part of the overall management framework you should put in place to get better results using the other techniques in this section.

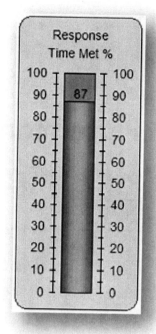

As you can see, the small, simple Overall KPI Result dashboard represents several types of information at once. It could represent an overall result as shown, or you could have a series of these dashboards, each showing the KPI result for the handful of KPIs.

Another snapshot dashboard element can be similar to a thermometer graph as shown to the right. This sample indicates the percentage of time the required response time is met for a service call. The scale can be changed to represent any measurement.

Simple Dashboards are not Enough

In addition to these, however, you must also have other types of measurements that provide more useable information. While this tells you what the result currently is, it doesn't provide any context or trending about whether the service is getting better or worst.

The full range of dashboards should include multi-period measures or simple trends. One example of a multi-period trend is for preventive maintenance, but you could do the same thing with the information from the thermometer graph.

The dashboard shown below represents the results for four quarters. This can be an annual report or a rolling report in which the results for each quarter replaces the previous year's results, always giving you the current plus three previous quarters to review. It would be even more useful if it showed the results monthly and compared it to the previous months.

Add Trends

Finally, trends are the most important performance measurement tools. They provide critical insight into the direction any given measurement is going, allowing you to take corrective action if the trend continues. You can also compare trends from previous years, or as shown,

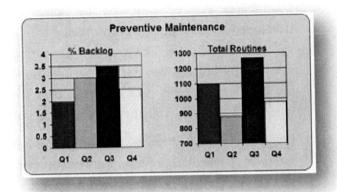

show the relationship of one measurement (percentage of abandoned calls) against other information (total number of calls).

While this dashboard shows two specific measures related to preventive maintenance, this type of dashboard element could represent any performance measurement.

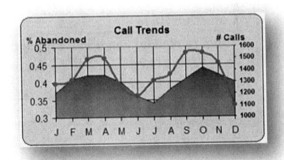

This indicates a trend. It can provide a rolling trend with the last 12 months. This gives you Y/Y comparison and can see where performance is heading and take corective action.

Combine Elements

The dashboard elements shown here can be combined into one page to give you a full view of all performance measurements or KPIs in one place.

These can be updated daily, monthly or quarterly as required. This small dashboard is only an example of the possibilities.

Since you are measuring performance, you should make sure the results are clearly and professionally displayed in a way that enables management decisions.

Software Solutions for Dashboards

Dashboards can be provided by some FM systems, by special software developed to consolidate performance results and show dashboards, or with spreadsheet software with graphing capabilities, which was used to create these samples. By linking the chart to the data itself, all you need to do is replace the old data with the new data and your charts will be refreshed. While it's a little more work, if it's the only option you have, you should use it.

Either way, a visual representation of the information can give you an overall reference, particularly of trends and comparisons between facilities, regions, staff and service providers. When used appropriately, these visual displays augment simple reports and numerical data and are an excellent way to represent this information to your staff, suppliers and most importantly to senior management.

Consider This

Visual references can also be a good way to explain a complicated FM decision to an approval authority who might not relate to the raw numbers.

Quick Summary

Key Points

➡ Dashboards should show trends to provide useful information.

➡ They augment reports and other performance data.

➡ They can be created with simple tools like Excel.

Executive Tips

➡ Use dashboards to demonstrate success to senior management.

➡ Dashboards are only one part of a performance management framework.

Traps to Avoid

➡ Don't rely on dashboards to manage results. They don't tell the full story.

➡ Don't just use dashboards that only show a point in time. You need trends and comparisons.

Your Strategic Plan

Based on this section, what strategic initiatives do you plan to implement that will help you manage your assets better and when do you expect to accomplish them?

What are you going to do?	When

Notes

Customer Service

Introduction

When many facility managers and their staff think of customer service, they think simply of the basic things such as being nice, satisfying the customer's needs and doing things on-time and with good communication.

The most important thing about good customer service in the delivery of FM services is much more tangible. Customer service is about providing the services and environment the occupants require for them to be productive and successful in what they are doing.

Whether you manage a corporate facility, a public facility or a commercial property, the principles of good customer service delivery are the same and include culture awareness, training, measuring and continually assessing and improving how you manage and deliver facilities services to your organization and the occupants and tenants.

42

Customer Service in Corporate FM

FM organizations are being driven to improve their customer service.

"If you're not serving the customer, your job is to be serving someone who is."- Jan Carlzon

Service is increasingly important to an organization's success and internal service from the FM department is part of this success by serving the internal customer, whether they are a tenant, occupant or colleague.

The tension between customer service and costs are complicated by the three levels of customer the FM serves: individuals, departments and the corporation.

Corporate FM organizations are being driven to review and improve their customer service to model that of the commercial service industry. Unfortunately, the dynamics of providing and managing space for corporate use doesn't exactly fit the commercial model, which is based on exchanging money for service. Even if you have some form of "chargeback" in place for the space and services you provide, internally transferred corporate costs occur in a closed loop, and any incremental costs affect the bottom line of the corporation as a whole.

The individual-, department - and corporate-level customer each have different expectations and needs, so serving them all at the same time requires the skills of a diplomat and the agility of a juggler. To do this successfully, you have to adapt your message, approach and delivery when dealing with their sometimes conflicting needs and goals. The most difficult task involves resolving the frequent conflict between the needs and expectations of the different levels within the constraints of the corporate culture, organizational hierarchy and funding.

This often puts FM literally "between a rock and a hard place" when providing customer service. While enhanced services may be what the individuals or departments want or need to do their jobs effectively, corporate policy or budgets may not allow for it. Proving revenue increases or cost savings as a result of your services are often impossible since they usually relate to productivity and efficiency, aspects that are difficult to measure. As well, your budget is rarely linked to the budget of the departments who may benefit from the increased service. While implementing a "chargeback" process may facilitate this issue, it will still exist to some extent.

The FM has to deal with these issues on top of the many day-to-day issues they have always had to handle, and they have to do it effectively. To be seen as a key element of the company's success is important and should be actively fostered. In addition to handling the customer service issues, you also need to become an advocate and salesperson for your FM initiatives.

What's Different about Customer Service for FM?

For true customer service, there is a direct link between the customer and the service through some sort of cost. With this link, the customer understands what they should be receiving, and the seller clearly understands what they can afford to deliver. This is an important aspect of successful customer service: knowing and meeting expectations. If the expectations are not well understood, then it is difficult to meet them. In FM, your job is even harder, since your customers expectations often outstrip your resources.

Some key differences between customer service in FM and traditional customer services are as follows:

- ✓ No direct link (if any) between the service and cost.
- ✓ Your customer is captive - they have no choice but to get their service from you.
- ✓ The corporate FM is often a gatekeeper for accommodation-related costs.
- ✓ Your customers are also colleagues.
- ✓ There are multiple clients with different needs and expectations.

Traditionally, the FM didn't actually serve customers. The employees who used FM were merely colleagues, and didn't merit the same attention and care that a customer deserved. This made them captive customers, since they couldn't get their services elsewhere. Often the facilities services and related space solutions were developed and managed based purely on cost and high-level corporate direction. The fact that individuals and departments using the space weren't seen as customers created obvious problems.

Those problems prompted increased focus on customer service within corporate FM and the shift signaled a new focus on how FM could "serve" internal customers, even though they don't have the look and feel of real customers.

This happened for two reasons. First, there was a better understanding of the "soft" management issues and the value in ensuring that employees have pleasant, productive environments to work in. With emphasis on the knowledge worker and an increasingly competitive market for employees, this is increasingly important in terms of how it impacts organizations. The second reason for the shift is rooted in what can be called the customer service chain shown further below that illustrates how the services provided by internal services such as FM can impact the external customer.

In addition, services provided by the FM have become increasingly professional and competitive. This has partly resulted from outsourcing, which ratcheted up the expectations by delivering better service and higher value. One advantage of outsourcing the FM function is that a customer service focus is easier to foster when the service is performed by an outside organization, rather than internal forces who are colleagues of the people they are serving. Contractually-binding performance measures have a tendency to solidify focus and get results.

The Multi-Level Customer

The facility manager has customers on three different levels. While the needs and expectations are different, they are usually linked together, even if the linkages are not formal or readily identified.

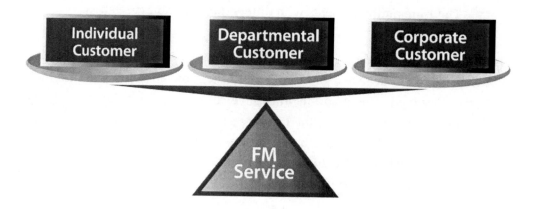

The three levels can be represented as follows:

Who	Their representation	Their Interests
Individuals	Employees at all levels occupying space	Personal space use, productivity and comfort issues
Departments	Managers responsible for a business unit	Business needs and issues related to their business unit
The Corporation (or Organization)	The executive / shareholders / stakeholders	Business needs and cost issues related to the corporation as a whole

Here, there is constant tension as FM tries to strike a workable balance between the needs of the three different customer types. The corporate needs usually prevail, and it is FM's job to make the best of things, including communicating effectively with the other customers, finding creative ways to meet their needs, and selling them on the merits of decisions they may not completely agree with.

The key to maintaining balance is to understand the difference between the customers and how their needs and expectations interrelate. The FM must have a very clear understanding of top-down corporate goals and expectations, so they can adapt their approach to suit all levels of customers. Ultimately, FM leaders must be able to use their understanding of each customer to influence and guide overall corporate direction so that it serves all the needs within the organization.

The Individual Customer

This is the end users whose needs are typically related to performing their jobs in relative comfort. They can be difficult to satisfy because of their diverse needs and expectations, many of which are not possible in the corporate environment. You can measure how well you are doing through satisfaction surveys, which can also be an effective tool for planning and communicating issues upward. If you implement surveys, design them carefully to measure both parts of the service ("soft" and "hard" issues) separately. The soft services are related to how you deliver service, while the hard services relate to corporate initiatives, policies and directives, including such things as space utilization standards and funding levels for office furniture, finishes and maintenance.

Successfully serving the individual customer will be easier if you consider the following:

- ✓ Understand the customer by determining their needs, anticipating and communicating issues, and be proactive.
- ✓ Be diplomatic and ensure that "the customer is always right" by using excellent communications and more effectively educating the customer.
- ✓ Manage the customer rather than allowing the customer to manage you.
- ✓ Develop efficient and effective service delivery methods at the lowest possible costs.

The Departmental Customer

Departmental customers represent the middle ground. The managers who represent the departments also have to deal with and reconcile the conflicting needs of their employees with corporate needs on many fronts, including difficult human resources issues. You can serve this customer best by understanding what they need to be successful and working with them to facilitate their own issues where facilities services have an impact.

Meeting the needs of the departmental customer will be easier if you consider the following:

- ✓ Understand what they need to achieve their business goals and work with them to provide it.
- ✓ Involve them in facilities issues up-front. This gains their buy-in and helps you serve the individual customer better.
- ✓ Communicate with them as well as the individuals. You should retain communications to the individuals, otherwise your communications may be filtered or mis-communicated.
- ✓ Enable departments to do their job by providing the services they really need and by helping to market and sell their needs to the corporation if necessary.

The Corporate Customer

While this is arguably the most important customer, there is a little bit of the proverbial "chicken-and-the-egg" involved when it comes to which level of customer truly impacts the bottom line. The reality usually requires you to consider this customer as the most important of the three. The key to being successful is understanding the corporate needs as well as the individual and departmental needs, and work with all of them together. For facilities issues, the FM is in the best position to see the big picture and influence corporate decisions in a way that will be positive to all levels of customer.

Satisfying the corporate customer will be easier if you consider the following:

- ✓ Clearly understand the corporation's priorities and goals.
- ✓ Have a firm understanding of the financial issues related to delivering facilities services and be able to communicate them to the corporation in a way they will understand.

✓ Develop a firm set of guidelines, practices and policies to ease service delivery to the departmental and individual customers once decisions are made by the corporate customer.

✓ Work with other senior positions in the corporation such as HR, IT, marketing, sales, etc. to ensure that facilities issues are well understood and support their own initiatives.

✓ Communicate effectively at the corporate level regarding facilities issues that affect all levels of the corporation.

Consider This

When it comes to customer service, FM leaders must perform a constant balancing act. By understanding the different customers and effectively managing their often conflicting needs, FM customer service can be successfully delivered to all levels while maintaining the balance that is crucial in the corporate environment.

The Customer Chain

Internal customer service impacts the external customer regardless of what your company is in business to do. The customer service food chain shown below shows how a break in customer service, even internally, can have a ripple effect on the external customers that are so important to the bottom line.

✓ FM organization

✓ Other internal service providers (i.e., HR, IT, purchasing, engineering)

✓ Sales, production, service, etc. delivering the product to the customer

✓ External customers

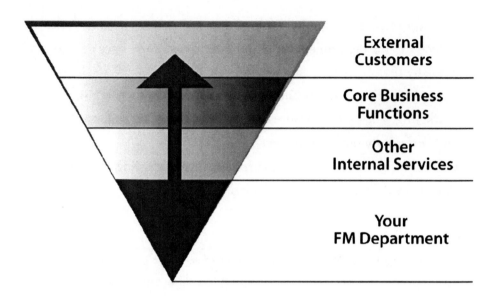

External
Customers

Core Business
Functions

Other
Internal Services

Your
FM Department

Quick Summary

Key Points	➡ Serving customers internally is important to your company's success.
	➡ You need to navigate multiple levels of interests.
Executive Tips	➡ Work with senior individuals and department managers to understand what they need from FM to meet their corporate goals.
Traps to Avoid	➡ Assuming all your processes enable good customer satisfaction.
	➡ Minimizing the level of support and training your staff need to be successful.

43

Delivering Customer Service

Meaningful customer service requires a sustained effort.

"The customer doesn't expect everything will go right all the time; the big test is what you do when things go wrong."
– Sir Colin Marshall

With a large number of internal and external resources providing services, developing an appropriate customer service culture and the mechanisms necessary to ensure everyone is doing their part to deliver consistently is even more important than ever. Simply understanding why customer service matters and measuring the results isn't enough – you need to deliver.

The problem with customer service is that every customer has a different idea of what it really means and every one of our employees or our subcontractor's employees also has a different idea of what customer service means. Adding the different levels of customers described above makes it even more complex.

The best way to deal with this is to develop parameters that can be used to deliver service so you deliver a baseline level of service while maintaining a consistently positive and productive attitude and approach by each of your team members.

As well, you need to provide flexibility so your team members feel comfortable in adjusting the services where appropriate and in dealing with issues and complaints so the customer feels that he's been dealt with fairly.

This includes training and having the policy and procedures to provide guidance. None of this should be done in isolation. How you represent the department and how you sell the FM department to other groups within your organization, or to your tenants, will shape their expectations and their satisfaction with what you ultimately deliver.

Of course, before you start developing or re-developing your customer service delivery, you need to know what works and what doesn't. Do a survey using the approach outlined later in this section and conduct one-on-one interviews with the main decision makers. Armed with this information, you will be in a better position to drive customer service in your department.

Developing a Customer Service Orientation

Customer service comes from two main things, effective processes for delivering service and the right attitude and approach from your staff. While knowing what processes work and fixing the ones that don't is one approach, a customer service orientation begins with your front-line staff. You need to instil a strong customer-focussed attitude, empowering them to identify areas where policies or processes need to be changed. Until they focus on customer service, the processes won't matter.

To be successful, you also need to implement an overall strategy with great communication and a steady, consistent approach that constantly reinforces the message and the behaviour. Otherwise, change won't be sustainable, so will lack lasting positive impact.

Training & Re-Training

With training, you begin to instil the right approach to service. More importantly, you arm your staff with the tools they need to effectively deal with service issues.

The reality is that no matter what you do, not everyone will be satisfied with your service. Other times, your processes will fail you. If your staff knows how to handle difficult customer service issues, they can confidently repair any situation that arises.

Training programs are available, but make sure the exercise is appropriate to the team. Some staff don't respond well to, or appreciate, some of the more "touchy feely" exercises included in some customer service training programs. Other programs can leave staff feeling like they are being treated like children. While the session and content may be developed to focus on soft issues with engaging exercises, it may not be well received by highly-experienced people in very technical roles. These kinds of programs are often delivered at such a low level of communication that participants feel like they are being told they don't know much about serving the customer. Beware of exercises that are at a low level and lack a direct connection to the topic. These are not good matches for anyone who wants to encourage positive changes to customer service within a professional FM working environment.

Consider This

Training is essential and good training programs foster increased success. The key lesson is that you need to consider the audience and don't include exercises and initiatives just because you think they are fun and engaging. Always test them with your audience and make sure they fit are a good fit.

It's also important to remember that good training goes beyond the actual training program. It can be delivered and forgotten. To be effective, regularly communicate with staff about quality customer service and provide refreshes as needed. Make sure staff understands why you are being repetitive. You aren't just afraid they'll forget what they learned, you want to re-emphasize the importance of the material to them and the organization.

Instilling the right culture

Culture is a very difficult thing to change in most organizations. To be effective you will need to make the cultural shift part of a concerted, ongoing effort and to communicate clear reasons for the change. One problem with customer service from the facilities department's perspective mirrors the same problem other internal service departments have: they don't look at their colleagues in the organization as customers. After all, their pay checks come from the same place.

One way to support your initiative is to look at what departments within your organization do to develop their customer service culture for their approach to their external customers. Whether you're a government, non-profit, corporate or commercial organization, there is always an external customer of some kind.

You may be able to use or adapt some of their training programs, communication material and even policies and procedures within the FM department. Have select staff sit in on the training so they can report back to your team about what others in the organization are doing. Use this information in your own customer service training program and communications to link what you do to how your organization delivers service externally. Always reinforce why it's important to your department.

Consider This

FM professionals must personally demonstrate good service and its importance by getting involved in the service delivery process. Where appropriate, personally follow up on specific customer service issues and share that experience with your staff whenever you can. Model quality customer service skills to effectively "set the bar" in terms of what you expect from staff.

Setting Customer Expectations

Good customer service means meeting the customer's expectations in addition to delivering the services they need for them to do their internal job within your organization.

Delivering adequate services is usually the easy part. Delivering them to the level the customer expects is harder unless you know what their expectation is. This is an area where you can control the expectation and make it easier to deliver the level of service that meets the organization's needs first and foremost. Keep in mind that the quality of customer service delivery is linked to organizational resources and the budget allocated to facilities services.

Documentation

The best way to set expectations is to document them. This way the customer knows what to expect and you can easily point to the standards when there is disagreement. Of course, your objective shouldn't be to simply ignore the requirements of individuals within your organization as there will be times when increased level of service is warranted or departments need something different. This makes flexibility a key attribute, since your service may directly impact their ability to perform their part within the organization.

Develop your standards based on current service delivery first by measuring and understanding what you are delivering. Decide whether they are adequate and if anything needs to be improved, take steps to implement the changes. Then produce a document, electronically or on paper, that outlines your standards. Make it short and easy to read and focus on the key services and deliverables that matter to your customers, not everything you do.

For instance, you can include the following types of information in a double-sided brochure:

- ✓ How to reach your services (email, web form, help desk).
- ✓ Response standards for responding to their request and for completing their request (by type).
- ✓ Frequency of various activities, such as vacuuming, mowing, window washing, etc.
- ✓ What services are provided by your department.
- ✓ Which services are free and which are billed back to the customer.

Managing Perception – It's more Important than Reality

Perception is a key hurdle when dealing with customers or occupants. With internal company employees and building occupants as customers, you will encounter customers who have a perception of your service that you don't agree with.

Your customers will see things differently based on their viewpoints or experiences, so you shouldn't be taken off guard. Just remember, their perception is reality to them and the key to great customer service is knowing how to deal with it, since changing their perception is not easy.

The customer's perception influences whether they think they're getting the service they expect or not. While the old adage "the customer is always right" can't be taken literally, you can use that perception to approach issues. Acting as if your customer has a legitimate problem to solve puts you in a better position to resolve the issue and convert the customer from foe to fan.

If you treat their perception of a problem as incorrect, you will fuel the fires of discontent, making it more difficult to deal with the real issue. The argument about whether the customer's perception is right or not overshadows the real issues and antagonizes customers, making it much more difficult to bring them onside as a satisfied customer.

Changing perception

Naturally, there are times when the FM needs to focus on changing a customer's perception. When this is the case, it should be done very professionally and diplomatically, without implying that the customer is wrong. Often the facts, carefully positioned, will help change their perception sufficiently to allow you to deal with the real issue at hand. They key is to let them change an inappropriate perception without you having to confront that perception head-on.

Consider This

Information changes the way people understand a situation. A proactive approach to customer service implies a willingness to make sure your customers have the information they need to develop accurate perceptions of what FM really does to make their working lives easier.

While this approach takes more time and a little more finesse, you will get better results. There will be times when you will need to accept that in the customer's eyes, you have not met their expectations. As it won't be possible to fix some customer's perceptions on some issues, these situations will demand a proactive attempt to fix the problem without fighting about it. Over time, your focus on constant improvement should bring even the most hard-nosed customer on board.

In one example, a facility manager said something in a meeting that was perceived by the customer very differently from what was meant. The customer was upset about what was happening with their project and escalated the issue. To resolve the situation, the facility manager apologized, acknowledging the customer's perception of what happened, and then clarified the real issue. The FM then provided information and facts to shift the customer's perception and resolve an issue rooted in a misunderstanding of information presented.

Rather than focusing on the fact that information was misunderstood or taken out of context, the FM delivered an apology that satisfied the customer, who was then much more receptive to the facts. Indeed, the apology enabled the customer to change his perception on his own. This resolved the problem in a positive, cooperative manner.

Accept the customer's perception as real

Effectively dealing with customer perception means accepting that the customer's perception is real to that customer.

Once you or your staff put up a defensive posture and move to defend your own position without acknowledging the customer's perception, you make the issue more difficult to solve. Realistically, the defend-first approach comes from a position of pride in the work you do. Keep that pride (and any associated attitude) in check when dealing with customers because a satisfied customer, whether internal or external, is more important to your organization and your career.

This approach underlines the fact that you should never argue with a customer's perception. The best way to deal with their perception is to resolve it as if it's a real issue. This gives you a chance to explain (or apologize) based on what the customer sees, not what you see. That will make it easier to get past their perception and deal with the real issue. As soon as you break down the perception barrier, you will find it easier to convey the facts, establish your position and solve the underlying issue.

Customer Service Processes

While good customer service is important externally and internally, consistency in that service delivery is just as important.

The best way to maintain consistency in how your occupants or tenants are dealt with by your staff is with training and establishing a quality customer service culture. Part of how you do that is with policies and processes that guide your staff and ensure consistency because everyone knows what is expected of them.

There are a few policies and procedures that you should develop for your operations. While your procedure will be different and more detailed to suit your specific operations and issues, here are some of the elements you should include in a service request management procedure.

Before you write your actual processes, review the suggestions in the section on communications. The information shown below includes some suggested content. You will need to format and structure your procedure along with the necessary flow diagrams, references and steps.

Naturally, each of your operational procedures should include customer service related processes and identify the customer interface and communications. Two specific processes are noted below, since service request management and complaint management and recovery are essential to a coordinated customer service approach, especially if that approach requires a change in an FM department's organizational culture.

Service Request Management

Customer service should be a priority from the moment a request is received to the moment it is completed and closed with the customer. Your help desk, service desk or call centre is often the first interface with your service for tenants or occupants. After that, you take action on the request and ultimately complete the activity, whether it becomes a formal work order or is simply a task assigned to one of your staff.

Your success depends on providing services to your occupants or tenants:

- ✓ A simple, easy avenue for customers to access services.
- ✓ Fulfill all requests in a way that satisfies the customer.

- ✓ Find out what they need and understand all the requirements in order to satisfy the request.
- ✓ Give customers feedback and do follow-up with the customers.
- ✓ Satisfy the customer by fulfilling their requirement to their expectations.

To do all this, you should have a procedure that outlines the overall process flow, touch points, activities to be done and the expectations, including service delivery standards such as how long a request should take.

Your processes should deal with the following five elements:

1. What does this practice accomplish

Outline what the practice accomplishes in concrete terms and why it's important. You can use some examples to illustrate the process and demonstrate the consequences of a failure of good customer service. Try to focus on the ultimate impact of service for the customer, whether they are tenants, corporate office workers, production line workers, faculty, doctors or data centre managers.

Essentially, this practice provides guidelines for all team members when responding to service requests to ensure a consistent approach to service delivery.

2. Roles & responsibilities

Outline the roles and responsibilities of everyone involved in serving the client. Don't limit it to front-line staff. Take the same approach internally as you do with your occupant and recognize there are internal customers that others within your organization provide services to. When they have a direct impact on service, add them to the process.

For instance, you can identify the general role for front-line team members:

- ✓ Responsible for receiving, responding and completing a customer request to the satisfaction of the customer.
- ✓ Identifying and escalating issues that prevent satisfying the customer request.

✓ Interfacing with colleagues, contractors, individuals, systems and / or tools to ensure customer requests are satisfied.

You should also establish the roles of supervisors and managers in the process, since they do have a part to play in both delivery and monitoring processes. Detail how you will:

✓ Support team members in delivering services to customers.
✓ Monitor all aspects of request management, including customer interaction, follow-up and completion of the request.
✓ Provide coaching and assistance to ensure that requests are efficiently and effectively fulfilled to the satisfaction of the customer.

Based on your own operation and processes, you would specifically define roles of individuals by title or job classification.

3. General approach

Outline the general approach and philosophy for delivering services. You can identify any specific service levels you have such as turn-around times, call response times, work order request completion goals, etc.

Don't forget to deal with the full range of services and separately identify them. You should also discuss service for visitors where applicable.

The goal is to ensure a consistent and effective customer service delivery from all your team members. By setting the stage, you let them know what you expect.

In this section, you can provide context to some of the formal processes. For instance, if you have a help desk, call centre or web request process and want to encourage use of those methods, identify them as the preferred approach.

4. Customer contact

Since customer service is partly based on first impressions and expectations, the initial contact with internal and external customers will influence whether they are well served. Follow-up contact should, of course, reinforce initial impressions.

Whether the customer forwards a request by phone or in person, team members should respond in a standardized manner, whether it is in the way they answer the phone or receive and address customers and vendors. While a centralized call centre of help desk will be preferred, if you don't have one, your front-line staff may be contacted directly.

Where team members are contacted directly for service by the customer, they should record the service requests which should then be entered into your FM system. At the same time, remind them of the proper method the next time they have a request, whether it's email, through the web or your call centre or help desk number. This proactive approach demonstrates to the customer our ability and desire to maintain and improve facility conditions.

Your process for customer contact should include follow-up and close-out for any type of activity. The feedback loop is always important and if you combine this process with a feedback process such as a transaction survey, you will get input that helps you modify your approach to improve it.

When establishing processes and approaches to dealing with customer requests or calls, you should establish classifications of the calls so they can be handled properly relative to their importance. A call classification system also communicates levels of service to the customer, helping them understand FM functions and priorities.

In addition, define the type and nature of calls and issues, including categorizing them into emergency, urgent and routine. This helps you communicate to the customer the timelines for completion. It also helps you guide customer expectations.

5. Customer follow-up

Customer follow-up is essential to customer satisfaction. Many times, customers call in a request and don't see it completed because the work was done at night or when they are away from their work area. Other times, you may need to wait for parts and a customer may assume you haven't made any effort to deal with the issue.

By establishing a routine process, you can satisfy the customer's desire to be kept informed. The simplest thing is to ask the customer whether they want a follow-up when they first call for service. Sometimes, a follow-up call won't be necessary unless there is a delay. Some software will automatically email the caller at key milestones. You could also provide access to the status through a web interface for your customers. The latter is a very passive method and it is always better to be proactive.

Another way is to provide your staff or service providers with small cards they fill in and leave on the desk of the caller when they attend to the problem if the caller isn't present when the work is done.

Complaint Management & Recovery

The simple fact is that you will receive complaints and there will be occupants or tenants who are not satisfied with your service delivery.

Complaint management and recovery is almost more important than the original service delivery. This includes addressing the original complaint and then making sure you have either a satisfied or neutral customer.

Putting a process in place that tracks and manages complaints also gives you valuable information you can use to improve your services. If you set it up so your staff and contractors aren't penalized for complaints, you will get results. If the culture is to penalize for failed service delivery, you may not hear about these issues until they have escalated. This makes customer satisfaction and complaint management much more difficult. The benefits of a complaint management process include:

- ✓ Identifying and rectifying gaps in service
- ✓ Ensuring customers have the services they need to do their job
- ✓ Protecting your organization's reputation
- ✓ Improving service response
- ✓ Preventing escalation.

Your complaint management process should include defining the different types of complaints and identifying what your staff should do about each type of complaint, including how to communicate effectively, what they can do to mitigate the problem and when to escalate.

If your staff is well-trained in how to deal with complaints, the complaints are more likely to be resolved to the satisfaction of the customer without needing much intervention or changing your overall approach to service delivery. Often it's a matter of setting expectations, communicating status and understanding the root of the complaint.

An appropriate response to a complaint includes the following progressive steps:

Immediate action

Take immediate response and, if possible, immediate action to reduce the impact and potential escalation of a customer complaint.

Provide the customer with a sense their issue is getting high-priority attention and will be addressed immediately. This often increases customer perception of quality service and enhances satisfaction.

Understanding

Understanding the basis and underlying reason or root cause for a complaint, in addition to the stated concern, positions your staff to effectively resolve the complaint instead of reacting only to what they are told.

Communication and follow-up

Communicating remedial action, resolution and subsequent follow-up to ensure customer satisfaction is imperative. Even where the customer's concern cannot be resolved due to technical, contractual or another similar reason, appropriate communication and response usually meets the need for customer satisfaction.

Escalation

Where it is not possible to resolve the customer's complaint, it is important to escalate the issue for awareness and possible solution as soon as possible.

Feedback to the customer about the escalation process communicates concern for customer satisfaction and demonstrates continued attention to customers' concerns.

Quick Summary

Key Points

➡ Develop a customer service culture within your group.

➡ Establish processes that make it easier to deliver services and deal with issues.

➡ Accept that the customer truly believes what they perceive. Clarify the facts, don't dispute their perception.

➡ Training will help your staff deal with complaints and service delivery problems.

Executive Tips

➡ Learn from service delivery mistakes and complaints to improve results, not punish staff and contractors.

➡ Clearly set customer expectations about your services to make it easier to satisfy them.

Traps to Avoid

➡ Don't let your staff's pride get in the way of good customer service or relations.

➡ Don't let your staff view customers as less important simply because they are internal.

44

Measuring Customer Satisfaction

Developing the satisfaction surveys.

"Your most unhappy customers are your greatest source of learning." – Bill Gates

Measuring satisfaction is critical to making decisions and implementing changes to improve your operations and deliver the services your company needs to be successful.

Understanding occupant or Tenant satisfaction will guide your initiatives to improve service. Measuring occupant satisfaction is key to ensuring the services and space you provide enables them to be successful, whether they are tenants in a commercial building or employees in corporate facilities.

As a management tool, satisfaction surveys allow you to change what doesn't work, improve what does and focus on the issues that matter.

Unfortunately, many surveys are designed and implemented without a clear idea of why the survey is being done and how the results will be used.

With a little planning, you can implement a strategic satisfaction survey that enables effective analysis and gives you valuable strategic information you need to take action.

Decision Making Goals

Start by establishing goals. Decide what you what to learn from the survey and what decisions you want to make with the results.

To compare satisfaction year-over-year, the questions you base your benchmark on must remain the same for each survey. The rest of the questions must focus on issues you want to know more about. Before developing the survey, establish the goals related to your specific objectives. This may be tenant retention, efficiency for employees or a pre-cursor to a relocation decision. Discuss these goals with other decision makers in your organization to validate their usefulness and the priority.

Questions

The questions must give you information that is easy to analyze and provide data you can act on to meet your goals. While asking general questions, such as overall satisfaction with cleaning, may be useful for benchmarking satisfaction levels, it won't provide information you can analyze and act upon. For action, you need more specific questions.

To get service-related feedback, phrase questions so you get feedback on the service, not the building systems. Asking about your response to hot/cold concerns is a service-related question, while asking about satisfaction with the temperature is a technical issue, not a service issue. If you already track complaints and service calls, you have data you can use to identify and act on technical problems in your building.

Questions related to individuals, especially if the occupants see those individuals face-to-face, often receive a higher positive response than questions about the service they provide. Carefully consider whether a question about individuals or staff members is worth asking, since there are often more relevant questions to ask.

Comments are a very important supplement to the question, and can help with the analysis of the results by giving you specific, situational examples. If possible, allow space for at least one general comment. An opportunity to comment about specific questions would be ideal.

Once you craft the questions to match your goals, randomly list your questions instead of grouping them by service area. The occupant will think about each question on its own, rather than taking the easy way out and providing a group of similar questions with the same answer.

Survey Methodology

Your goals will dictate whether to use a targeted or mass sampling method. For a large organization's portfolio, where you want satisfaction results from all the occupants, a non-targeted sampling is appropriate.

To gather input from a smaller number of individuals, such as one specific group or department managers, a targeted approach is best. Either way, work to get a high response rate. For targeted sampling, contact the individuals directly and influence their participation.

Effective survey methodology is essential for accurate, relevant results. You also want a survey that is easy and efficient to administer. Along with good questions, the end result will be valuable management information you can analyze and act upon in order to increase satisfaction.

Sampling

The sample size is important, since it influences the validity of the results. The sample size also influences whether to use a targeted, random or mass sampling method. For a large organization's portfolio where you want satisfaction results from all the occupants, a non-targeted sampling is appropriate. The same applies to other properties where your tenant's employees are the survey target.

If you need to gather input from a smaller number of individuals, such as the tenant representatives, department managers, etc., then a targeted approach is more appropriate.

Either way, ensure your response rate is as high as possible to get statistically-relevant results. Dissatisfied people tend to fill in surveys more often than satisfied people, so a higher response rate will moderate the effect. For targeted sampling, you have more control over response rate, since you can contact the individuals directly and influence their participation.

Regardless of the method, include tracking information on the survey to facilitate analysis. This includes data such as the building name, the individual's department, floor or other key information that will help you analyze the information and make decisions.

Distribution

The distribution method depends on the sample size and level of effort required. The options are telephone, paper or web-based. Telephone surveys work for small sample sizes, and can result in high response rates. Paper-based surveys can be manually or automatically tabulated (with scanning technology), however compilation of the comments could be time consuming, so this option is not effective for larger surveys.

A web-based survey is efficient since the system itself collects and tabulates results, including comments. It does have challenges, however. In a commercial building environment, your tenant's employees may have varying access to the internet, and your ability to send notices and reminders about the survey will be limited. This is easier for corporate facilities, since the entire organization is linked through one system. Access to the internet by all employees shouldn't be assumed, and a detailed discussion with your IT department is necessary.

If you can't use a web-based survey, cconsider using a third-party service to administer your survey. They have the systems in place to manage distribution and compile of results, and will provide the respondents with an assurance of anonymity.

Response Scale

The scale you use for the responses is very important, and can influence the results as well as your ability to analyze the results.

A four-point scale forces the occupant to identify whether they are satisfied or not, eliminating the use of a "neutral" option when they are not sure. However, since some occupants will not be able to respond to the question for various reasons, you may want to use a four-plus-one scale by adding "insufficient information" or "don't know." These additional options are better than using "neutral" as they reflect the fact that the occupant may truly not know how to respond to some questions.

The scale would look like this:

Question	Very Dissatisfied	Dissatisfied	Satisfied	Totally Satisfied	Don't Know
Question 1					
Question 2					
Question 3					
Question 4					

Analysis

Once the results of the survey are tabulated, the next step is to analyze the results. Where possible, individuals involved in delivering the services should be involved in the analysis, providing additional insight and facilitating the development of action plans.

To create a benchmark, calculate the satisfaction level for the questions identified as benchmark questions, and establish an average overall satisfaction level. You can refine the benchmark by building or type of building.

For analysis that allows you to take action, look at each question separately and assess the results of the four response options instead of simply analyzing a single number that shows percentage satisfied. This provides more information on the degree of satisfaction, which is important in determining the extent of any problems.

In the example below, both graphs show that 65% of the occupants are satisfied to some degree. The first graph shows a reasonable distribution of responses, however the second graph shows a distribution more heavily weighted to "'Very Dissatisfied." This points to a more significant problem.

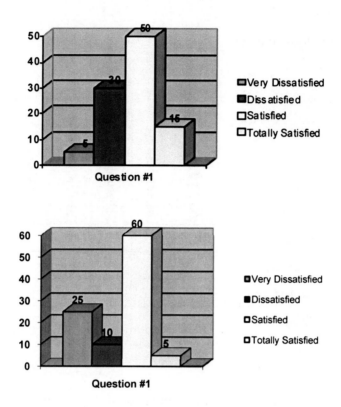

If you have a more detailed breakdown - by building, tenant or department, for instance – it is easier to pinpoint the issue. Comments also help pinpoint actual events or issues, enhancing your ability to develop an action plan that results in change.

In addition to reviewing the data question-by-question, analyze the results between related questions. This validates the results and pinpoints issues. For instance, if the occupants are satisfied with the service from the call center, yet not satisfied with the results of their service request, you can eliminate the call center as a source of dissatisfaction and focus on other areas of the service management process

Action Plans

Just measuring satisfaction isn't enough. You need to take action based on the results.

Start by developing an action plan that tackles a small number of important issues rather than tackling every issue and diluting your efforts. Focus on the areas of highest impact and questions with the lowest satisfaction, as long as you have the ability to make the changes necessary. If you don't, document the reasons and understand the limitations so you can inform and educate others in your organization.

Read the comments in conjunction with the percentage responses to get a better feel about the issues, being careful not to let them overshadow your own observations and understanding. Comments are valuable, but they sometimes represent extreme opinions.

Use the process outlined in the Health Check portion of the *Strategic Management* section to drill into the processes, procedures, tools and resources that impact the particular result. Figure out what needs to change and develop your plan to change it, using the strategic management tools presented in this book. Involve and engage your staff or suppliers in identifying the issue and developing an approach to improving results. If relevant, speak directly with a number of tenants/occupants about the issue to get their feedback. Identify what should be done, what could be done and what can't be done, then prioritize them based on the impact it will have and the cost/resources it will take. Sometimes you can't make enough change to justify the cost or effort involved.

Communicating Results

Whenever you conduct a survey, it's important to communicate the results and your plans to the participants. This shows you are listening, identifies the value in filling out the survey and tells them what you are going to do.

Communicate openly and honestly. Celebrating your success is important, but being honest about low satisfaction levels and telling the occupant what you plan on doing about it is more important in the long run. If there are things that are beyond your control, explain them but don't make it look like it's an excuse.

Your communication should be tailored to your audience. How and what you communicate will depend on the message you want to deliver. What you say to corporate occupants will be different from tenants. How you represent information will be different when reporting upwards within your organization versus directly to the survey participants.

Your message to senior management should highlight your successes and also make the case for additional resources where results are poor or declining. Be prepared to demonstrate that you've done everything you could with your own resources, however, before making your case.

Quick Summary

Key Points	➡ Don't measure satisfaction unless you will do something with the results
	➡ Ask the same questions year-over-year to see a trend, adding other questions as needed.
	➡ Ask for comments as they help you understand the issues.
Executive Tips	➡ Understand what your goal is before you measure satisfaction results.
	➡ Only ask questions that you have control over and can do something about.
Traps to Avoid	➡ Don't over-survey your tenants, occupants or customers.
	➡ Don't misinterpret response data or simply use it to justify the status quo.

45

Satisfaction Survey Examples

Developing the satisfaction surveys.

"Quality in a service or product is not what you put into it. It is what the client or customer gets out of it." -- Peter Drucker

You shouldn't just use one survey to gather information and opinions about your service delivery and facilities. Since you have different levels of customers and types of services, use several approaches.

Here are three different types of surveys you can use, covering different types of customers and different issues.

The occupant satisfaction survey is the typical one used by facility managers and gives you feedback from the general occupants in the building.

The decision maker survey targets key individuals who have influence or are senior members of the organization. The questions you ask will be different and your survey methodology should target the individuals specifically instead of a sampling method you would use with the occupant survey. Asking the opinion of the decision makers moves you one step closer to a better relationship with them. It also builds awareness on their part about what you do for them and how you help them be successful.

The transaction survey can be used for work orders, moves, projects, reprographic services or any other tangible service you deliver for an individual in the organization. The individual requesting the service or for whom the service was delivered is surveyed about their experience and satisfaction specifically with that service.

Occupant Satisfaction Survey

This should be distributed electronically or by paper to all occupants. You will probably get a relatively small percentage back. For maximum effect, communicate with them before you send the survey and then give them a reminder of the deadline shortly after you distribute it.

Change the questions to fit your specific requirements, services and issues.

The survey is designed to gather opinions from and gauge the level of satisfaction of general occupants, whether they are organization staff or tenants, to understand their perceptions and pinpoint areas where improvement is required.

Aim to balance survey detail and length. Since the key purpose is to address service delivery, focus the questions on elements which will provide information that helps develop solutions. Questions can be segmented into clear areas of services, service qualities, department and staff. They can also address the office environment and general physical condition of facilities.

Survey Content

For each question, ask the level of importance for better analysis of results.

Information for sorting and analysis only:

Please identify your location	(drop down list)
Please identify your department	(drop down list)
Please indicate your job function	(radio button list or drop down list)
How often do you interact directly with a Facilities employee or services?	(radio button list)

Your satisfaction with our services:

Please indicate your level of satisfaction with the services provided by the physical plant department by selecting the appropriate choice for each service along with how important each service is to you.

Services	Highly Satisfied	Satisfied	Dissatisfied	Highly Dissatisfied	Not Applicable	Importance (1-5)
	1	2	3	4	(NA)	1-5
Grounds (grass, plants, trees, roads, parking lots, snow removal, etc.)						
Maintenance (plumbing, electrical, walls, etc.)						
Renovations (office relocations and remodeling, built-in cabinets, walls, etc.))						
Custodial services (cleaning, recycling, garbage pickup, etc.)						
Miscellaneous requests (keys, signs, electrical outlets, painting, etc.)						
Others (add as appropriate)						

Please share your comments about how we can improve your satisfaction with our services:

Text Input
_____

Your opinion about the qualities we demonstrate:

Please indicate your level of satisfaction with the following service qualities demonstrated by the physical plant department.

Qualities	Highly Satisfied	Satisfied	Dissatisfied	Highly Dissatisfied	Not Applicable	Importance (1-5)
	1	2	3	4	(NA)	1-5
Communication & updates						
Timely response						
Timely completion of work						
Quality of work						
Availability of staff						
Others (add as appropriate)						

Please share your comments about how we can improve your satisfaction with our service qualities:

Text Input

Your opinion about the department and our staff in general:

Please indicate your opinion of the plant services department and staff.

Qualities	Highly Satisfied	Satisfied	Dissatisfied	Highly Dissatisfied	Not Applicable	Importance (1-5)
	1	2	3	4	(NA)	1-5
We make it easy for you to know who to contact						
Our resources are available and accessible						
We appear to have the technical knowledge necessary to deal with your issues						
We are able to satisfy your requirements						
We are responsive and provide timely service						
We appear professional						
Others (add as appropriate)						

Please share your comments about how we can improve your satisfaction with our department and staff:

Text Input

Your opinion about your office environment:

Please indicate your level of satisfaction with your office environment and general building condition.

Qualities	Highly Satisfied	Satisfied	Dissatisfied	Highly Dissatisfied	(NA) Not Applicable	Importance (1-5)
	1	2	3	4	(NA)	1-5
Parking						
Security						
Signage & direction						
Lighting levels						
Indoor air quality						
Washrooms						
Lounges / common areas						
Vending services						
Cafeteria services						
Elevators / escalators						
Building appearance (interior)						
Site appearance (exterior)						
Cleanliness (interior)						
Others (add as appropriate)						

Please share your comments about what would improve your satisfaction with your office environment and general building condition:

Text Input

Decision Maker Survey

Decision makers can be emailed the survey or sent a paper copy, depending on your approach. Send a reminder to them before the due date. If possible, communicate with them in advance, such as speaking to them at a senior management meeting. This helps them understand the survey's importance. You can also personally visit or call them.

Change the questions to fit your specific requirements, services and issues.

The survey is designed to understand the needs of decision makers and get their opinions of our services and hear their priorities. Since they will also receive a general occupant survey, this survey focuses on strategic information. The survey is kept short and focused.

Survey Content:

The Physical Plant department serves several levels customers. Please rank the relative importance of these four categories of customers with respect to the services we provide.

Customer	1 (highest)	2	3	4 (lowest)
Students				
Administrative departments/staff				
Academic departments/staff				
Overall Institutional interests				

For you to be successful, what do you need from the plant services department? Please rank them for us.

Service	1 (highest)	2	3	4 (lowest)
Fast service				
Flexibility				
Low cost services and cost savings measures				

Communication of issues and activities				
Consultation and advice related to space				
Renovation & renewal initiatives				
Etc. (add as appropriate)				
Additional Services (please identify)				
Other (please identify)				

Please share your comments about what we can improve upon to serve your needs:

Text Input

If you were to prioritize the responsibilities of the physical plant department, what would be the relative importance of each one?

Responsibilities	1 (highest)	2	3	4 (lowest)
Grounds (grass, plants, trees, roads, parking lots, snow removal, etc.)				
Maintenance (plumbing, electrical, walls, etc.)				
Renovations (office relocations and remodeling, built-in cabinets, walls, etc.))				
Custodial services (cleaning, recycling, garbage pickup, etc.)				
Miscellaneous requests (keys, signs, electrical outlets, painting, etc.)				
Others (add as appropriate)				

Please rate degree to which you feel your department and functional needs are supported by the following services.

Responsibilities	Fully Supported	Partly Supported	Not Supported	N A
Grounds (grass, plants, trees, roads, parking lots, snow removal, etc.)				
Maintenance (plumbing, electrical, walls, etc.)				
Renovations (office relocations and remodeling, built-in cabinets, walls, etc.)				
Custodial (cleaning, recycling, garbage pickup, etc.)				
Miscellaneous requests (keys, signs, electrical outlets, painting, etc.)				
Others (add as appropriate)				

Please indicate why the services provided by the Physical Plant are important to you and your department:

Text Input

Transaction Survey

Service response card can be left with the customer for them to return by internal mail. You can also phone, email or send a web survey to them after their work order is closed.

The survey is designed to get their opinion of the transaction with simple yes/no responses instead of a scale, since with a transaction, they are either satisfied or they are not. If they aren't, it is more important to understand why, which is the reason for the text input.

The survey is kept short to increase the likelihood that they complete it. This also helps focus the results on service delivery through the help desk and work order process itself.

Survey Content:

You are a valuable customer and we value your opinion on how well we are meeting your needs. Please take a moment to answer the following questions.

	Yes	No	Not Applicable
Were you satisfied with how your request was received and handled by our help desk staff?			
If not, please explain:			
Did we communicate the status of your request to your satisfaction?			
If not, please explain:			
Was your request completed on-time?			
If not, please explain:			
Was your request completed to your satisfaction?			
If not, please explain:			
Please tell us what we can do differently:			

Quick Summary

Key Points	➡ Survey information enables you to make decisions that improve service.
	➡ Include a general survey, transaction survey and decision maker survey.
Executive Tips	➡ Carefully develop questions that give you the information you need to make changes.
Traps to Avoid	➡ Don't overdo the surveys — occupants can get survey fatigue.
	➡ Letting respondents select a neutral option doesn't tell you anything about the service.

46

Walk of the VIP

A critical look from your customer's perspective.

"Organizations have more to fear from lack of quality internal customer service than from any level of external customer service." – Ron Tillotson

Everyone gets a little complacent when they have been in the same place for a while. It's as simple as seeing something deteriorate very gradually over time — you don't usually notice the change.

By getting someone else to use a fresh, critical eye, you will catch things that you may not have recognized as problems or have filtered out for various reasons. It's especially relevant for visible services and conditions that we see every day.

This simple three-step process will help you assess the general condition of your facility from an outsider's perspective and highlight the things that need the most attention.

Even if you can't fix everything you're the visual inspection finds, you will now have a list for your annual planning process.

Here are the three steps involved in the Walk of the VIP:

Step 1: Choose a VIP

This person is to assume the role of a Very Important Person. Imagine them as either the most important tenant in your building, or as a member of your organization's senior management team.

Your VIP should represent your most scrupulous customers, occupants or decision makers. What do they see as they walk through your buildings? What route do the VIPs normally take from the time he or she enters your building until they arrive at their office? Where do they go and what route do they take for lunch, parking and other business?

Where possible, the VIP should not be part of your FM team or be directly related to the building. You want someone who isn't familiar with your facility, but it must be someone who will be very observant and not hold anything back.

Prepare them by explaining the purpose and using a checklist to record observations, similar to the one below. Your VIP can identify the priority for each item using a scale such as 1 (high) to 3 (low).

Executive Tip

The VIP is an extension of the "secret shopper" approach used in the retail industry. The VIP should have a list of things to check and rate and the information they provide should guide FM management decisions.

Step 2: Visit the Building

Accompany the VIP to the building, taking at least two paths most-commonly travelled into the building by the occupants, such as from the front entrance and from the parking garage. Also visit the most frequently-used common areas (i.e., lounges, hallways, parking, cafeteria).

Your job is simply to lead them through the building and give them access. Refrain from making comments or influencing what your VIP observes.

Step 3: Look, List, Plan, Do

Look

During the visit, the VIP uses a critical eye and lists their observations (dirty floors, untidy lobbies, poor lighting, squeaky doors, leaky pipes, uncomfortable temperatures ...), no matter how small or insignificant they appear. They should give enough information to indicate where the issues are.

This includes all visible building elements as well as the services, on-site staff, project activity, etc. in the building.

In addition to the detailed list, they should provide their general observations.

List

During the walk-around, record everything the VIP identifies. This allows them to focus on their inspection. Since you are writing down the information, it will be easier for you to understand what they are identifying when you review it later.

Plan

The next step is to develop an action plan to address each of the items on the VIP list, categorizing the items as follows:

- ☐ Immediate quick fix; you or your contractor does them right away.
- ☐ Do-able in time / no new cost; make plans for them to be done.
- ☐ Do-able in time / additional cost, assess funding.
- ☐ Divine intervention; schedule at your earliest convenience.

Do

Implement all items that are immediate quick fixes and do-able in time/no new cost. Build all the other items into future budgets.

Things to Consider

Focus on areas most often missed by you and your FM staff on a daily basis. You are may be missing issues, since many develop over time and it is hard to notice incremental changes. This approach also helps you consider items or issues you may have "filtered out" because constraints have limited your ability to deal with them. Potential problem areas include main and back entrances, parking-related entrances, stairs and hallways, corridors, stairwells, lunch areas and lounges and the paths your tenants, executives and customers take when they approach, enter and move within your building.

Sample VIP Form

Here is a simple form you can fill in based on what your VIP sees as you accompany them on their inspection. Take a few pages and a clipboard with you to make it easier.

General Observations	
Specific Observations	**Priority**
1	
2	
3	
4	
5	
6	
Etc.	

Quick Summary

Key Points	➡ Get someone else to help you see things that need improving
Executive Tips	➡ Draw on others to help you be successful. ➡ Focus on some of the most visible elements and paths in your facility.
Traps to Avoid	➡ Small changes in condition over time are hard to see.

Your Strategic Plan

Based on this section, what strategic initiatives do you plan to implement that will help you manage your assets better and when do you expect to accomplish them?

What are you going to do?   **When**

_____ | _____

_____ | _____

_____ | _____

_____ | _____

_____ | _____

Notes

_____

_____

_____

_____

_____

_____

_____

_____

_____

_____

_____

_____

Costs and Productivity

Introduction

Whether we like it or not, dealing with cost pressures is a fact of life. As professionals, we must always balance cost management with service delivery, risks and long-term impacts. At the same time, we also have a responsibility to spend money wisely for our organizations.

While you can reduce costs and improve productivity by conducting benchmarking, doing a health check and procuring services effectively as described in previous sections, there are other ways to approach value and cost.

This includes understanding costs and ensuring the rest of your organization understands the costs through communication and even a chargeback approach. You can also engage those around you, including service providers, to get their help and expertise to reduce costs by managing services, adjusting scope and understanding the cost drivers. Always take the long-term view of the total cost of ownership instead of just focussing on today.

47

Facility Cost Allocation Drives Behavior

Whether you implement chargeback or not, tracking and reporting costs will change behavior.

"People don't change their behavior unless it makes a difference for them to do so." - Fran Tarkenton

Real estate costs money and money is the bottom line for any company. Facilities managers who recognize this can raise their profile and contribute to the success of the company by accurately establishing facility costs and positioning the information for better corporate decisions.

Facility Cost Allocation (FCA) is often associated with a chargeback model. Charging users for services and space is just a tool and should not drive the FCA model.

With an effective costing system in place, facility managers can communicate the cost information in a meaningful way to the facilities group, user departments and other senior decision makers in the organization. By doing this, the facility manager also plays a larger role in future decisions and ensures they will be consulted about major decisions that impact facility costs.

Costing systems are referred to by a number of different terms, including transfer pricing, chargeback, activity based costing, cost accounting and others. Using a more generic term such as FCA to describe the practice in FM is more appropriate, since while the mechanism and techniques to implement and manage a costing model can vary considerably, the underlying principles are the same – identify and communicate costs to drive behavior and ensure the most effective and efficient use of real estate resources in support of the corporations core business.

It's this principle that should dictate how facility managers implement FCA and how it is managed, since success depends on FCA being a management tool rather than simply another accounting process.

Setting Goals for Chargeback

While many facility managers immediately associate FCA with some form of chargeback model, actually charging users and departments for the services and space you provide is simply a tool within FCA. It should not drive your FCA model.

The goal is the efficient and effective use of real estate resources with information that drives decisions and behaviors that benefit the corporation.

The ultimate goal of any FCA model is the efficient and effective use of real estate resources. However, when developing FCA, facility managers need to refine the goals to a more direct and actionable level that meets the specifics of their own situation and allows FCA to work within the existing framework of the corporation.

To do this, facility managers must clearly understand the issues and the implications before establishing goals. This includes current funding and budgeting processes, establishing how and where decisions that affect real estate are made and understanding the current mechanisms in place for measuring the performance of individuals and departments.

By identifying all the goals and then focusing on a few which will help gain support for the FCA initiative, it is possible to start with more straight-forward and less controversial elements, then work towards full implementation by building on the successes and learning from the problems and issues encountered.

The initial goals may be as simple as providing facility-use options and the related costing impacts, identifying the costs of providing work-order services to various departments, establishing benchmarking information that show the differences in costs to provide space for various departments or functional areas, or determining whether services are delivered efficiently.

By successfully implementing the initial goals and proving added-value information for organizational decisions, it will be easier to move to a more full-fledged model that encompasses a more broad based allocation of costs.

Costing

FCA includes a management and a costing component, both of which are required to effectively influence behavior.

The costing component enables accurate and effective calculation of the costs to own and/or operate the facilities on a unit basis and establish the cost of providing specific services based on their own unit of measure, such as mail costs per employee, move costs per work station, etc.

To be useful, costing must go beyond simple budget numbers and the chart of accounts. Accounting packages and integrated FM software can help establish the costs, although it takes some planning and forethought to ensure the results are accurate, timely and structured enough to be useful and meaningful within your organization. Only then can they be used for asset analysis, cost control and to drive behavior both within the FM department and throughout the organization. Techniques for doing this are well documented and are used successfully in many other industries. The most recognized methods include activity based costing and traditional cost accounting methods. The most basic difference is how overhead and other non-transaction costs are allocated.

Influencing Decisions

The management component of FCA provides facility managers with the influence they need to effectively drive behavior. While the cost accounting component of FCA is relatively straight forward, the management component can be much more difficult, since it needs to be developed and supported in a way that ensures attention is paid to the results. It must be established well before you start developing costing models, since your costing models must support the management objectives.

While a common approach is to charge departments and other users for the space they occupy and the services they use, this can complicate the underlying objectives and introduce behaviors that are not in the best interests of the organization as a whole. Alternatives to charging should be carefully considered before implementing a chargeback mechanism. It may be better to begin the process from a reporting and management basis and integrate the information into the decision making process. With the right support, implementing a direct chargeback mechanism can be avoided while achieving the behavior changes at the same time.

Both the implementation and the communication of FCA must be structured to ensure better decisions and to support policy decisions such as corporate occupancy standards as well as provide support for facilities-driven initiatives that reduce costs. Facility managers can do this by showing a direct impact on departments and to the overall corporation.

To be successful, FCA must have full support within the organization and must be included on the executive agenda and business plans in order to drive real estate decisions. At the same time, care must be taken to ensure that costs are not the only factors used in decision making, since costing information taken on its own could influence poor decisions, especially where an isolated decision does not consider the impact on the organization as a whole.

Implementation

Effective implementation of the costing and the management components of FCA are just as critical as the actual components themselves, since even a brilliantly-designed system will fail if it is ineffectively implemented.

This is true from a business process and a communications perspective. The business processes, as mentioned earlier, must dovetail into existing processes and support or complement the current decision making and measurement tools within the organization. You can implement these using a building block process or all at once, depending on your organization's culture, level of support and the complexity of the FCA system you design and the existing business processes. The building block process allows elements to be implemented in stages, giving you time to gain acceptance and prove their usefulness within the corporation before implementing the next element. Regardless of your approach, gaining visible support from the necessary decision makers is part of the business process element.

Communications is also important, since the processes involved and the intended goals of FCA must be shared and understood. Your own situation will dictate how best to communicate, but decision makers will need detailed explanations about FCA, how it affects them and how they should use the information to their advantage. This communication may be direct if the facilities department has a strong hand in real estate decisions and policy. The information must be handled more delicately if individual departments have a great deal of autonomy in how they use real estate services.

Benefits

While implementing chargeback can be difficult, there are a number of benefits if you implement it carefully to meet your goals, not just to shift responsibility or budgets. These benefits include:

- ✓ Provide support for consolidation initiatives.
- ✓ Place the accountability for miscellaneous work order costs back on the department using the service.
- ✓ Improve space utilization.
- ✓ Increase support for cost savings measures by showing how it will impact the bottom line of every department involved, and therefore the company as a whole.
- ✓ Put facilities costs in front of the decision-makers.

Behaviors you can change

In addition to the benefits above, chargeback systems can influence the behavior of occupants at your facilities. Keep in mind that sometimes behaviors can change in ways you don't expect, especially if you implement systems in a way that makes the occupants think they are in a "free market" and can make all their own decisions about facilities services and space to benefit their own department with little regard for the overall impact.

Take care to avoid:

- ✓ Ignoring the cost of real estate when making operational decisions.
- ✓ Not planning changes for maximum real estate savings.
- ✓ Inefficient use of facilities services and resources.
- ✓ Lack of coordination between departments regarding space usage.
- ✓ Failure to fully cooperate in cost saving / environmental activities (such as energy / recycling).
- ✓ Resisting significant facilities-driven consolidation and planning measures.

Conclusion

Implementing and managing an FCA system is fraught with challenges and will take incremental resources to make it work. If your goals are clearly identified and well-supported organizationally, it will be worth the time and effort and place facility management in a more influential role within the organization. It will ultimately ensure that the real estate resources are efficiently and effectively used to support the organization's core business and contribute to its success.

Quick Summary

Key Points	➡ FCA can provide you with information to make decisions.
	➡ FCA can enable you to support initiatives based on cost mitigation.
Executive Tips	➡ Get buy-in at the senior levels and demonstrate the value of your costing information for decision making.
	➡ FCA should influence behaviors and ensure facility costs are considered when corporate decisions are made.
Traps to Avoid	➡ Don't implement chargeback first. Instead, use the information to raise awareness and drive behavior.

48

Lifecycle View: Total Cost of Ownership Saves Money

Are you wasting 85% of your building's total costs?

"For tomorrow belongs to the people who prepare for it today."
– African proverb

Initial costs represent only 15% of a building's total cost. If you ignore this when developing a building, you are wasting the other 85% of your costs. Keeping the initial capital cost as low as possible seems right, but it's costing you a lot more over the life of the building.

The problem is visibility. The initial capital cost is the most visible part of the decision-making process. Ergo, the long-term high cost of bad decisions is seen only after the building is occupied.

Visibility into the total cost of ownership is one way to address this. Justification and decisions should be based on the total cost of ownership, not just initial costs.

Estimate the total cost of operating over the life of the facility and use this information as part of the budgeting and decision-making process to arrive at better decisions that include more up-front funding to design and build a more efficient building.

Using a lifecycle costing (LCC) approach can help reduce short and long term costs.

LCC goes beyond when to replace a particular piece of equipment or building component; it's about taking a systematic approach to balancing maintenance costs, operating costs and replacement/refurbishment costs over the life of the asset. While it may seem complicated, in practical application, it is very simple.

The benefit of using LCC is that it combines cost information with hands-on FM experience and provides FM professionals with one more good reason to take a closer look at some of your costs, which you can then work towards reducing. It also provides financial information you can use to make decisions.

The concept is simple. LCC includes all costs associated with building assets from acquisition to disposal/replacement of the building itself. For practical reasons, a typical lifespan is often used, such as 30 years or 50 years, depending on your organization and the type of facilities you own.

For costs measured in future years, adjust upwards for inflation each year and then adjust downwards for the real value of money in that year compared to today's money, which is easy to do with most spreadsheet's built-in formulas.

What does this Mean for you?

Initial costs of a building represent only 10-to-20% of total cost, depending on the life span you assume for the building. Privately-owned buildings have a shorter lifespan, while government and institutions have a longer lifespan.

The rest of the cost, an astounding 80% to 90%, is for maintenance, operating and refurbishment/replacement of components over the building's lifespan. Ignoring this large proportion of costs means you may be wasting money.

How can you use Lifecycle Costing for new Facilities?

While minimizing the initial capital cost of a new building seems right, that save-now approach could cost a lot more over the life of the building.

The initial capital cost is the most visible and easily measured part of the decision-making process, yet the high cost of bad decisions is only seen in the future.

Justification and decisions should be based on the total cost of ownership, not just initial costs.

Implement techniques that drive down the total cost. Use effective financial analysis to illustrate the benefits and shift the behavior of decision makers.

By estimating the total cost of operating over the life of the facility based on a more efficient design and by using this information as part of the budgeting and decision-making process, you will arrive at a better decision. It may include higher costs to design and build a more efficient building, or to purchase more expensive, yet energy efficient and longer-lasting components.

The easiest way to reduce total costs is to build operating efficiency into the design and construction of the building using existing techniques, many of which are well developed but not always used. Here are some of the more useful ones.

Green Initiatives

Use green standards and initiatives to lower ongoing energy costs. This includes how the facility is designed and the energy efficiency of the equipment. It's politically and socially correct while contributing to a lower total cost of ownership.

Facility operations input in design

Involve facilities staff and service providers such as custodial, grounds, mechanical/electrical service contractors to provide guidance on design to minimize operational costs.

Value engineering

Value engineering goes beyond financial analysis and assesses the design, including materials, equipment and functional requirements to eliminate or modify design elements and reduce unnecessary costs.

Commissioning

Commissioning ensures the building is performing as it was designed, meets specifications and the effort you put into the design to reduce costs will be realized.

How can you Reduce Operating Costs at your Current Facilities with Lifecycle Costing?

Your existing facility has an operating budget and a capital replacement budget. You can manage down these costs with a LCC approach, which could include extending or advancing their replacement based on the information you collect. The best part of the process is it forces you to understand your current operational costs and the alternatives.

The most important thing is to understand the costs of your major systems. This includes regular servicing and preventive maintenance, ongoing repairs, consumables and energy costs. With the right software or for smaller portfolios, an up-to-date spreadsheet, you can have the information you need.

Secondly, you need to have information on the condition of your equipment, which is closely related to reliability, maintenance/repair costs and energy consumption, not to mention the required replacement timeframe.

Since LCC includes operating costs, look closely at maintenance schedules related to your repairs and the risk of failure of that equipment. In a portfolio, if you are doing the same routines at the same frequencies on all your equipment yet they are operating in different conditions, look closer and adjust frequencies for conditions to reduce costs. A chiller operating in a constantly hot, humid city will require different routines and frequencies than one operating only during the summer season. Similarly, if you are changing HVAC filters based on the calendar instead of pressure drop, get feedback on the condition of the filters when they are changed and extend filter changes based on conditions.

With your maintenance costs under control, look at your older equipment and using LCC, estimate your current costs, replacement costs and timeframes. Re-do the assessment with earlier replacement that includes lower operating costs, including energy, and make decisions based on that information.

Analyze the replacement and what the reduced operating costs, particularly energy, would be over the life of that equipment or your specific planning horizon versus the current equipment. This will tell you whether you will get the lowest total cost from replacing it sooner, or whether it can run well past its theoretical life, saving you the cost of replacement.

In some cases, even if the equipment can last longer, it is prudent to replace it sooner in order to reduce operating costs. Equipment that consumes a lot of energy is a particularly good target for this.

Using the LCC approach will provide you with the financial information you need for an informed decision. It also makes you look at all your costs much more closely, thereby helping to reduce current and future expenses.

Reducing Total Costs through Design and Construction

The easiest way to reduce total costs is to build operating efficiency into the design and construction of the building using existing techniques, many of which are well-developed, but not always used.

The caveat is that these techniques may extend the total project time, increase consulting/professional fees up-front and may result in design changes that increase initial costs. Build these techniques into the initial schedule and budget and then use the results, along with the related financial analysis, to justify increased construction costs that reduce ongoing costs.

Multi-Disciplinary Approach to Design

The design of the building has an ongoing impact on costs. Many disciplines involved in the design process, which is usually led by architectural considerations, followed by system design by mechanical, structural and electrical engineers, to name a few.

Involving the full range of disciplines throughout the design process, versus an architect-led approach, enables better integration of the disciplines. The end result is driven by solutions rather than design.

Green Initiatives

Green buildings are expected in the current economic and political climate, especially for public facilities. Using green standards and initiatives typically result in slightly higher initial costs, but lower ongoing energy costs. This is politically and socially correct and contributes to a lower total cost of ownership.

The increased costs of a green building, especially when it is LEED certified, are usually easier to justify and get approved. Some levels of government are already mandating or encouraging green buildings. Keep in mind that while formal standards and initiatives such as LEED carry the green label, other techniques should also be used to reduce costs. When justifying the increased cost under the banner of green initiatives, be sure to take the full benefits of energy reductions from all initiatives into account.

Facility Operations Input in Design

It is rare during the design phase of a new project for facility professionals to be consulted for input on the design regarding ways to minimize future operational costs.

Since the ongoing costs are up to 85% of the total costs of ownership, this is a significant oversight. If you have adequate internal operations resources with the time and experience necessary, this is a very low-cost method to save money. That said, you may need to augment internal resources with external resources or consultants for certain areas. For instance, involving service providers for janitorial, grounds, maintenance, security and other services will provide invaluable guidance on design elements that can reduce operational costs.

Examples include designs that enable easy access for maintenance, surfaces with low maintenance and janitorial costs and physical design and technology that reduce the need for guards. Other considerations include adequate space that is efficiently located for maintenance and janitorial services to reduce labor needs, and modern building automation that enables efficient ongoing management and maintenance of systems, including energy conservation.

Since operations and maintenance staff can be a significant operational cost, design and equipment selection that can reduce staff requirements should be included.

As always, the earlier decisions and initiatives are taken during the design phase, the easier they are to include in the final design. Include the facility operations input from the start.

Consider This

Treat requests for professional input into facility design very seriously. This is the FM professional's chance to showcase his technical and managerial expertise. By providing solutions to problems the organization may not yet have encountered, you are establishing your credentials.

Lifecycle Costing Calculations

The LCC analysis takes four key cost components into account to determine the lowest total cost of design alternatives. It's a well-established economic analysis that takes a component-by-component approach to the initial cost as well as maintenance, energy and replacement or renewal costs of the equipment over the life of the building. The analysis is rigorous, taking into account the time value of money and inflation to develop a net present value for the total cost of the components over their entire life cycle.

This technique enables effective decisions related to design and equipment selection alternatives and options. This ensures the best choices for total cost of ownership, not just initial construction costs. This technique provides the information and evidence you need to influence decision making if the final design exceeds budget but demonstrates the lowest total cost of ownership.

This technique can be used for a design/build tender to achieve the lowest total cost rather than the lowest initial construction cost. By requiring LCC analysis by a third party at part of each submission and using the results as a basis for final selection, you can make the best financial decision.

The formula for total costs is simple:

	Initial/capital cost
+	Maintenance cost
+	Operating cost (consumables, utilities, staffing)
+	Refurbishment/replacement costs (reduce by salvage value, if any)
=	Total Lifecycle Cost

Put all your costs in a row in your spreadsheet, inflating your operating costs (especially energy) each year.

Use the net present value (NPV) formula in your spreadsheet software to calculate the real cost of the replacement and operating costs over the anticipated lifespan. Copy it and make changes based on earlier or later replacement and reductions in operating costs to determine the best option.

Value Engineering

This tool is closely related to LCC and they often work together. Unlike LCC, value engineering goes beyond purely financial analysis and assesses the design, including materials, equipment and functional requirements. The intent is to eliminate or modify elements of the design that are either not required to achieve the functional requirements or add unnecessary costs.

This isn't engineering in the same sense as mechanical, structural or electrical engineering for building systems. It is engineering in the broader sense, including quantifiable elements such as equipment and materials, plus non-quantitative aspects like productivity, aesthetics, occupant comfort, performance and functionality.

Generally, value engineering will drive design and equipment selection alternatives. LCC will then analyze the total economic impact of those decisions

Commissioning

Even if the design reflects the best value in initial and total cost of ownership, the actual implementation of the design during construction needs to be validated against the design specifications. Payback on commissioning costs for energy alone is under five years. This has a huge impact on the total benefits over the life of the building.

Commissioning is a quality assurance process that verifies that the systems installed during construction meet the original design criteria through testing and documentation. This process is conducted by third party commissioning consultants throughout the construction process.

Commissioning can be conducted on a system-by-system basis or a total building commissioning. The level of commissioning depends on the mandate given to the commissioning consulting and the costs you are willing to incur.

A total building approach includes a broader range of systems on an integrated basis, not on a system-by-system basis and is the preferred approach to ensure the lowest total cost of ownership.

Commissioning should include functional performance testing and documentation of the design intent, operating parameters and sequences. This can also include developing system operations manuals to provide guidance on efficient operations for the facility staff.

The commissioning consultant should be involved in the design phase of the project so they are fully aware of the design intent and can develop their commissioning plan with full knowledge of the system design decisions. Commissioning should start as soon as possible during the construction phase.

To get the best value from the commissioning process, the FM staff should be involved in the commissioning and receive training on the systems during the construction phase. Since the cost of operations is by far the largest part of the total cost of ownership, it is critical to give operational staff the knowledge they need to operate the facility efficiently in accordance with the design intent.

Corporate facilities present a unique opportunity to focus on the total cost of ownership rather than simply the initial cost. The long life and ownership of a typical corporate facility makes this stewardship even more important.

Quick Summary

Key Points

➡ Reduce total cost, not just construction costs.

➡ Use existing tools to save operating costs with good design.

Executive Tips

➡ Demonstrate the impact of efficiency with facts and financial information over the life of the building.

Traps to Avoid

➡ Don't focus on the initial construction cost.

49

Talking Numbers with your CFO

How to see facilities the way your chief financial officer and the finance department do.

"If you wish to converse with me, define your terms." - Voltaire

To get results, you need to get attention and approval for your initiatives from the decision makers at your company.

Since facilities cost money and money is the bottom line for any organization, the chief financial officer (CFO) is a key decision maker. Unfortunately, the drivers at the executive level of your organization may not line up with how you think about facilities costs.

If you are going to get the CFO's attention, you need to know how to assess the financial impact of decisions and present them in a way your CFO understands and cares about.

Avoid Being a Cost Centre

Facilities are often seen only as a cost to the company, so the pure expense side of the equation is usually the focus of financial analysis. In fact, a much broader and more strategic approach is needed.

This includes efficiency gains, revenue increases, cost avoidance, risk mitigation, future value and replacement costs, total cost of ownership, return on investment (ROI) and more.

Understand how to Look at Money

Before you begin to look at your facilities in these terms, however, you need to clearly understand how your company looks at money. Corporate finance can be complicated and may lack obvious links to the expenses you control. This includes taxation issues, capital versus operating expenses, the debt/equity ratio, expected ROI and margins for the main business line, financial liability and many other issues.

Only when you understand how your CFO looks at finance issues will you position facilities-related initiatives and opportunities in a way that is meaningful to them and likely to get attention and approval.

Consider This

By successfully representing the impact of facilities in a way that matters to the corporation, you increase your ability to sell your initiatives and be consulted about major decisions that impact facility costs.

The first step is to learn more about how your company looks at and assesses financial issues. You can do that by talking with your CFO or other key members of the finance group. In addition to learning about the specific approaches necessary within your company, you should also teach yourself about general corporate finance.

Here are 11 questions that will help you do that. Before you ask them, do a little homework on the general issues around the financial terms so you will understand the context.

If you're unsure about the answer you get, ask for clarification so that you understand the implications about how you run your facilities department.

Most importantly, build a relationship so that you can test your ideas and continue to learn from your CFO.

Eleven Questions for your CFO

After you do your homework, learn the answers to these questions by talking to your CFO or someone in the finance group:

1. How are facilities-related costs (capital and expense) accounted for relative to the company's other costs and revenue. Are they distributed to divisions and products or maintained as a central cost?

2. How are assets and liabilities (i.e., leases) for facilities accounted for on the company's balance sheet, and what is the impact of increasing or decreasing assets or liabilities?

3. How are the company's taxes affected by capital investment related to facilities?

4. How does the company deal with exchange rates? Does it hedge, and if so, what impact can it have on procurement and expenses (for companies with facilities in other countries)?

5. What is the amortization / depreciation approach for assets and how does it impact the company's results, including tax liabilities?

6. What is the company's cash position and how do facilities costs affect this?

7. What is the company's cost of borrowing?

8. What is the expected return on investment or payback period required to justify capital expenditures? Is it different for energy/environment/sustainability initiatives?

9. What is the proportion of capital and expense budgets for facilities relative to the overall corporate costs?

10. What is the target debt/equity ratio, and how does increased investment in facilities impact the company?

11. What model is used to analyze investment and other financial decisions? Is there a process or spreadsheet?

Quick Summary

Key Points	➡ Understand how expenses and capital affect your company.
	➡ Build a relationship with your finance group.
Executive Tips	➡ Build ROI into every business case.
Traps to Avoid	➡ Make sure your numbers are precise and accurate. Errors put everything into doubt.

50

Boost the Bottom Line with Cost Reductions

Learn to balance costs and services.

"You must consider the bottom line, but make it integrity before profits." – Denis Waitley

Facility managers can take a leadership role in reducing costs for their organizations by examining areas that may not have received much attention before.

A key responsibility of facility managers has been to provide the physical environment and related services that enable your organization to be successful at its core business. The focus is frequently on achieving the lowest possible costs to boost the bottom line or divert an organization's funds to core business.

You can demonstrate the value of a professional FM and add a key accomplishment by closely examining areas where you can reduce costs and by taking decisive action - especially in areas that may not have been considered before, or may not have received much attention in the past.

There are several opportunities you can consider, depending on your portfolio. They all relate to money going out the door to landlords, suppliers, utility companies and others.

Some of those costs can stay out, while others should be put back in eventually, otherwise you may end up with additional long-term expenses. Immediate cost reductions are certainly the goal, but don't pass over good opportunities just because the rewards will be months out. The need to lower costs will continue.

Space Costs

First, the physical space itself is a significant cost where you can benefit if your company's situation has reduced space requirements. Examine your leased space, the markets you are in, the termination dates and renewal options. While you may not realize significant benefits, consider it a cost avoidance initiative; even a sublease at net rent will relieve you of the operating cost portion of the rent. Work with your landlord to negotiate reductions in energy and cleaning costs for vacant space and ensure they are doing what they can to reduce their operating costs in the building. Get them to pass those cost savings along now, not next year during the annual CAM adjustment exercise.

Beware, however, of long-term fixes that may box you in when the economy picks up and you need to be nimble to respond and beat your competition. What's important is that you squeeze whatever you can out of the portfolio - and are seen to be proactively addressing the situation.

For owned space, consolidate and shut down unused offices to save operating and energy costs while you carefully examine the operating expenses. Have a discussion with your service providers and get them to identify areas where they can reduce real costs, such as reducing some services or cutting back on scope. This can include stretching out periodic activities, for instance, to reduce the total annual cost.

For larger portfolios, an often overlooked item is late fees for utility payments and even inaccurate utility readings. Set up a process to ensure prompt payment and review utility readings carefully, including the price and calculations.

There may be some services you can eliminate while also being environmentally sensitive. These include eliminating bottled water, reducing the frequency of garbage pick-ups, requiring occupants to bring their recyclables to a central depot and more. Do some of this in conjunction with your service providers to implement it with little or no cost.

Suppliers, Subcontractors & Service Providers

Are they just contractors or are they partners and a key part of your overall service delivery? Always remember, if your subcontractors fail to perform, so do you.

Don't use old-school approaches. They are important to your success, so manage them to improve performance. Use their skills and knowledge. Communicate about problems and give them a chance to propose solutions and provide action plans.

Implement measurements but put away the sledgehammer and start formal performance management meetings that focus on resolution and improvement rather than penalties. Implement regular performance feedback. As with employees, regular feedback is the best approach to get results.

Take a good look at your procurement approach for key service contractors. Do you focus on price and specifications or are you focusing on fit, past performance, sophistication and skills, their ability to recommend leading practices and share their own cost-cutting initiatives?

Balancing subcontracted services with in-house resources is important. Take a look at what your staff are doing compared to what is subcontracted and you may be able to shift some of the low-value activities to a subcontractor while you and your team focus on the high-value and strategic aspects of your responsibilities.

Look at your cost base and rationalize it to ensure you are efficiently using your suppliers and not paying more than you should. Examine your spending patterns across all your facilities and with all suppliers and service categories. While small transactions may seem trivial to deal with, they can add up and now is the time to do the analysis. You may see opportunities to consolidate vendors or provide volume to existing vendors in exchange for more favorable rates. By managing miscellaneous work orders, you may be able to group some work together and provide more lead time to contractors, resulting in lower costs.

When dealing with suppliers to explore cost reductions, you need to reduce the disincentive. Ask them to cut their profit margins or fixed overhead components and you won't get much help. Ask them to cut costs without adjusting performance standards or expectations to match those cuts, and you will get blank stares.

If you ask them to identify areas where their expertise suggests savings are possible and ask for reductions in real costs rather than those based on unit pricing rates (which include profit, overhead, risk, etc.), you are more likely to get help, which will reduce costs and mitigate service impacts. Sweeten the exercise with an extension or renewal and they will be even more receptive. Providing a contract extension may also result in reduced pricing, since they will avoid the cost and risk of a procurement process and may be able to eliminate some or all of the amortized costs they have built into the existing contract.

Recognize your suppliers as skilled and knowledgeable partners rather than an as adversaries and you can reap the benefits. Consider their business needs as well as your own and you can develop win-win situations that get you results and reduce costs.

Here are three examples of how you can put this approach into action:

1. Janitorial reductions: review specifications and identify cost-saving initiatives where changes wouldn't have a large impact; also consider frequency/service reductions to save costs by reducing hours.

2. Landscaping: review specifications and look for alternatives. If a specification calls for 22 cuts per season across a portfolio and those aren't needed due to growing conditions, the supplier can cut their costs based on the skipped costs, yet retain their profit and overhead.

3. HVAC: review "by the book" routines. Are they too frequent based on environmental conditions and the run-time of the equipment? A good HVAC contractor can identify where frequencies can be stretched or routines skipped in a particular period, saving costs without affecting the equipment or service.

In some cases, you'll have the data and information you need to analyze space and costs and to make decisions and establish strategies or take action to reduce expenses. The likelihood is great, however, that you will have to make decisions without solid information. While you are going through this exercise, consider the type and nature of information you could have used to better analyze your costs. Then develop a plan to get that information and use it improve a current cost crisis, or to better manage your portfolio after the dust settles.

Quick Summary

| Key Points | ➡ Cost savings need to be balanced with services required by the core business. |
| | ➡ Space and service provider costs are two key areas to look for reductions, in addition to energy. |

| Executive Tips | ➡ Use your service provider's knowledge and make it beneficial for them to help you save costs, not just cut service. |

| Traps to Avoid | ➡ Don't arbitrarily reduce supplier costs in critical areas without understanding the impact of the cost cuts. |
| | ➡ Carefully consider increased future costs that may result from inappropriate cost reductions. |

Your Strategic Plan

Based on this section, what strategic initiatives do you plan to implement that will help you manage your assets better and when do you expect to accomplish them?

What are you going to do?	When

Notes

Reference Information

Introduction

Learning from others is a way to enhance your own knowledge, discover solutions you didn't know about and share your own successes with colleagues.

Associations, magazines and conferences are an excellent way to learn from and share with other facility managers.

Magazines provide ideas, lessons learned and examples from others that you can apply or adapt to your situation.

Associations, both local and national, are either general to facilities or property management, or are specific to a certain type of facility. They usually provide publications and other information as well as seminars, networking events and conferences.

Conferences are sometimes affiliated with an association, but not always. Either way, they provide an opportunity to network with others in your field, learn about new products or services and take seminars by leaders in the industry.

References

The following organizations have been referenced in this book either as a good source for information or some of their material has been used with permission.

IFMA – International Facility Management Association
www.ifma.org
IFMA is the largest association for facility managers in the world and is affiliated with a variety of other FM associations in many countries. The FM competencies discussed in the *Management & Leadership* section were developed by IFMA. They have many research reports available for both members and non-members.

Human Synergistics
www.humansynergistics.com
If you are interested in the teamwork exercise discussed in this book, visit their website to find out how you can use it with your team. You can hire a facilitator or use their Leader's Guide and other material to conduct the simulation yourself.

The Checklist Manifesto
www.thechecklistmanifesto.com
By Mr. Atul Gawande and published by Macmillan, this book explores the value of checklists and how to implement them so they work. Checklists are a useful tool in facility management, so this book is worth reading.

Other FM Related Books

This is a short list of books focusing on specific areas of FM. Explore them and others to expand your knowledge and build your skills in all areas of FM

Improving Your Project Management Skills
www.amacombooks.org
By Larry Richman and published by AMACOM, this book is based on an American Management Association Project Management Seminar and covers all stages of projects from concept to planning, budgeting, design, implementation and close-out.

Innovations in Office Design – The Critical Influence Approach to Effective Work Environments
www.stegmeierconsulting.com
By Diane Stegmeier and published by Wiley, this book focuses on the difficult yet critical area of resistance to workplace change. Based on the author's 10-year research study of the collaborative workplaces of 140 organizations in 24 diverse industries, the book is a compilation of case studies and best practices in change management.

Lifecycle Costing for Facilities
http://rsmeans.reedconstructiondata.com
By Alphonse Dell'Isola and Steven Kirk and published by RSMeans, this book provides the theory of lifecycle costing along with information needed to apply it from a practical standpoint, including maintenance and repair costs for building elements.

Facilities Manager's Desk Reference
www.wiley.com
By Jane M. Wiggins and published by Wiley-Blackwell, this book is a detailed reference guide for FM practitioners covering many practical areas and the services typically under the responsibility of facility managers.

Facilities Planning and Relocation
http://rsmeans.reedconstructiondata.com
By David D. Owen and published by RSMeans, this book covers space needs as well as the scheduling, budgeting, design, installation, move and post-occupancy processes.

Facility Manager's Maintenance Handbook
www.mhprofessional.com
By Richard P. Payant & Bernard T. Lewis and published by McGraw Hill, this book focuses on detailed steps to plan, design and execute maintenance and operations procedures for building systems.

The Facility Management Handbook
www.amacombooks.org
By David G. Cotts, PE, CFM and Richard P. Payant, CFM, CPE, and published by AMACOM, this third edition covers a broad range of areas the typical facility manager should know about, including a new section on sustainability and security concerns.

Magazines

Some of these magazines are free to qualified subscribers in the magazine's home country and some are only available to members of the parent association, however most have some free content that can be accessed on their web sites, including complete digital editions.

Building Magazine (Canada)
www.building.ca
Covers the building development and management industry in Canada. Provides building developers and managers, contractors, architects, engineers and specification writers with the latest news and information.

Buildings Magazine (US)
www.buildings.com/
Helps building owners and facilities managers make decisions relevant to the construction, modernization and management of their facilities. Provides content that enlightens and inspires. Award-winning editorial content.

Building Operating Management Magazine (US)
www.facilitiesnet.com/bom
Covers technology and management issues for building owners and facility managers responsible for large office, educational, healthcare, government, retail, hospitality and other commercial/institutional buildings.

Canadian Facility Management & Design
www.cfmd.ca
For facility managers and the designers of workplaces, educational institutions and healthcare facilities. Focuses on leading-edge developments in energy management, sustainable design, products, ergonomics, outsourcing, technology and managerial skills.

Canadian Healthcare Facilities
www.mediaedge.ca/ches.shtml
Canadian Healthcare Facilities is the official publication of the Canadian Healthcare Engineering Society (CHES) and is a vital information source for 2,500 readers who are actively involved in healthcare facility operation and management.

Canadian Property Management Magazine
www.canadianpropertymanagement.ca/
Brings industry news from one end of Canada to the other along with pertinent and timely features, technical articles and case law reports.

Cleaning & Maintenance Management Magazine (US)
www.cmmonline.com/
Provides balanced editorial that is focused on product application as well as the business management needs to the most diversified group of end users within the cleaning and maintenance market.

Condo Business (Canada)
www.condobusiness.ca
For developers, property managers, condominium boards and those directly involved in the industry. Provides a mix of feature articles, news commentary and expert advice on everything from maintenance to legal issues to be competitive in this dynamic market.

Facility Care (US)
www.facilitycare.com
Provides information on quality operation, design and maintenance of healthcare facilities as well as a shared community of healthcare facility experts who explore and analyze issues that affect your facility and its environment of care.

Facilitator Magazine (US)
www.rfmaonline.com
By the Restaurant Facility Management Association, a resource for news, educational articles, up to date developments and the very latest trends in the world of restaurant facility management.

Facility Management Magazine (Australian)
www.fmmagazine.com.au
An information resource servicing professional facility managers. Readers are managers of Australia's built environment, responsible for the sustainable and efficient operation of office buildings, schools, hospitals, retail complexes and civic structures of all kinds.

Facilities Management Magazine (Middle East)
www.fmmagazine.net
A quarterly FM magazine on the GCC's built environment including green buildings and environmentally friendly technologies. Integrates disciplines involved in making an infrastructure, pleasant, functional, and manageable places to live and work.

Facility Management Journal (US)
www.fmjonline.com
The publication of the International Facility Management Association. FMJ has been written specifically for professionals involved with developing and maintaining productive workplaces. The FMJ is a resource for those in the built environment.

Facility Manager (US)
www.iaam.org
The International Association of Assembly Managers' publication includes articles from practitioners and experts that shape the industry, association news and announcements and well as industry trends and solutions.

FM Quest (India)

www.aifmi.in

This is a new quarterly publication from the Alliance of Infrastructure and Facility Managers of India association that focuses on the association's and members areas of interest in facilities and infrastructure in India.

FM World (UK)

www.fm-world.co.uk/

From the British Institute of Facilities Management, it aims to keep those interested in facilities management, workplace and property issues up-to-date with the latest developments and thinking and provides a forum for topical debate.

Health Estate Journal (UK)

http://www.healthestatejournal.com

The Journal of the Institute of Healthcare Engineering and Estate Management with news about the institute, a broad range of product and industry news and in-depth technical articles. Covers issues in the UK and abroad.

Health Facilities Management (US)

www.hfmmagazine.com

Produced by the American Hospital Association, provides coverage of the unique challenges facing health facility design/architecture, construction and operations communities. Reports on trends in hospital construction and renovations.

Journal of Property Management (US)

www.irem.org

Offers coverage of the real estate management industry with expert insights on trends and issues affecting all property types. Includes industry advice on maintenance, sustainability and overall management practices for real estate managers.

The Leader

www.corenetglobal.org

Published by CoreNet Global, covering corporate real estate trends and practices with a focus on the workplace and occupiers of leased space.

Maintenance Solutions (US)

www.facilitiesnet.com/ms

Provides articles, columns focusing on products and solutions for technical and maintenance across all types of facilities.

Maintenance Technology Magazine (US)

www.mt-online.com/

Maintenance Technology magazine is a business and technical information source for managers, engineers and supervisors responsible for plant equipment maintenance & reliability as well as asset management.

Premises & Facilities Management Magazine (UK)
www.pfmonthenet.net
Provides best practice guidance, service suppliers, products and applications, news and jobs.

Practical Facilities Management Magazine (UK)
www.practicalfm.co.uk/
Articles reflect a multitude of disciplines, with an extensive news section leading each issue and business news and product showcases highlighting the diversity of the industry.

Professional Retail Store Maintenance (US)
www.prsm.com
PRSM's official publication, it covers maintenance issues and information for the retail industry.

Qube Magazine (UK)
www.qubeonline.co.uk
A merger of two magazines, Building Maintenance and Services (BMS) and Total Facilities Management (TFM), this magazine offers facility managers information for interior and exterior products, services and solutions.

RFP Office Space Magazine (Hong King)
www.rfpmagazine.com
Focusing on corporate real estate, workplace, design and office management for corporate end users, developers and investors, architects and designers. Includes timely and essential articles, informative interviews, trends and industry intelligence.

Today's Facility Manager Magazine (US)
www.todaysfacilitymanager.com
Up-to-date articles on the latest practices, products, and services in the field with strategic and product focused editorial.

Online Portals

While many magazines include free online access to articles and information and some associations also have useful on-line resources for both members and non-members, here are some other on-line only portals with information and resources for Facility Managers. For some content, you will need to sign-up.

FacilitiesNet
www.facilitiesnet.com
By the publishers of Building Operating Management magazine, provides articles, product information, webcasts and other resources. U.S. Based.

FM Link
www.fmlink.com
With daily news, association information, regulation, news, reports, benchmarking and surveys, including an FM forum where you can post questions and answers to FM issues. U.S. Based.

i-FM
www.i-fm.net
Provides on-line daily news, articles, research and resources. UK based.

International Journal of Facility Management
www.ijfm.net
An on-line journal devoted to the science, technology and practice of facility management. Through research and practice papers, the journal shares new theories, research, experience and best practices for building and workplace strategy, design, management, operations, use and disposition. U.S. Based.

Associations

This is a list of national and international associations. Some of these associations have local or regional chapters and there are other associations that operate locally or regionally and cover all types of facilities.

Some associations have their own annual conferences, produce magazines for their members and provide reference material and resources for members and non-members. Where the association has provided information, it has been included below, edited for length.

ABRAFAC - Associacao Brasiliera De Facilities (Brazil)
www.abrafac.org.br

AFE - Association for Facilities Engineering (US)
www.afe.org
For facilities engineers and operations professionals, helps members grow professionally through quality networking, knowledge sharing, certification and other resources. Promotes the facilities engineering profession.

AIFMI - Alliance of Infrastructure and Facility Managers of India
www.aifmi.in
An industry-managed organization, playing a proactive role in India's Facilities Management community. Sets a common voice for the industry and enhance the credibility of IFM, promoting FM in the public and private structures.

APFM - Association of Property and Facility Managers (Singapore)
www.apfm.org.sg
Promotes the standard and practice of property and facility management in various sectors of the industries. Provides for exchanges among members and dialogues with the authorities and other allied professional bodies.

APPA - Association of Higher Education Facilities (North American)
www.appa.org
Promotes leadership in educational facilities for professionals seeking to build their careers, transform their institutions, and elevate the value and recognition of facilities in education.

ARSEG - Association des Responsable Services Généraux. (France)
www.arseg.asso.fr

BGFMA - Bulgarian Facility Management Association
www.bgfma.bg

BIFM - British Institute of Facilities Management
www.bifm.org.uk
Provides information, education, training and networking services individual professionals and organizations. BIFM's mission is to advance the profession and consolidate FM as a vital management discipline.

BOMA - Building Owners & Managers Association (International)
www.boma.org

CCFM - Conference for Catholic Facility Management (US)
www.ccfm.net

CHES - Canadian Healthcare Engineering Society
www.ches.org
Helping members manage the environment which is essential for healthcare delivery. Members are directly involved in, or responsible for the full range of functions including plant, maintenance, facilities, clinical engineering, safety, construction, security, support services, environmental management, and waste management.

CREW Network - Commercial Real Estate Women (North America)
www.crewnetwork.org
The industry's business networking organization influencing the success of the commercial real estate industry women. A commercial real estate network in major North American markets representing every discipline within commercial real estate.

CRFC - Canadian Recreation Facilities Council (Canadian)
www.crfc.ca

CoreNet Global
www.corenetglobal.org
A leading professional association for corporate real estate and workplace executives, service providers, and economic developers. Publishes LEADER Magazine covering corporate real estate trends and practices and conducts 5 Global Summits annually

EuroFM - European Facility Management Network
www.eurofm.org

FMA - Facilities Management Austria
www.fma.or.at

FMA - Facilities Management Association (UK)
www.fmassociation.org.uk
Members represent all sectors of the industry and get involved, because they want to grow their business and because they want to make sure their voice is heard by government, industry and the media.

FMA - Facility Management Association of Australia
www.fma.com.au

FMN - Facility Management Nederland
www.fmn.nl

FM-ARENA (Switzerland)
www.fm-arena.ch

GEFMA - German Facility Management Association
www.gefma.de
The leading German network for executives in facility management including external and internal service providers representing the full range of facility services. Includes in-house facility managers as customers, investors, property owners and the public sector.

Global FM
www.globalfm.org

HEFMA - Health Estates & Facilities (UK)
www.hefma.org.uk

HEFMA - Higher Education Facility Management Association of Southern Africa
www.hefma.org
The objective is to develop and maintain high quality standards in the management, maintenance, operation, planning utilization and development of the physical infrastructure of higher education institutions.

HKIFM - Hong Kong Institute of Facility Management
www.hkifm.org.hk

HFMS - Hungarian Facility Management Society
www.fmportal.hu
To develop FM as a business area of strategic importance, maintain and develop world class domestic professional excellence, create rules to govern facility management activities and represent the professional and economic interests of its members.

IAAM - International Association of Assembly Managers (US)
www.iaam.org

IAAPA - International Association of Amusement Parks and Attractions (US)
www.iaapa.org

IHEEM - Institute of Healthcare Engineering and Estate Management (UK)
www.iheem.org.uk
A specialist institute for the healthcare estates sector. Approximately 10% of members are based overseas. Its primary purpose as an a professional development organization, is to keep members up to date with developing technology and changing regulations.

IFMA - International Facilities Management Association
www.ifma.org

The world's largest association representing professional facility managers in 78 countries. Certifies facility managers, conducts research, provides educational programs and produces the World Workplace conference.

IPFMA - Irish Property & Facility Management Association
www.ipfma.com

IREM - Institute of Real Estate Management (US)
www.irem.org

Education, resources and information for real estate management professionals. Affiliated with the National Association of Realtors, IREM serves the multi-family and commercial real estate sectors in the U.S. and around the globe.

ISSA - Worldwide Cleaning Industry Association
www.issa.com

JFMA - Japan Facility Management Promotion Association
www.jfma.or.jp

MEFMA - Middle East Facility Management Association
www.mefma.org

Unifying the facility management industry in the Middle East and promoting excellence in the management of facilities. Conducts research, provides educational programs and helps FMs develop strategies to manage human, facility and real estate resources.

MFS - Maintenance and Facility Management Society of Switzerland
www.mfs.ch

NAIOP - National Association of Industrial & Office Properties (US)
www.naiop.org

NARPM - National Association of Residential Property Managers (US)
www.narpm.org

NPMA - National Property Management Association (US)
www.npma.org

PMI - Project Management Institute (US)
www.pmi.org

PRSM - Professional Retail Store Maintenance Association (US)
www.prsm.com

Helping retail facilities professionals make informed business decision by delivering best practices, education, forums and partnerships. Its active retail and vendor membership works together to meet the ever-changing demands in retail facilities.

RICS - Royal Institution of Chartered Surveyors (UK)
www.rics.org
With membership that includes Facility Managers and Property Managers, RICS is the world's leading professional body for qualifications and standards in land, property and construction. Attaining RICS status is the recognized mark of property professionalism.

ROFMA - Romanian Facility Management Association
www.rofma.ro

RFMA - Restaurant Facility Management Professionals (US)
www.rfmaonline.com
Representing restaurant facility professionals and vendor companies. Helps to define the core competencies for meeting the high standards of knowledge and skill that have become critical to the success of the restaurant facility management industry.

SAFMA - South African Facilities Management Association
www.safma.org.za
Represents the FM industry with a diverse membership comprising of FM organizations, in-house operatives, consultants, training organisations and service providers. Supports, represents and advances the FM industry through awareness and a common voice.

TEFMA - Tertiary Education Facilities Management Association (Australasian)
www.tefma.com
Represents members in university, polytechnic, technical and further education institutions in Australia, New Zealand, Hong Kong and Singapore. Workshops for FMs, an annual conference, benchmarking survey, publishes guides and a newsletter.

Conferences

This is a list of national and international conferences. Some are affiliated with associations listed earlier in this section and some are stand-alone conferences. Visit the association's websites for other local or regional conferences.

Most conferences provide both a trade show and an educational stream, in addition to networking, awards and social events. Descriptions are a combination of information provided by the conference organizers and information from the conference website.

AFEC - Advanced Facilities Management and Engineering Conference (US)
www.afec.biz
Dedicated to increasing the skills and knowledge of Facility Managers and Engineers in the Rocky Mountain Region, preparing them to meet the demands of their occupation, today, tomorrow, and into the future

BIFM - Annual Conference (UK)
www.bifm.org.uk
Includes a wide range of speakers and delegates. Available to anyone who has an interest in the wide-ranging facilities management industry. It attracts 1,200 of the industry's key decision makers and includes an awards dinner with high profile entertainment.

BOMA - International Conference & The Every Building Show (US)
www.bomaconvention.org
Brings together experts and resources in the commercial real estate industry. Building owners and managers from across the U.S. and around the world come together to discuss current trends, best practices and learn from industry leaders.

CHES - Trade Show and Education Forum (Canada)
www.ches.org
Includes keynote presentations, workshops, educational programs and a trade show. Participants receive updates on codes and standards, discuss sustainability and hear presentations on applying technology appropriately to enhance patient experience.

Conference for Catholic Facility Management (USA)
www.ccfm.net
A forum and network for professionals whose responsibilities include real estate, construction, property management, and real properties for the Roman Catholic Church.

Cityscape Dubai Facilities and Asset Management Conference
www.cityscapeglobal.com
Offers an opportunity for facility managers to see and meet real estate companies showcasing their latest projects and services, as well as offering a platform to meet with industry peers.

CoreNet Global

www.corenetglobal.org

Conducts five global summits annually in Asia, Australia/New Zealand, Europe and North America for managers of real estate, real estate service providers, including design, construction and landlords as well as other asset management functions.

Crew Network Convention & Marketplace (US)

www.crewnetwork.org

This three-day event is dedicated to providing attendees with critical business networking and development opportunities, comprehensive market forecasts, cutting-edge education and professional development training.

EFMC European Facility Management Conference

www.efmc-conference.com

Provides speakers, best practices and networking from Europe and abroad for the full range of professionals involved in the facilities, real estate, asset management, architecture and construction fields.

Facility Decisions (US)

www.facilitydecisions.com

Held in Las Vegas every fall, includes educational courses presented by industry experts providing insight and information on a wide variety of topical subjects. Includes top suppliers showcasing the latest products, services and technologies.

Facility Management Exhibition & Conference (Germany)

www.fm-messe.de

A combination of exhibition, conference and networking events for FMs as well as academics from applied research. Offers an overview of products and services, a user-oriented conference with experts from industry and science to share knowledge.

Facility & Property Management Conference (Romania)

www.facilityconference.ro

Specialists in the field provide a rich analysis of the present challenges together with the latest trends and technological innovations that influence the management of building services to identify practices and solutions for operations and maintenance activity

FM Expo (Middle East)

www.fm-expo.com

Provides a roster of speakers from international industry experts, post-conference workshops, a trade floor with suppliers and solutions as well as networking and learning opportunities.

FM Ireland Exhibition & Conference

www.fmireland.com/Conference.asp

For directors and managers responsible for retail, industrial, commercial, residential facilities and public buildings. An opportunity to network with others in the industry and learn how to design and run your facility efficiently, safely and sustainably.

Healthcare Estates (UK)
www.healthcare-estates.com
Bringing together delegates speakers and exhibitors from all areas of the Healthcare Estates Sector. Designed for everyone involved in the planning, design, construction, management, maintenance and operation of healthcare facilities.

Healthcare Facilities Symposium & Expo (US)
www.hcarefacilities.com
Brings together the entire team who designs, plans, constructs and manages healthcare facilities. Focuses on how the physical space directly impacts the staff, patients and their families and the delivery of healthcare.

HFMC - Hungarian Facility Management Congress
www.hfms.org.hu
A national conference of the Hungarian Facility Management Society, this conference provides networking and education on a variety of FM topics with a different theme each year.

Venue Connect: IAAM Annual Conference and Trade Show (US)
www.iaam.org
Brings together FM decision makers and companies providing products or services to the industry. Dozens of educational sessions by industry experts providing education, networking opportunities and access to the latest trends, topics and solutions.

IIDEX / Neocon Canada
www.iidexneocon.com
With a focus on suppliers and seminars for furniture and office interior design products and services, this conference also includes Facilities and energy/environment related seminars and vendors on the trade floor.

IFMA World Workplace (US)
www.worldworkplace.org
A three-day educational and networking event focused on the future of the built environment. Includes a conference focused entirely on education and an exposition incorporating product demonstration and instruction.

Integrate (Asia)
http://ifma.org.hk
Integrate is one of the largest annual FM conference in Asia providing the industry with the best opportunity to gather with peers and colleagues in the FM profession. The event is publicized to the FM industry globally and attendees are from every continent.

IREM iCon (US)
www.irem.org/icon/
Features inspiring speakers, educational experiences and association with people who will expand your perspective and professional vision. Build community and connectivity that reaches far beyond a physical gathering.

MEED Facilities Management (Middle East)

www.meedconferences.com/facility

Addresses strategic developments in the expanding facilities management sector related to identifying strategic partners, assessing the full costs of ownership, addressing sustainability issues in all sectors.

NeoCon World's Trade Fair (US)

www.neocon.com

Primarily for design professionals and those who use design services and products, includes showrooms and exhibitors, seminars, tours and educational programs as well as networking with industry players.

NFMT Exhibition & Fair (US)

www.nfmt.com

For non-residential building owners; facility managers; maintenance engineers; directors of sustainability; planning; operations and management, provides interaction with suppliers and educational tracts focusing on key strategic areas of FM.

PM Expo (Canada)

www.pmexpo.com

Through seminars and suppliers, facilitates the exchange of ideas, best practices, and product knowledge that provide strategies and cost effective solutions for managing and operating your buildings.

PRSM Conferences (US)

www.prsm.com

For the retail industry, this educational event boasts more than 35 education sessions and over 300 exhibiting companies. A mid-year conference is also held in September each year and is an excellent opportunity to learn about current facility industry issues.

RFMA Annual Conference (US)

www.rfmaonline.com

Industry restaurant facility professionals meet for education programs with over 20 technical sessions designed to increase the knowledge of facility professionals. Exhibits vendors with solutions for the challenges of today's restaurant facilities.

Stadium Management Conference (US)

www.iaam.org

Provides relevant industry topics, trends, challenges and solutions through dozens of sessions taught by industry experts. Also enables networking with your colleagues and service providers.

The Workplace & FM Asia Summit

www.facilityone.cn/events

For key decision makers and influencers among Asia's growing base of Facility Management practitioners, this conference includes over 60 and panellists who will introduce cutting edge sustainable FM concept and practices.

Designations

Designations are one way to promote your skills and capabilities with your employer or in the marketplace. They usually require you to demonstrate industry experience and take specific training. Most also require you to maintain your designation through additional continuing education. These designations are either general FM or industry / facility type specific.

BOMI – Building Owners Managers International
www.bomicanada.com
RPA (Real Property Administrator)
FMA (Facilities Management Administrator)
SMT (Systems Maintenance Technician)
SMA (Systems Maintenance Administrator)

CoreNet Global
www.corenetglobal.com
MCR (Master of Corporate Real Estate)
SLCR (Senior Leader of Corporate Real Estate)

IFMA – International Facility Managers Association
www.ifma.org
CFM (Certified Facility Manager)
FMP (Facility Management Professional)

IREM
www.irem.org
CPM (certified property manager)
ARM (Accredited Resident Manager
AMO (Accredited Management Organization)
ACoM (Accredited Commercial Manager

NAHB
www.nahb.org
RAM (Registered In Apartment Management)

NAA - The National Apartment Association
www.naahq.org
CAM (Certified Apartment Manager)
CAPS (Certified Apartment Supervisor)

NARPM - The National Association of Residential Property Managers
www.narpm.org
RPM (Residential Management Professional)
MPM (Master Property Manager)
CRMC (Certified Residential Management Company)

CSS (Certified Support Specialist)

PRSM - Professional Retail Store Maintenance
www.prsm.com
RFMP (Retail Facility Maintenance Professional)

RFMA – Restaurant Facility Management Association
www.rfmaonline.com
CRFP (Certified Restaurant Facility Professional).

Index

About the Author

Michel Theriault is Principal of Strategic Advisor, an independent Facility & Property Management consulting firm providing strategic and management support that helps managers assess, analyze, develop and implement initiatives to get better results.

Other books by the Author

"Win More Business - Write Better Proposals"
Published March, 2010

"The Built Environment" Blog

www.thebuiltenvironment.ca

Contact Information

Please feel free to connect with me on Twitter or LinkedIn

Web: www.strategicadvisor.ca

Twitter: www.twitter.com/micheltheriault

LinkedIn: http://ca.linkedin.com/in/micheltheriault

Email: michel@strategicadvisor.ca

Online Bonus Content

www.thebuiltenvironment.ca/fmbookbonus

Lightning Source UK Ltd.
Milton Keynes UK
10 December 2010

164145UK00001B/22/P